Repairing the U.S. Social Safety Net

Also of interest from the Urban Institute Press:

Reshaping the American Workforce in a Changing Economy, edited by Harry Holzer and Demetra Smith Nightingale

International Perspectives on Social Security Reform, edited by Rudolph G. Penner

Helping America's Homeless: Emergency Shelter or Affordable Housing, by Martha Burt, Laudan Y. Aron, and Edgar Lee, with Jesse Valente

Repairing the U.S. Social Safety Net

Martha R. Burt & Demetra Smith Nightingale

THE URBAN INSTITUTE PRESS
WASHINGTON, DC

THE URBAN INSTITUTE PRESS
2100 M Street, N.W.
Washington, D.C. 20037

Library of Congress Cataloging-in-Publication Data

Burt, Martha R.
  Repairing the U.S. social safety net / Martha R. Burt and Demetra Smith Nightingale.
    p. cm.
  Includes bibliographical references and index.
  ISBN 978-0-87766-761-2
  1. Public welfare—United States. 2. United States—Social policy. 3. United States—Social conditions. I. Nightingale, Demetra S. II. Title.
  HV95.B867 2009
  362.5′5680973—dc22

                                                                    2009028784

Printed in the United States of America

12 11 10   1 2 3 4 5

THE URBAN INSTITUTE is a nonprofit, nonpartisan policy research and educational organization established in Washington, D.C., in 1968. Its staff investigates the social, economic, and governance problems confronting the nation and evaluates the public and private means to alleviate them. The Institute disseminates its research findings through publications, its web site, the media, seminars, and forums.

Through work that ranges from broad conceptual studies to administrative and technical assistance, Institute researchers contribute to the stock of knowledge available to guide decisionmaking in the public interest.

Conclusions or opinions expressed in Institute publications are those of the authors and do not necessarily reflect the views of officers or trustees of the Institute, advisory groups, or any organizations that provide financial support to the Institute.

Contents

Acknowledgments

The idea for this book began when the two authors were invited by the World Bank's Safety Nets, Social Protection, and Labor group to create a course on the U.S. safety net through which moderate-income countries could learn about safety net and antipoverty programs and consider how they might mount similar programs of their own. Margaret Grosh and John Blomquist of the Social Protection division were the first to invite us to attempt this course; Emil Tesliuc, also in Social Protection, was the one that made it happen. Emil's comments, suggestions, and input throughout the project were vital to our work; we learned from him that similar social problems exist in many countries and that cross-national policy lessons should be shared more often.

The World Bank has elaborated on the course we developed until it is now a week-long distance learning course with numerous other contributors. The course has been translated into Portuguese, Russian, and Spanish so far and attended by hundreds of people from at least a dozen countries. As we participate in the daily question-and-answer sessions for these courses, we have learned a great deal from all the participants as we hear their questions and concerns and, to answer fully, have to push ourselves to explain how U.S. programs work and why they are structured the way they are. Common questions from locales as diverse as Uruguay and central Russia have helped us focus on the most important aspects of U.S. programs and the ones that need the most explaining.

Theresa Jones of the World Bank's Latin America and Caribbean division further expanded the reach of the course and our cross-national perspective, organizing and convening forums, lectures, and exchanges for administrators and officials from nearly every Latin American and Caribbean country.

The next stimulus came from Kathy Courrier, vice president of communications at the Urban Institute. Even before the World Bank course became a reality, Kathy was encouraging us to turn our work into a public policy book. Her enthusiasm as well as her periodic queries as to "how we were coming along" brought us through the final push after numerous postponements.

The Urban Institute's president, Robert Reischauer, and the committee that annually chooses projects to support with the Institute's general support funding responded enthusiastically to our proposal to write the book with a generous account that kept us going long after we had spent it all.

Many individuals helped at various points. Pamela Holcomb and Amber Sears participated fully in the early stages as we developed the World Bank course, prepared extensive annotated bibliographies, and compiled background materials. Ajay Chaudry and Kathy Courrier reviewed drafts of some chapters and provided helpful comments as we revised. At the Institute for Policy Studies at Johns Hopkins University, Maura Hardy and Sarah Hutcheon helped draft some early chapters; Matthew Maronick edited sections of some chapters; and Burt Barnow reviewed sections and offered useful suggestions. The final book benefited greatly from the thoughtful comments of two anonymous reviewers, whom we thank for their suggestions.

The book also benefited greatly from students in the Masters of Public Policy graduate course in social policy at Johns Hopkins University from 2003 through 2008. Their questions, discussions, and opinions led to several revisions of key sections. Each year, the students' enthusiasm, intensity, and commitment prove there is hope for improving American public policies in the future.

Both of us had the opportunity to visit Argentina, Chile, and Russia as part of World Bank missions on social assistance, homelessness, and employment policy. Special acknowledgments are due to the dozens of national, regional, provincial, and local administrators and staff who met with us, explained their policies, and let us observe their programs and to the World Bank staff in Moscow and Buenos Aires who facilitated our visits. We are particularly grateful to insights, knowledge, and cooperation we received from Boris Sergeevich Mozgolin, then-head of the Department of Economy and now vice-governor on economic issues, and Irina Pavlovna Titarenko, deputy head of the Department of Economy in Tomsk Oblast (Siberia, Russia), Eva Raskovsky and Claudia Berra of the Ministry of Labor in Argentina, and Patricia Jara and Andres Agurto from the Ministry of Planning in Chile.

Finally, we thank our personal safety nets. Betty Carol Sellen and Clay Nightingale bore with us over many months as we finished the book. Gregory Nightingale reviewed, commented on, and sometimes edited sections of the book, challenging us to clarify our points and polish our words. Finally, Peter Maravell Smith (1949–2007) provided a personal glimpse into a social safety net stretched beyond the limit in post-Katrina New Orleans.

We greatly appreciate the contributions, support, and encouragement of all these individuals. We, though, assume responsibility for any omissions or errors. And of course the opinions and recommendations are ours alone and do not represent positions of the Urban Institute, Johns Hopkins University, the World Bank, or their funders or trustees.

Preface

The U.S. social safety net changes continuously, as do the problems it addresses. Changes in the economy, politics, and society as a whole all affect the specific details of programs discussed in this volume. Radical change may also stimulate significant program reorientation and give birth to entirely new programs. As this book goes to press, the United States faces the most serious challenges to its economy and to the well-being of its people since the Great Depression of the 1930s. It also has a new presidential administration in the beginning phases of what many believe will be a watershed change in social policy. Many of the serious national policy challenges facing President Barack Obama fall squarely within the purview of this book, even though it was written before he took office. The volume should thus provide a useful historical and operational context for a range of programs and policies affecting the lives of poor and vulnerable persons, as well as a baseline for documenting changes pursued by the Obama administration.

1

U.S. Social Policy
and the Social Safety Net
in Historical Perspective

From the earliest days of human life on Earth, individuals have come together, first in hunter-gatherer groups and later in increasingly complex communities, to do together the things that one person, or even one family, could not do alone. They have organized to hunt, farm, and defend. They have cared for the young, the sick, the old, and the vulnerable. And they have developed mechanisms—government in one form or another—to decide how these things should be accomplished and how to make them happen. When the biblical Joseph advised Egypt's pharaoh to save grain during the seven fat years so that the population would not starve during the coming seven years of famine, he was setting social policy to provide a safety net for a whole nation. Implicit in this Old Testament story is that it was the pharaoh's responsibility to see that the people did not starve and that it was within his authority to order that surplus grain be delivered to the government and saved for the time when it would be needed.

Every modern nation has some form of a social safety net. In some, including many European countries, the net is extensive. In others, it is rudimentary, as it is in much of the developing world. But even in countries with a rudimentary safety net, official policy statements show that they *aspire* to being able to provide a better safety net for their people. A country's values, history, resources, and social and economic conditions determine the scope, shape, focus, and functioning of its social safety net—a generalization that is as true for the United States as it is for other countries. This book is about the social safety net in the United States in the early 21st century. By examining the values, history, and social and economic conditions that have helped define and shape it into today's set of programs and practices, this chapter provides the foundation for understanding that safety net.

Defining Social Policy and the Social Safety Net

In the United States, the term *social safety net* is typically applied to the set of social programs that are primarily or totally focused on less-advantaged and more vulnerable Americans, including those with short-term crises and those with long-standing issues. Safety net programs are designed to serve people with little money, inadequate education, poor health, or physical or mental disabilities or those living in situations where they risk abuse or neglect.

Public social safety net programs are established and created by government action through laws, regulations, program rules, funding priorities, and the like. The public policies are also affected and refined by agency officials and staff who must turn those policies into action. One way to understand where social safety net programs are located in the broad context of public policy is to consider three interrelated spheres of public action: social policy, economic policy, and (for simplicity) all other public policies, as depicted in figure 1.1. Social policy is defined here as the category of *government actions related to social activity and conditions of individuals, families, and the communities or institutions in which they function*—including education, work, health, housing, and social insurance (that is, essentially mandatory contributory government programs that provide individuals with insurance to mitigate certain risks, such as unemployment or pensions for retirement). Economic policy refers to *government actions related to financial and economic activity and conditions*, including tax, financial, business, commerce, monetary, and fiscal policies. "Other" policies address all other public actions, including public works, defense, transportation, immigration, energy, the environment, and security. Social and economic policies, as well as most other public policies, affect all segments of society—at all socioeconomic levels and in all personal situations—and influence income, assets, health,

Figure 1.1. Where Social Safety Net Policies Fit in the General Spheres of U.S. Public Policy

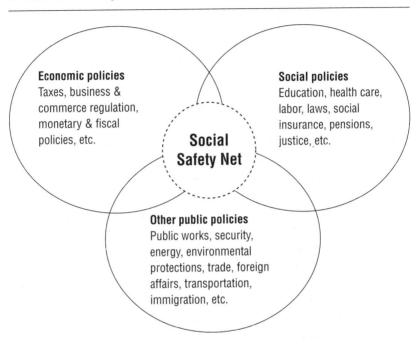

housing, wealth, work, retirement, security, and access to education and other opportunities.

Figure 1.1 shows the social safety net at the intersection of the three public policy spheres. Programs and activities of the social safety net—including social services, income transfers, and assistance—appear as components of social and economic policies related to vulnerable segments of the population or persons in vulnerable situations: people whose incomes are low, those with disabilities, abused or neglected children, the economically disadvantaged, the elderly, and those affected by disasters or crises. Safety net policies also involve or are affected by policies in other areas, such as transportation, environmental protection, and immigration. Thus, the social safety net encompasses many programs and activities established by a host of public policies, including those specifically related to poor and vulnerable people as well as those focused more broadly on the entire society.

Policy Framework

In this book, we use the generalized conceptual framework shown in figure 1.2 to help describe social safety net programs and policies in the United States. We also use it to make occasional comparisons to safety net policies in other countries, to give the reader some context in which to understand the ways that uniquely American assumptions and values shape the nation's social safety net policies.

To understand the American social safety net, one must first recognize that it grows out of the history of the United States, including its political culture, the governance structure of federalism, prevailing economic and fiscal conditions, and societal needs. That history shapes our national values and assumptions, which in turn lead us to select certain goals for our social policies (philosophical premises) and to construct them in certain ways (policy mechanisms). The result is our current unique combination of programs and policies to protect, support, and assist the poor and vulnerable members of society.

The U.S. social and economic safety net has evolved over nearly a century through government policies related mainly to three general goals—providing basic financial security, protecting vulnerable populations, and promoting equality of opportunity—shown in figure 1.2. The programs and policies developed to pursue those goals are shaped by the core American values of individualism and freedom, self-reliance and independence, the work ethic, fairness, and the primacy of family and community. These values have led the nation to choose particular philosophical premises as the basis for safety net programs, including offering certain benefits or supports as a right, others as something one can earn, and some that are given by the society to deserving people who can show need—basically, as charity. Finally, the combination of all three factors (values, premises, and goals) has influenced the choice of policy mechanisms for carrying out our safety net programs. We address each of these components of the policy framework in detail below, beginning with American societal values and assumptions.

Values and Assumptions Underlying U.S. Safety Net Policies

The political and social culture of a nation determines which of many assumptions or concepts dominate at a particular time in history, and the assumptions in turn define the scope and nature of the policies devel-

Figure 1.2. Social Safety Net Policy Framework

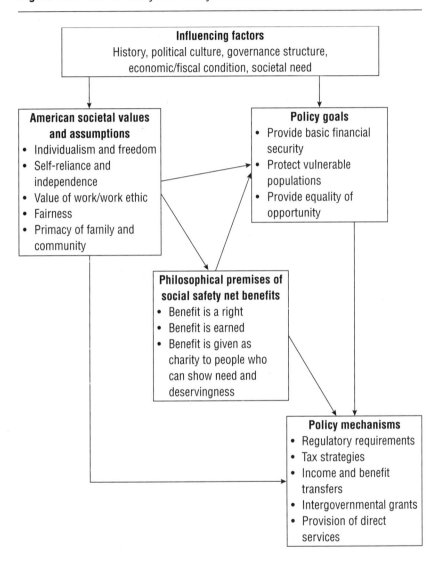

oped to reach societal goals. Ellwood (1989) explains that the complex American national psyche is constantly struggling with some powerful but potentially contradictory shared values that define how the national culture regards people living in poverty. Compassion, fairness, and a willingness to help those in need are a part of the American sense of community and dignity. At the same time, these values conflict with others held just as strongly: the importance of work and the work ethic, the sanctity of family, and the importance of independence and self-reliance.

Implicit in Ellwood's analysis but not stated overtly is a negative corollary, growing out of both the Calvinist origins of much American social thought and its social Darwinist extension (Katz 1990; Trattner 1998): that is, that if one is poor, it is one's own fault and that poor people are somehow *less worthy, less blessed, less "chosen," and also less "fit"* than those with money. Calvinist religion (the religion of the Puritans who were the first Europeans to populate New England) held that individuals were obliged to pursue secular work with determination and perseverance. Such commitment to work would lead them to accumulate money, but they were also to live an abstemious life and not squander their resources on luxuries, so that the excess could go back into their businesses. Economic success was understood as a sign that one was among the "chosen." In the Calvinist view, poverty arose generally from laziness and refusal to follow religious injunctions to work hard and was thus something one brought on oneself. Because giving money to the poor directly or through charitable institutions could encourage laziness, it was, therefore, acceptable only in dire situations. Families and local communities had the responsibility to provide that help. In the latter part of the 1800s, social Darwinism layered the concept of survival of the fittest onto the earlier Calvinist beliefs and supported the idea that easing the conditions or disadvantage of poverty would interfere with "nature's way," because biological and genetic factors were what made some less adept or "fit" at surviving and succeeding in society (Patterson 2000).

These same values about the work ethic and individual responsibility are evident in the concept of the American dream, which in many respects evolved from the earliest days of the nation's efforts to grow economically. Inherent in the American dream are the assumption and expectation that individuals, through their own initiative, can achieve economic success and upward mobility and, through their individual efforts, contribute to the nation's success. To some degree, one extension of such thinking is that only those truly unable to participate economically deserve assistance. Echoing a liberal perspective, Katz attributes this aspect of the nation's cultural identity, which justifies social assistance only for the deserving poor and refuses to help the undeserving poor, to fundamental principles of capitalism that have guided the development of the nation:

> The culture of capitalism measures persons, as well as everything else, by their ability to produce wealth and by their success in earning it; it therefore leads naturally to the moral condemnation of those who, for whatever reason, fail to contribute or to prosper. (1989, 7)

Conservative scholars contend that social factors explain more about poverty than capitalism does. But they also acknowledge, even justify, that work is a key part of responsible civic behavior. Some, like Lawrence Mead, strongly contend that work is a main source of dignity in society and that behavioral and psychological deficiencies and lack of individual responsibility are the primary causes of not working. Since individual dysfunctional behavior, and not the nature of capitalism, is the primary cause of not working, Mead implies that perhaps the "moral condemnation" described by Katz is justified: "I believe that dysfunctional poverty threatens the traditional politics of justice and that only if it is overcome can a debate about justice resume" (Mead 1997, 197). He goes on to say that "only if order is restored in cities, and especially if work levels rise, could the poor become more self-respecting. Only then could they stake claims on the collectivity as equals, rather than seeking charity as dependents" (230).

Debates, sometimes passionate, continue about the relative contributions of capitalism and individual behavior to poverty. There are, though, many points of agreement: U.S. culture stigmatizes poverty; much of the stigma is associated with work status and the societal value placed on work; and the nation has struggled—and continues to struggle—politically in establishing coherent policies to provide a social safety net.

According to Ellwood, three basic conundrums explain the extreme difficulty of reconciling the inherent contradictions in antipoverty and safety net policies.

- *The security-work conundrum:* the desire to provide economic security but not reduce individual initiative and work effort
- *The assistance–family structure conundrum:* the desire to help poor people, especially children, and protect their well-being but not encourage or endorse poor decisions or irresponsible behavior by parents or other family members

- *The targeting-isolation conundrum:* the desire to target public resources and services to those who need them the most but not isolate or stigmatize people because of their assistance status

Policies that emphasize one of America's core values may mean ignoring
others considered equally important. Policies designed to provide all persons with a decent standard of living, for example, may serve as a disincen-
tive to work and go against the ideological heritage described above.
Attempts to balance competing values inevitably lead to compromises of
one or more values and result in program complexity. Eligibility for assistance can be made conditional on certain behavioral expectations ("we'll
give you money, but you must take concrete steps to get a job"), or benefit levels may be adjusted by formulas designed to create financial incentives to work ("we'll set benefit structures so that even though you are on
welfare, you are always better off if you also work"). Assistance can be
restricted to those poor households that are deemed "worthy" (e.g., having a disability that makes it impossible to work), or quality control procedures can be developed to counter potential fraud or abuse.

Ellwood's three conundrums, for which there are no perfect solutions,
weave throughout the discussions in the following chapters, highlighting the American struggle to support poor and vulnerable people within
the context of core values.

Particularly since the great expansion of social safety net policies and
programs beginning in the 1960s, these conundrums and the tensions
among several strongly held but conflicting American values have been
central to policy and political debates. In the late 1990s and early 2000s, for
instance, a high priority was placed on promoting work through welfare
programs and on strengthening traditional family structures by reducing
out-of-wedlock childbearing and removing any disincentives to marriage
in tax and transfer programs (referred to as "marriage penalties") (Weil
and Finegold 2002). These values and behaviors are also typically the focus
of much of the social science research and evaluation of the effects of programs and policies on individuals, communities, governments, and society.

Philosophical Premises of Safety Net Programs

A society's values influence the premises on which it structures its social
safety net programs. We can classify any country's policies and programs
regarding poor and vulnerable people according to three alternative

philosophical premises—whether a support or benefit is offered as a right, as something to be earned, or as charity.

- *Rights—people receive benefits as a right:* Some countries offer many of their safety net activities as a right, such as a right to housing in Scandinavian countries or to health care in all industrialized countries other than the United States. Countries may articulate rights even if their economies cannot sustain them as yet—most countries in the world other than the United States have ratified the United Nations Convention on the Rights of the Child, which declares that children have a right to survival; to be protected from harmful influences, abuse, and exploitation; and to develop to the fullest, among more than 50 other rights.[1] With few exceptions (such as public education for school-age children and health care through Medicare for anyone 65 or older), U.S. safety net programs in general do not operate on the assumptions of rights.

- *Earned benefits—people receive a benefit because they behave in certain ways:* A social contract is common in many countries, reflecting a reciprocity between government responsibility in some areas (e.g., education, public safety, standard of living, child care, health care) and individual responsibility (e.g., good citizenship, compliance with laws and taxation, working to support oneself and one's family) (Zunz, Schoppa, and Hiwatari 2002). In the United States, the social contract and reciprocal social insurance benefits are usually earned through *employment*—working for at least a minimum length of time (Bawden 1989). Social Security is the primary American example in numbers of people, dollars distributed, and antipoverty effect. People must work at least 40 calendar quarters (10 years) to qualify for Social Security benefits when they retire. The earned income tax credit (EITC) is another example, offering low-income workers a cash supplement in the form of a refundable tax credit conditional on having income from employment during the preceding tax year.

- *Charity—benefits are neither earned nor a right:* Receipt of assistance or benefits depends on governmental attitude, usually reflected in program rules and regulations, eligibility criteria, and funding levels. Being "poor enough" is almost always a requirement. Most U.S. safety net programs for vulnerable and disadvantaged people are of this type and are usually referred to as "means-tested" programs because the application procedure assesses whether one's means—income and assets—are low enough to qualify. We designate many U.S. safety net programs as "charity" to reflect the attitudes that surround them—they are offered grudgingly, with suspicion that recipients are not really worthy, and in amounts that are deliberately kept below the level that would meet basic needs—even though those who qualify may be entitled by law to receive their benefits.

A group of people with a particular characteristic might be affected by programs in all three categories. For example, policies for persons with disabilities include earned benefits through the Social Security Disability Insurance component for workers who have contributed enough in Social Security taxes before they become disabled. At the same time, there is a large set of programs and laws, particularly those enacted with the Americans with Disabilities Act, that guarantee disabled persons some important rights in education, health, employment, and other domains. Yet a third set of programs provides disabled people with income and supportive services if they are poor and disabled *enough*—these programs are means tested and fall under the category of charity as we use the term. The three-part categorization provides a useful conceptual framework for thinking about the complex mix of social policies and programs in the United States.

Goals of Safety Net Policies

Now that we have shared some concepts for understanding the characteristics of U.S. safety net programs, we return to a discussion of policy goals and begin to see how American values and philosophical premises have shaped the approaches selected to reach them.

Providing Basic Financial Security

The first goal, providing basic financial security, acknowledges that government has a responsibility to ensure a minimal living standard for people who find themselves impoverished. In the United States, the additional caveat is that those ensured a living must be deserving of public support. That is, financial security may be provided to those who are impoverished through no fault of their own and who are doing, or have done, everything possible to support themselves. In a real sense, U.S.

income assistance and safety net policies are targeted mainly toward "deserving poor" people and operate under the philosophical premise of charity even when they are legal entitlements.

Debate has continued over the years about who is "deserving," resulting in a complex set of program factors that determine who is eligible and under what conditions. Some groups have fairly automatic eligibility for benefits (e.g., the elderly); others have conditions that must be met before they qualify to receive benefits. Conditional eligibility components are a form of social contract, specifying that individuals or families may receive public assistance if they fulfill certain requirements. The requirements may include behavioral or reciprocal activities that in and of themselves ensure that the individual is in fact "deserving" of assistance—being willing to work, participating in specified social services programs, or, most recently for example, guaranteeing that one's children attend school or receive immunizations.

Financial security policies in the United States take the form of both cash and in-kind assistance. The primary forms of cash assistance are Social Security pensions for the elderly; Social Security Disability Insurance for persons who work and contribute to the insurance and then become disabled; Supplemental Security Income (SSI) for low-income elderly, blind, and disabled people; and cash welfare, currently through the Temporary Assistance for Needy Families (TANF) program. The first two are "earned" benefits, while the latter two fall under the premise of charity. In-kind assistance is offered in health care (Medicare for the elderly, *a right;* and Medicaid for the poor, *charity*); food assistance (the Food Stamps Program, *charity*); and rent subsidies or vouchers (housing assistance programs, *charity*).

Progressive tax policies complement direct cash transfers. The federal income tax system, for example, has a redistributive effect because various tax credits and tax deductions are based on income. These include the largest income assistance program in the United States, the refundable earned income tax credit (EITC), which operates as a form of negative income tax for low-income workers, particularly those with children.

Protecting Vulnerable Populations

The second goal of safety net policies is to protect vulnerable populations. In the United States, it is generally accepted that the government has the responsibility to provide support for some groups of people with particular vulnerabilities who are unable to care for themselves. Here again, the most deserving poor and vulnerable are easiest to identify—malnourished children, children at risk of abuse and neglect, abandoned or orphaned children, persons with disabilities that render them unable to care for themselves, and low-income seniors.

Support services and in-kind assistance to vulnerable groups often supplement cash assistance. Child welfare programs, for example, intervene with families in which children are at risk of abuse or neglect, providing family services if appropriate and out-of-home residential placement for children if the family cannot be immediately stabilized. Vouchers for food, nutritional education, and food subsidies for senior centers, schools, and day care centers are provided for the elderly, for children, and for low-income pregnant mothers.

Other vulnerable and destitute groups, such as homeless people—even those who are mentally ill—are more controversial in the United States because some personal behaviors such as alcoholism or drug abuse may make them appear somewhat less deserving.

Promoting Equality of Opportunity

The third goal of safety net policies is promoting equality of opportunity, particularly for those groups or communities that are or have been persistently economically or socially disadvantaged and for those with special circumstances, such as persons with disabilities. Since the 1960s, there is general recognition in the United States that some people, especially those with intergenerational histories of poverty and disadvantage, may need compensatory assistance to survive, thrive, or advance in society. Similarly, some communities such as those with high concentrations of poor persons, high unemployment rates, high shares of substandard housing, or very poorly performing schools may need compensatory assistance in various social or economic areas.

Compensatory policies in the United States include supplemental funding for elementary and secondary education for children living in high-poverty areas, job training programs in communities with high rates of unemployment or where a major business has closed or moved, and community and economic development in places that otherwise are not developing.

Target areas are often defined geographically as those of high and persistent poverty (over 40 percent) or schools with high percentages of poor children. Unlike many other safety net programs, which provide benefits or services directly to individuals and households, programs promoting equality of opportunity tend to go to localities with very high need and to serve all area residents. Primary examples are job training programs (usually run by government training institutes or nongovernmental training or human services organizations), compensatory programs for children in elementary and secondary schools (usually run by local school districts), and community and economic development programs (typically operated by nonprofit or local government agencies).

Policy Mechanisms

Any government has at its disposal a variety of mechanisms it can use to turn policies into practice. The United States uses a range of policy mechanisms for its social programs in general and its social safety net programs in particular. These include the following:

- Income and benefit transfers, mainly monthly cash payments, vouchers, or in-kind benefits
- Insurance (the principal mechanism for Medicare and Medicaid)
- Intergovernmental transfers—block grants or formula grants to state or local governments, often requiring state or local matching funds, which are used to fund services and supports
- Public-private transfers—contracts with nonprofit and for-profit agencies
- Government regulations, such as rules governing nursing homes and child care centers to ensure minimal levels of safety and quality
- Tax strategies, including EITC and other tax credits, to provide incentives to work or attend school
- Provision of direct services such as employment assistance, child care, remedial education, counseling, crisis intervention, or emergency shelter

Many programs use more than one strategy or policy mechanism. For example, Temporary Assistance for Needy Families, the primary welfare program for families with children, provides direct payment of monthly cash grants combined with direct services to assist individuals in obtaining a job as well as child care and other support services to enable a parent to work. In addition, most states have incorporated a benefit formula that provides a financial incentive to work. Financial work incentives are also provided through the separate federal EITC refundable tax credits for workers with low incomes; many states also have similar state tax credits.

Literally hundreds of federally funded programs make up the U.S. social safety net; this chapter has mentioned many of the major ones, and subsequent chapters discuss some in more detail. States and some local jurisdictions also have their own state- or locally funded safety net programs in addition to programs in which they partner with the federal government.

The Major U.S. Safety Net Programs

Table 1.1 summarizes the major U.S. federal safety net and related social programs, showing the philosophical premise on which they are based (right, earned, charity), whether they are universal or targeted to particular groups such as poor people or poor families with children, and whether they are open-ended funding commitments for all eligible people or capped at a specific level regardless of whether the amount covers everyone who qualifies. For programs that began in the Great Depression or later, the table also provides the year the program was first authorized, recognizing that in many cases subsequent legislation has substantially changed the program. The table starts with the only two programs that have a *right* as their philosophical premise (elementary and secondary education and Medicare), then shows several programs for which the philosophical premise is an *earned benefit* (Social Security, the earned income tax credit, and Unemployment Insurance), and continues with the many programs that operate from a means-tested or charity perspective.

For targeted programs, table 1.1 then describes the basis of targeting, which in addition to income may include disability status, age, victimization, or community of residence. Finally, the table shows whether funding for the program is open-ended or capped. Under an open-ended funding arrangement, government has an obligation to provide funding for all who qualify, so program costs are likely to rise in periods of hard economic times when more people will have lower incomes and fall as the economy gets better and incomes rise. The reader may begin to sense from table 1.1 how hard it is to describe U.S. safety net programs simply,

(text continues on page 19)

Table 1.1. Selected Major U.S. Social Programs, Grouped According to Whether They Are Right, Earned, or Means-Tested; Universal or Targeted; or Open-Ended or Capped Federal Funding

Program category	Right, earned, charity	Universal or targeted	Open-ended or capped federal funding
Education			
K–12 school	Right	Universal for school-age children.	Public education is a right; funding is mainly from state and local sources; some capped federal funding is available for special purposes.
Compensatory (1965)	Right	Targeted to localities with high proportions of low-income students.	Capped federal funding is specifically for compensatory education for local districts with high proportions of low-income students; that funding is capped annually.
Health insurance			
Medicare (1965)	Right	Universal for everyone 65 and older.	Open-ended entitlement; mandatory contributions by workers—for all seniors and those receiving SSDI.
Medicaid/SCHIP	Charity/means-tested	Targeted to low-income elderly and disabled adults, TANF recipients, and children.	Open-ended entitlement, federal/state matching funds for all who qualify; some states limit SCHIP enrollment.
Indigent Care	Charity/means-tested	Targeted to low-income without other health insurance, in some states.	State option with state funding; some states do not offer the program.
Social Security programs			
Social Security (1935), SSDI (1935)	Earned	Universal for those with enough quarters of earnings.	Open-ended entitlement for those who qualify based on work and mandatory contributions.

(continued)

Table 1.1. *(Continued)*

Program category	Right, earned, charity	Universal or targeted	Open-ended or capped federal funding
Earned Income Tax Credit (1975)	Earned	Targeted to low-income households, primarily those with children.	Open-ended—federal government has an obligation to provide funding for all who qualify by reason of work and pretax income level; many states have similar and complementary provisions.
Unemployment Insurance	Earned	Targeted to those unemployed who have worked enough in recent quarters in jobs covered by the insurance program.	Open-ended entitlement for those in jobs covered by the insurance and for whom tax contributions were made—employer-funded state trust funds, 26 weeks basic, extended benefits during recessions.
Cash assistance AFDC/TANF (1935/96)	Charity/means-tested	Targeted by individual characteristics (income plus disability or age for SSI).	Open-ended entitlement for families with children below a certain income; federal and state funding.
TANF (after 1996)	Charity/means-tested		Capped federal funding with lifetime eligibility limited to 60 months.
SSI (1974)	Charity/means-tested		Open-ended entitlement, federal funding for low-income blind, elderly, and disabled people.
General assistance			State and/or locally funded and administered cash assistance for poor persons who do not qualify for federal programs; usually open-ended funding but many states do not have programs and make eligibility temporary (e.g., fewer than 12 months per year).

Food

Food Stamps (1964)	Charity/means-tested	Targeted by household characteristics (income, assets, number in household).	Open-ended entitlement for all who qualify; federal funds pay for all benefits, while a federal/state match pays administrative costs.
School lunch/breakfast (1946–66)	Charity/means-tested	Free or reduced-price school meals for children in families whose income is low enough. Also extra resources for schools with high percentage of qualifying children.	Capped federal funds; entitlement for those who qualify; plus distribution of surplus food and other food purchased by the Department of Agriculture.

Housing

Public Housing (1935), project- and tenant-based rental assistance (1968–74), and tenant assistance	Charity/means-tested	Targeted by household characteristics (income in relation to area median income, assets, number in household).	Capped; only enough funding to cover about a third of all who would qualify.
Employment and training	Charity/means-tested	Historically, targeted to lower-skilled persons and displaced workers; now targeted to meeting labor needs of local employers.	Capped.
Child care	Charity/means-tested	Targeted to families with a working parent while on TANF and for some time thereafter, and in some states, to more low-income families.	Capped entitlement. Not enough money, so not all who need get.

(continued)

Table 1.1. *(Continued)*

Program category	Right, earned, charity	Universal or targeted	Open-ended or capped federal funding
Child protective services	Charity, but not means-tested	Targeted to abused and neglected children.	Capped for services; open-ended entitlement for out-of-home placement and foster care.
Special rural programs (health, housing)	Charity	Targeted by type of community and poverty level.	Capped, not entitlements.
Economic development	Charity	Targeted by type of community.	Capped, not entitlements.
Homeless assistance (1987)	Charity	Targeted to homeless people.	Capped, not entitlements.

even for an overview. The table reveals a few of the complex choices involved in responding to need in the context of American values.

Historical Perspective

A brief historical overview of the major safety net programs will help place the discussions in subsequent chapters into context.[2] Policies designed to protect or support needy populations in the United States have their roots in the colonial era. Local communities and new colonial governments were assumed to have responsibility for the poor in their midst. Some adopted "poor relief" approaches similar to those existing in England at the time, including operating homes for the poor or requiring work in exchange for assistance. Initially, community provision of charity was the norm for caring for the poor, particularly for those considered "deserving," such as widows, the elderly, and orphaned children. Over time, as states joined the new federalist nation, constitutions in such states as Indiana, Massachusetts, and New York, among others, included provisions requiring state or local governments (usually counties or municipalities) to assume responsibility for the welfare of poor and destitute people. From the beginning, the federalist structure of the United States produced variation across states in the generosity of support for poor people and the scope of responsibility taken by state and local governments in this arena.

The U.S. Constitution reinforced the primary role of states in many areas of public policy, giving authority to the national government only in specific areas. Article X of the Constitution states that "all powers not delegated to the United States [national government] by the Constitution, nor prohibited by it to the states, are reserved to the states respectively, or to the people." Until the mid-1900s, most safety net policies and responsibilities for the poor rested with states. While recognizing the strong role of states' rights in the United States, however, the preamble to the Constitution also includes among the purposes of the national government the responsibility to "protect the general welfare" as well as to "establish justice" and "provide for the common defense." While the present social safety net system reflects a gradual expansion of the federal role in protecting the general welfare, the important role of states in the federalist structure is also very evident in the cross-state variations that still exist in some safety net programs. A brief discussion of a few of the main historical developments regarding social safety nets provides useful context for understanding the current programs and policy issues addressed later.

Policies for Veterans Came First

The constitutional responsibility for general welfare and defense provided an avenue through which the national government's role in social policy gradually emerged. The first national social and safety net policies were targeted toward war veterans and their families, beginning with a small program for Revolutionary War veterans. As an incentive for men to join the Continental Army during the revolution, the Continental Congress enacted veterans' pensions. Then, in 1811, the U.S. Congress authorized the first hospital and residential facility for disabled veterans, although the states continued to be responsible for their direct medical care and services to veterans (Scokpol 1995).

The national government's role expanded greatly after the Civil War ended in 1865, establishing a fairly large program of benefits for Civil War veterans and their survivors. The aftermath of each subsequent war brought further expansions. After World War I, disability payments, health insurance, and vocational rehabilitation services were added to veterans' pensions and health care. The Servicemen's Readjustment Act of 1944 (known as the G.I. Bill) expanded benefits beyond the safety net to include postsecondary education tuition benefits, job training, housing purchase subsidies, and employment preferences. Together, veterans' pensions and education, rehabilitation, health, and survivors' benefits and services eventually formed the basis of the federal government's social policy sphere, from which subsequent safety net, social advancement, and employment programs evolved for veterans and nonveterans (Patterson 2000; Scokpol 1995).

Aside from veterans' benefits and support, safety net policy remained the responsibility of states and localities throughout the 19th century and into the 20th century. Policies and programs varied across states in their scope of support and assistance. Some states provided cash assistance to poor mothers (mainly widows) or their children, and some did not; some states or localities supported child welfare orphanages and "poor farms" for destitute elderly and disabled people, while others did not.

Race and Inequality

A central theme in any examination of U.S. social policy and safety net programs is race. Although a full treatment of the historical import of race and racism in the United States is beyond the scope of this book, an appreciation of the lingering effects of slavery, racial disparities, and inequality is critical to understanding both the nature of programs and public attitudes toward the poor (Patterson 2000; Scokpol 1995; Trattner 1999).

Our strong federalist and representative structure of government allows a high degree of state autonomy in most policy arenas. As the nation developed and expanded in the 18th and 19th centuries, regional differences in economic and social structures emerged, some of which still exist. The nation was torn apart politically by the issue of slavery, which had been a critical feature of the economic development of the agricultural South as distinct from the emerging industrial North. The abolition of slavery at the end of the Civil War led the way for gradual progress in civil rights, equal opportunity, and racial integration. While the nation has made great progress toward alleviating racism and discrimination and increasing equality and opportunity, much inequality and discrimination still remain, along with an undercurrent of discomfort among policymakers in dealing directly with the problems of racism.

In fact, while cross-state variation in the generosity of public social assistance exists because of the federalist governance structure that gives states considerable autonomy, the variation across states has had the (unintended) effect of contributing to racial inequality in access to social services and benefits. Historically speaking, the nature of American federalism in the post–Civil War era permitted some southern states to adopt laws and policies designed to allow some interests to cling to the prewar economic structure. Some laws curtailed the early advancement of African Americans in the South, including former slaves, who were emerging politically and economically during the period of Reconstruction. On the national front, partisan politics reinforced the resurgence of prewar southern political and economic class lines as both major political parties sought electoral support from the southern states. As indicated in later chapters, many political compromises on social policy throughout the 20th century yielded to states' rights and strengthened regional and state social structures, sometimes to the detriment of poor people and minorities (Scokpol 1995).

Protection for Workers

In the first three decades of the 20th century, many states enacted public social policies related to work in the industrial era, such as workplace safety, minimum wage, and unemployment insurance; placed limits on child labor and made education compulsory; and established income replacement for workers injured on the job. Many policies adopted in a few states gradually expanded across the nation. For example, over half the states enacted workers' compensation laws between 1910 and 1915, under which individuals injured at work or contracting illnesses related to the nature of their job were entitled to financial benefits or reimbursement for medical costs. By 1948 all states had such laws (Patterson 2000; Trattner 1999).

Building on these state-initiated policies, the foundations of the modern national safety net system for poor and vulnerable people began in earnest during the administration of President Franklin D. Roosevelt in the 1930s at the height of the Great Depression. At that time, the national government enacted major social and economic laws, broadly referred to as the New Deal, including Social Security pensions for the elderly and private mortgage insurance for residential property ownership. Two New Deal programs that formed the basis of the expanding national safety net for the poor were the Aid to Dependent Children (ADC) program enacted as part of the Social Security Act of 1935 and housing assistance enacted in the Housing Act of 1937.

Neither ADC nor housing assistance was conceived as "poor relief" at the time of their passage but as support for families who had lost the income of workers or for low-income workers. In an era when women were expected to stay home and raise children, ADC (soon amended to become Aid to Families with Dependent Children, or AFDC) was intended to help them do so when their husbands—the breadwinners—had died or otherwise left the family. Even housing assistance was initially part of a broader set of policies designed to provide public employment for unemployed workers, in this case by expanding the housing production sector through subsidized construction projects. The 1937 act thus authorized public housing (social housing, in European terminology), created local housing authorities, gave them capital resources to construct housing, and provided operating subsidies that helped maintain rent levels affordable to poor working people. To qualify for the subsidized residential units produced, households had to meet an income floor high enough to pay the rent.

Antipoverty and Social and Economic Opportunity

The basic design of most of the safety net programs that exist today was set in the 1960s and 1970s. The social safety net established early in the century, particularly in the 1930s, acknowledged the importance of work to economic livelihood and provided basic support and protection to workers and their dependents. In the latter half of the 20th century, cultural, political, economic, and demographic trends ushered in a new era of social policy in the United States that included policies to reduce poverty and prevent conditions that lead to poverty. Recognition of widespread poverty among family households at a time when the nation was experiencing unprecedented economic growth and prosperity in the post–World War II period prompted enactment of a number of laws and programs, particularly through the Economic Opportunity Act of 1964, that together are often referred to as the War on Poverty. Federal programs supplying or subsidizing child care, social services such as family counseling and crisis intervention, remedial education, and health care for the elderly and disabled were all enacted in their earliest forms during the 1960s. To ensure an educated workforce and maintain the nation's economic competitiveness, the federal government expanded its role in elementary and secondary education, provided financial aid for low-income students to attend college, and funded job training and retraining. The civil rights movement, which began in the early 1960s, led to the subsequent expansion of laws prohibiting discrimination in employment, housing, education, and other areas.

A watershed year in the War on Poverty was 1965, when Medicare for the elderly and Medicaid for poor and disabled people became the nation's chief publicly funded health insurance programs. Medicare, along with simultaneous administrative improvements and benefit expansions in Social Security, greatly reduced poverty, hardship, and risk among elderly citizens. These developments left children, especially those in female-headed households and ethnic minorities, as the largest poor group in the United States, which they remain today.

During the 1970s and thereafter, the main public assistance programs for the poor—AFDC, Food Stamps, and Medicaid—grew and changed as the categories of people entitled to benefits expanded greatly and as experience with programs suggested the need for change or reform. For instance, the Kennedy and Johnson administrations in the 1960s initiated food vouchers as a pilot program in 1961 and codified it into law in 1964, with a requirement that a household purchase a certain amount of food stamps whose value expanded when they were redeemed in grocery stores. Recognizing that many poor households eligible for food stamps did not use the program because they could not afford the stamps even at the low cost set by the government, 1977 legislation eliminated the purchase requirement and thus opened the program to greatly expanded enrollment.

The 1970s also saw the greatest expansion and change in housing assistance, both in number of households covered and in assistance mechanisms. Income floors were eliminated and various forms of certificates and vouchers for housing creation or rental assistance were introduced rather than funding only housing owned and operated by public housing authorities. In the short run, "tenant-based" strategies were more cost-effective on a per unit basis because they did not involve construction costs. But one consequence was that the government largely got out of the business of producing affordable housing, contributing to today's crisis of affordable housing as one result.

Thus, the expansion of social policies in the 1960s and 1970s was broad, not limited to antipoverty and safety net programs. The antipoverty programs intermingled social safety net strategies with economic opportunity and social insurance strategies for poor and nonpoor alike, vulnerable or not. Food Stamps and Medicaid for the poor were enacted along with Medicare for all elderly people. Child care, youth development programs, and neighborhood and community programs targeted mainly the poor, and new federal financial aid was established for higher education for students of all incomes.

As discussed in the next chapter, these poverty reduction and prevention goals have only been partly reached. But the policies introduced in the 1960s and 1970s undoubtedly form the basis of today's complex and interwoven social policy system that includes social insurance, employment security, equal opportunity, and social safety nets.

Efforts to Reform or Reshape Social Welfare

The expansion of programs in the 1960s and 1970s and the complex set of benefit formulas, incentives, and eligibility rules raised increasing concerns. Were the programs effective, particularly since poverty seemed to persist? Were the eligibility rules the right ones? How fair was it to allow welfare mothers to stay home with their children when more and more mothers in society were working? Were there unintended negative consequences, such as the increasing number of children born out of wedlock or the high concentrations of poverty in inner cities? We examine the facts related to these questions in chapter 2. Before doing that, however, we examine how the questions themselves increasingly began to stimulate attempts to reform policies in the 1980s and early 1990s, with a focus on two examples, welfare reform and "last resort" emergency and crisis intervention programs. Reforms in both areas resulted partly from social, economic, and budgetary trends in the nation as a whole. As the country moved toward perhaps well-intended reforms, various unintended policy challenges emerged.

Soon after the major expansions in social policies in the 1960s and 1970s, important social and demographic trends affected how elected officials and the general public viewed some of the programs, particularly those under the rubric of the War on Poverty. Some of these trends and shifts in public attitude eventually culminated in reforms introduced in the 1980s and 1990s that in some ways attempted to reverse or redefine the program expansions.

The first important trend was the continuing increase in women's participation in the labor force that had begun during World War II and rapidly increased in the 1970s. In 1998, about 60 percent of women over the age of 16 were in the labor force, compared to about 38 percent of women in 1950 (Mosisa and Hipple 2006). Political and popular support for allowing poor women to stay home with their children and receive welfare payments deteriorated as more and more mothers in the general population were working even when they had pre-school-age children.

Second, caseloads in the AFDC program, originally enacted to assist widows and their children, increased exponentially and by the 1960s consisted mainly of divorced or never-married women and their children. The number of single-parent families, divorce rates, and nonmarital childbearing had increased substantially. In 1968, about 12 percent of children under 18 lived with just one parent; the rate has steadily increased so that by 2005 about a third of all children lived with only one parent (U.S. Bureau of the Census 2004). Some observers expressed concern that the welfare rules and incentives were partly to blame for the high rates of welfare dependency and nonmarital childbearing.

Third, in the last quarter of the 20th century, a wave of immigration from Central and South America, especially Mexico, as well as from many other countries, created an impact on the country equivalent to the massive European immigration of the 1880s through the 1910s (Borjas 2007).

The characteristics of workers, particularly low-wage workers, and the poor had changed. Some observers argued that the generous welfare state was attracting illegal immigrants.

Fourth, geographic and spatial shifts in residential patterns occurred, leaving high concentrations of persistently poor persons in economically declining old industrial inner-cities and new employment and middle-income populations in suburban areas and in the South and Southwest. Urban decay was a visible sign to some that the massive investment of the 1960s and 1970s in poor communities and persons had not been effective.

Finally, double-digit inflation in the late 1970s was fueled by escalating housing costs, plus other factors, that continued to rise without apparent regard to economic cycles until about 2008. Housing cost increases have changed the distribution of household expenses, with the greatest impact on poor households that had to spend increasing proportions of their income for housing but were not entitled to any subsidy to offset those outlays. High inflation along with the end of the post–World War II economic boom also posed serious fiscal problems for federal and state government budgets.

In response to these trends, challenges, and constraints, a number of significant public policy developments related to social policy, antipoverty strategies, and social safety net programs occurred.

Reforming "Welfare"

While welfare, meaning cash assistance benefits, is not the only safety net policy, its history exemplifies the nation's shifting priorities and values regarding social assistance and family support. Cash assistance is also often the focus of attention when the public starts to criticize people who receive government help, even though it is by no means the most expensive government program in the social safety net. Since the AFDC program was enacted in 1935, numerous reforms have occurred, some expanding coverage and scope and others changing services offered to recipients and expectations required of them. AFDC was established as an entitlement program, meaning any family with children that met the established criteria (mainly based on low income) received cash assistance. Until the 1950s, states determined who was eligible for AFDC and how policies were implemented. Great variation existed across states, both in how families qualified for assistance and how much assistance they got if they did qualify.

In the 1950s and 1960s, national welfare reforms expanded the role of the federal government, which assumed much of the cost of the cash benefits and related social services such as child care. States continued to have discretion in setting the amount of the benefits and the income cutoff for qualifying, but the federal government's funding of food stamps and social services tended to smooth out some of the variation in total benefits across states.

Although efforts to reform welfare began in the late 1960s, major national reform, described in chapter 3, did not come about until 1996. Reform proposals offered by both Republican and Democratic administrations that attempted to enact policies to guarantee income or jobs were regularly defeated (Burke and Burke 1974; Cottingham and Ellwood 1989; Katz 1989). But some changes made between the mid-1960s and the mid-1990s gradually strengthened work requirements as a condition of receiving welfare, reinforcing long-standing American beliefs about both individual responsibility and the centrality and value of work for achieving social dignity and economic success. Welfare reforms in 1968 added financial and nonfinancial incentives to encourage welfare recipients to work, including education and training, child care services, and earned-income incentives. The first work *requirements* were added in 1972; recipients of AFDC whose youngest child was at least six years old were required to register and cooperate with Work Incentive (WIN) programs that operated in all states to prepare individuals for employment and place them in jobs. Later, in the 1970s, the earned income tax credit was enacted as part of the nation's income tax system to reinforce the importance of work and reward working. During the 1980s, the Reagan administration further strengthened work requirements, added financial penalties for not complying, and for the first time allowed states to require welfare parents to work in exchange for their welfare check (i.e., "workfare").

The work and work requirement programs in the 1980s and early 1990s were precursors to the first major welfare reform legislation in 60 years. Temporary Assistance for Needy Families was established in 1996, replacing the 60-year-old AFDC program. Unlike AFDC, TANF is not an entitlement. Instead, it is time limited (five years in a lifetime), and it is a block grant from the federal government to the states, meaning that the federal government funding levels are capped at the established block-grant funding level rather than being open-ended as they had been for the entitlement nature of AFDC.

The changes introduced with TANF have had major effects on the social safety net: no longer are poor families with children guaranteed public assistance. Work, not welfare, is considered the core of the safety net. Individual effort is stressed, requiring individual welfare recipients to assume more responsibility for searching for work than in the past. Some public supports for workers can continue in the form of health insurance, child care, and food assistance for some (usually short) period of time. This work emphasis and the practices established to support working raise anew many critical concerns, discussed in chapter 3, about the changes in the industrial structure of the U.S. economy, the nature of work, the balance of work and family responsibilities, and work-based employee benefits, such as health insurance, education and tuition assistance, and retirement plans.

Reshaping "Last Resort" Programs

Unlike TANF and other cash and benefit assistance programs for the poor, "last resort" public programs, such as child welfare and emergency and crisis services (e.g., for homeless people and those with serious mental illness or substance abuse problems), have not followed a steady path of development. But they, too, offer examples of how policies intended to solve one set of problems may give rise to new problems.

Children's homes and orphanages, for example, became common in the United States after the Civil War, which orphaned large numbers of children. State mental institutions housed many ill and disabled people when families or communities could not care for them. Many small towns had vagrants or itinerant hobos temporarily or permanently living near roads and railroad tracks, evoking an almost idealistic counterculture image of freewheeling wanderers. Economic distress, the hardships of urban industrialization, and the resulting urban slums, however, made the problems of neglected children and homelessness much more visible and urgent. Local organizations such as the Children's Aid Societies in the 1800s, for example, embarked on nationwide efforts to raise awareness of the plight of neglected and orphaned children, adapting strategies that had been applied to protect animals from cruelty. Other groups and church organizations initiated early versions of foster homes, relocating impoverished children from urban slums to families in other communities and smaller towns. Private and religiously affiliated rescue missions and soup kitchens became active in the cities, providing the most basic services to alcohol-ravaged vagrants on city streets.

Policies and safety nets for vulnerable children and homeless people each in its own way received new federal attention and investment beginning in the 1960s, in response to the increased consciousness about the problems. While well intended, policies in both areas uncovered new problems, child welfare policy priorities increasingly shifted to the importance of family reunification whenever possible, rather than placing children into orphanages, resulting in complex and bureaucratic public systems of temporary foster care and family services. And a movement to deinstitutionalize people with mental illness in favor of more community-based arrangements, which started in earnest in the mid-1960s with the availability of Medicaid to help pay for it, had the unintended consequence of moving large numbers of persons with mental health and substance abuse problems from hospitals to unprepared communities, where many ended up homeless.

Social policy discussions of the 1960s and 1970s were mainly about the government's responsibility for alleviating poverty and increasing economic opportunity. In a real sense, the policy deliberations at the beginning of the 21st century recall previous eras much more than they do the 1960s and 1970s. They are focused on individual and community responsibility for improving one's own situation, work as a route off of welfare and out of poverty, and funding for social services and income support only for those who cannot work and for emergency and crisis intervention for those at risk of harm or victims of neglect and abuse. The ways that some of these policies have changed, particularly the reforms adopted since the 1970s, are the focus of chapter 3. Before describing those, chapter 2 provides an overview of poverty and poverty-related issues, since reducing or eliminating poverty and its effects is the central goal of social safety net policies and programs.

2

Poverty

U.S. social safety net policy aims primarily to alleviate poverty, help poor people, and compensate for disadvantages arising from poverty. In chapter 1, we examined the history and initial motivations for the major U.S. social safety net programs. Before we review the major changes in these programs during the past decade, which we do in chapter 3, let us take the time to understand important aspects of poverty in the United States, including its various definitions, how it is measured, and key recent trends. Of particular importance are childhood poverty and the feminization of poverty, issues related to the working poor, and geographic areas of concentrated poverty or concentrated problem behaviors.

What Is Poverty?

Most people intrinsically understand what it means to be poor, which serves well enough for everyday discourse. These understandings will differ from person to person and also from place to place and time to time. Some will define poverty in terms of money; others, in terms of access to food, shelter, and other necessities; and still others, in terms of community resources or social pathologies. But administrators of social safety net programs need to know whom to serve; they need a definition of their target group precise enough to allow staff to interview an applicant

NEW YORK INSTITUTE OF
TECHNOLOGY

and know whether or not that person is eligible for assistance under the program. Getting to such a precise definition is not simple, either conceptually or operationally.

Two broad approaches to poverty definition and measurement can be summarized as "income based" and "consumption based." Official poverty measurement in the United States has always focused on income. Both approaches are ultimately concerned with the well-being of some households relative to others. But one assumes that the amount of cash income a household brings in during a year is a good index of well-being, and the other recognizes that much income in the informal economy is not reported and that access to basic necessities such as food and shelter may not always come through purchase. Definitions of poverty that include the value of goods and services, such as food and health care, provided by government programs begin to look more like consumption-based definitions. We look first at the official definition of poverty in the United States and then at some alternative definitions and their consequences.

Oddly, federal law in the United States has never established a universal meaning of *poverty* or *need* for social safety net programs. For example, the 1935 statute establishing Aid to Dependent Children, the program that epitomizes "welfare," conditioned eligibility on the absence of a parent and spoke of "needy families." But the statute left the definition of need up to the states, where it resides to this day, despite countless program changes, including the program's demise and replacement by Temporary Assistance for Needy Families.

The Official U.S. Poverty Definition

The definition of poverty—and its translation into the poverty thresholds and poverty guidelines that drive practice in today's social safety net programs—was developed at the Social Security Administration by Mollie Orshansky in 1963 and 1964 to assess economic well-being and risk, purposes quite different from the uses to which they are now put (Fisher 1997). Federal government agencies had created many earlier versions of minimum budgets, minimum market baskets, and the like for specific uses, starting in 1905 (Fisher 1996), but none became an official governmentwide measure until Orshansky's.

Orshansky started with data from a U.S. Department of Agriculture survey on food expenditures conducted in 1955 showing that households used about a third of their annual after-tax household income for food purchases. She then consulted several food plans the department had developed and selected two, the "low-cost" and the more stringent "economy" food plans, to determine the actual dollar value of the food that would be needed to eat according to these plans. She calculated these costs for families of different size, age composition, and residence (farm/nonfarm) and then multiplied these costs by three to reach two sets of poverty thresholds, one set based on the low-cost plan and the other based on the economy plan. She also consulted a 1960–61 national survey of household expenditures conducted by the Department of Labor, which showed food costs at about one-fourth of after-tax household expenditures rather than one-third. She decided to go with multiplying by three rather than four (Fisher 1997), with the long-term consequence that the poverty threshold for future generations remains 25 percent lower than if she had chosen to multiply by four.

Shortly after Orshansky published her thresholds in 1963, many new federal programs were enacted to address and alleviate poverty and provide a social safety net, including Medicaid, Supplemental Security Income, major revisions to the Food Stamp Program, and the many programs under the auspices of the Office of Economic Opportunity (OEO). All of these programs needed guidelines to determine whom to serve. In 1965, OEO adopted Orshansky's lower set of thresholds—based on the economy food plan—as its working definition of poverty. By 1969, the Bureau of the Budget had declared slightly revised poverty thresholds derived from the economy food plan to be the federal government's official definition of poverty.

The poverty threshold varies by age, number of persons in the household, and number of children, with the threshold increasing for households with more children or other family members. Poverty thresholds also vary by household type; for instance, households with only elderly members are assumed to need less food and accordingly are assigned a lower poverty threshold. For a number of years, the cost of the economy food plan was recalculated annually, and poverty thresholds were adjusted accordingly. But since 1969, the thresholds have simply been adjusted for inflation based on the consumer price index (CPI).

What poverty thresholds do *not* do is vary by local cost of living. Poverty is defined in exactly the same way everywhere in the country. A family of three comprising a parent and two children that earned less than $16,242 in 2006, $16,705 in 2007, or $17,600 in 2008 was officially poor, but the case is easily made that such a family living in a small rural community in

a home without a mortgage or rent expense is likely to be materially better off than the same family living in a very high-cost city, such as New
York or Los Angeles.

Most U.S. safety net programs still establish their eligibility for benefits in relation to these poverty thresholds, even though few use the
threshold itself as their eligibility cutoff.[1] Housing assistance is the major
exception, as described below. Every year, the Bureau of the Census calculates poverty thresholds and issues poverty rates based on data collected
through the Current Population Survey. Questions based on this definition are built into data collection in numerous other surveys. The method
has prevailed, with occasional small revisions, despite the many issues
associated with this way of calculating poverty thresholds and the numerous reviews by commissions and task forces that have recommended
changes (two recent ones are Citro and Michaels 1995; Ruggles 1990).

Alternative Poverty Definitions

Anything as challenging to a society as poverty, and as central to policymaking, is bound to generate controversy (Blank 2008). Eligibility for billions of public dollars hinges on household poverty status. Legislative and
executive decisions about increasing or decreasing investment in safety net
programs depend on perceptions of whether poverty is getting better or
worse and whether particular program configurations are contributing to
the change. Since high and rising poverty rates tend to elicit stronger public response while low and dropping rates may trigger reductions in safety
net programs, a lot is riding on such definitions and measurement. With
that in mind, we briefly consider some alternative definitions and discuss
their implications.

Modified Inflation Adjustment

One alternative poverty definition derives from a technical change in the
way inflation is measured. As noted above, since 1969, poverty thresholds
have been adjusted annually in relation to inflation rather than to the
actual cost of food. In 1983, the Bureau of Labor Statistics changed the way
it calculated the housing component of inflation to reduce the sharp
annual increases in the inflation rate that had resulted from the rapidly
increasing value of home sales.[2] Using the new formula to calculate poverty
thresholds reduces the number of people considered poor and hence

affects poverty rates. This technical adjustment produces a poverty rate approximately 1.4 percentage points lower than the official rate. Using adjusted rates instead of the original rates, without any other changes in program rules or regulations, fewer low-income households qualified for public programs. Therefore, states and localities received fewer federal dollars, since their allocation depends on the number of poor people within a jurisdiction or sometimes on the poverty rate. It is easy to see why state and local interests would resist such a change and why some national politicians might favor it.

Increasing What Is Counted as Income

Other definitions of poverty derive from expanding the items included as income. All such items increase income and thereby reduce the number of people considered poor. Official poverty calculations include only earned cash income and exclude cash income from government transfer payments, such as cash assistance (welfare), workers' compensation, or Unemployment Insurance. Some have argued that income used to determine whether a household is above or below the poverty line should include such cash transfers (Blank 2008; Cellini, McKernan, and Ratcliffe 2008). Others argue that *all* government cash transfers should be included, whether they come from safety net programs (e.g., welfare, cash aid to the blind and disabled poor, EITC) or social insurance (e.g., Social Security, Unemployment Insurance, veterans' benefits). Still others argue for including all income enhancements reported to the Internal Revenue Service, including capital gains, interest, and dividends, although including such items would not have much effect on poverty levels because few people in or close to poverty have much income from those sources. Since none of these alternatives involve raising the actual dollar value of poverty thresholds and all propose to count at least some income in addition to what is now counted, all would result in classifying fewer households as poor.

A third approach would include the cash value of noncash benefits, including those for which a household must meet low-income eligibility criteria (e.g., food stamps, Medicaid, free or reduced-price school breakfasts and lunches, and rental or housing assistance) and those with no income limits (e.g., Medicare or the value of employer-provided health insurance).

Rather than accepting them as definitions of poverty, we may best use these alternative measures to show the poverty-reducing effects of the different social insurance and safety net programs. Such effects become clearer as we look at the poverty gap, which we discuss below.

Absolute or Relative Poverty?

An *absolute* poverty threshold does not change in "real" dollars from year to year, although its nominal dollar level changes through adjustments to reflect rises in the cost of living or inflation. The real purchasing power of the dollars is presumed to stay the same. The federal poverty line in the United States is thus an absolute measure of poverty. While a *relative* poverty threshold would change to account for inflation, it would also change in real terms as standards of living or average wealth changed. A relative poverty line would be higher in real terms in 2008 than it was in 1965 because standards of living and real disposable per capita income have expanded in those 40 plus years, and it takes more money now to keep the lowest rungs of the household income ladder in the same *general* position relative to the top rungs as they were in 1965.

In arguing for various ways to update and change the way that poverty is calculated in the United States, some policy analysts have proposed making the measure a relative one. In fact, until the Orshansky poverty thresholds became official federal policy in 1965, numerous poverty lines had been calculated for policy purposes from 1905 through the early 1960s. Fisher (1996) summarizes the ways these poverty lines changed in real terms, with the "minimum budget" rising 0.75 percent for every 1 percent rise in real disposable per capita income. Only with the Orshansky approach and its subsequent adoption by the Bureau of the Budget did the meaning of poverty in the United States become absolute, with the consequence that people qualifying as poor today are considerably *more poor* relative to other households than they were four or five decades ago.

Another way of thinking about poverty as relative or absolute notes that most poor people in the United States enjoy a standard of living far higher than that of the poorest people in most other countries in the world. The U.S. poverty threshold in 2008 was $17,600 a year for a family of three, in contrast to incomes of $100 to $300 a year for the poorest people in the poorest developing countries. In that sense, the U.S. poverty line is relative, because it defines what it takes to provide a family in this country with the "minimum necessities" of a standard of living far higher than that in most other countries.

For Housing, a Different Approach

The U.S. Department of Housing and Urban Development (HUD) does not use "poverty" as the determinant of eligibility for its housing assistance programs. Recognizing that housing is probably the biggest cost item in a family's budget and that housing prices vary dramatically across communities, HUD uses a *relative* measure of well-being to determine eligibility. It calculates the median income of all households in an area and establishes eligibility as incomes below 80, 50, or 30 percent of area median income (AMI), depending on the program. On average, official poverty thresholds approximate about 30 percent of AMI. But in some wealthy communities, the federal poverty line would be around 15 percent of AMI, while in others with high poverty rates, someone at 45 or 50 percent of AMI would be poor by federal definition. Just as HUD eligibility criteria are pegged to the local cost of living, its benefits are geared to local housing costs and helping households to afford "fair market rents," which HUD calculates and publishes annually for each local area.

This approach to eligibility determination produces a more realistic benefit. It cannot be used to produce national poverty figures, however, since all AMIs are relative. To assess housing problems, therefore, HUD researchers calculate "worst-case housing needs" and the level of resources needed to alleviate them. Most households with worst-case housing needs qualify because their income is at or below 50 percent of AMI and they spend half or more of it for housing. About 4.9 million households had worst-case housing needs in 2003, a proportion that had not changed significantly for the previous decade. The situation had worsened considerably by 2005 (the latest year available), however, when 5.5 million households were judged to be "worst cases"—an increase of 12 percent in just two years after a decade of stability (HUD 2005, 2007).

The relative approach that HUD uses to identify the low-income population eligible for its programs is similar to that used in cross-national studies of income and well-being. In the data from the Luxembourg Income Study covering many of the world's developed nations, for example, the threshold for poverty is the proportion of a population or subpopulation living in a household whose income is 40 percent or less of the national median household income. Thus, poverty is defined relative to the standard of living in each country, as indicated by the income of the median household in that country.

How Much Poverty?

Using the official poverty thresholds, the Bureau of the Census routinely publishes information about how many people are poor, their character-istics, and poverty rates for different groups. Figure 2.1 shows fluctuations in the number of people in poverty (top line) and the poverty rate (bot-tom line), from 1959 through 2008 (U.S. Bureau of the Census 2009). Also shown, as gray bars, are periods of recession, during which the num-ber of people in poverty generally increases as people lose jobs and are unable to find others. At the beginning of this period, 39.5 million peo-ple were poor, constituting 22.4 percent of the population. Both numbers and rates had dropped dramatically by the mid-1960s, aided by changes in Social Security that moved many elderly people out of poverty and by generally strong economic times. Figure 2.1 shows the rates fluctuating between 11 and 15 percent of the population. They stayed around 11 or 12 percent throughout the 1970s, but by the early 1980s both the number of people in poverty and the poverty rate increased, not falling to below 12 percent again until 1999. Poverty rates at or above 15 percent were seen in 1982 and 1983 and again in 1993. The economic downturn of the past few years is showing up in poverty statistics, as might be expected; the

Figure 2.1. Number in Poverty and Poverty Rate: 1959 to 2008

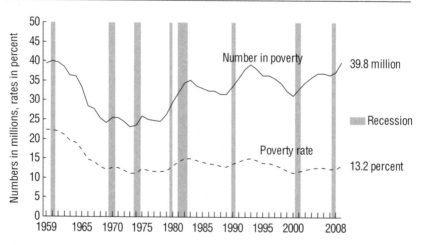

Source: U.S. Census Bureau, http://www.census.gov/hhes/www/poverty/poverty08/pov08fig04.pdf.

poverty rate for 2008 stood at 13.2 percent, up from 11.3 percent as recently as 2000; it is likely to rise again in 2009.

Figure 2.2 shows poverty rates by age, revealing the contribution of poverty reduction mechanisms among people age 65 and older to the substantial drop in poverty rates between 1959 and 1970. Today, people 65 years and older enjoy the lowest poverty rates of any age group in the United States. Children were *less* likely to be poor in the 1960s than seniors, but that situation had reversed itself by 1974. Now children are almost twice as likely as seniors to be poor, and that situation is an improvement over what prevailed during the 1980s and 1990s.

The Poverty Gap

Identifying a person or household as having income on one side or the other of an official poverty "line" is one way to think about poverty. But it does not reveal the depth of poverty—how far below the line a person's or household's income is. Nor does it adequately identify the number of people who may be just over the line but who still experience considerable material hardship.

Figure 2.2. Poverty Rates by Age: 1959 to 2008

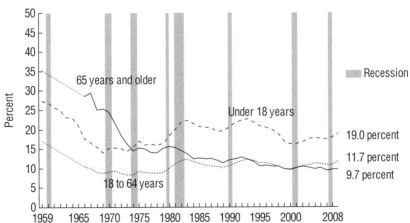

Source: U.S. Census Bureau, http://www.census.gov/hhes/www/poverty/poverty08/pov08fig04.pdf.

Note: Data for people age 18 to 64 and 65 and older are not available from 1960 to 1965.

One way to describe the depth or intensity of poverty is to use fractions of the poverty level to describe a population—for instance, looking at how many have incomes below 50 percent of poverty (often referred to as "deep poverty"), between 100 and 150 percent of poverty, and so on.

Table 2.1 shows this distribution for all people in families and in female-headed families in 2006, for all races and ethnicities combined. The table reveals considerable depth of poverty for all families, with 19 percent of all families below poverty having incomes of no more than 50 percent of poverty. For female-headed families the situation is far more extreme, with half of all such families who are poor reporting incomes that are only half the poverty level.

Another way to characterize the depth of poverty is to calculate the "poverty gap"—how much it would take to bring all households with below-poverty incomes up to the poverty line. If all households below poverty are only a little below poverty, the poverty gap will be small. But it will be huge if substantial numbers have little or no income. Difficult economic times also cause the poverty gap to increase, as more households find themselves with below-poverty incomes.

The U.S. House Committee on Ways and Means was one of the first to use analyses of the poverty gap in assessing the effectiveness of social

Table 2.1. Intensity of Poverty for All People in Families and for People in Female-Headed Families, 2006

Income-to-poverty ratio	All People in Families		People in Families with Female Head, No Husband Present	
	Percentage	Cumulative percentage	Percentage	Cumulative percentage
Below 50%	4.2	4.2	14.5	14.5
Below 75%	7.3	11.5	8.7	23.2
Below 100%	10.6	22.1	7.3	30.5
Below 125%	14.6	37.6	8.3	38.8
Below 150%	18.7	55.4	6.6	45.4
Below 200%	27.6	83	12.2	57.6
200% or more	17	100.0	42.4	100.0

Source: U.S. Bureau of the Census, Detailed Poverty Tables 2006, based on August 2007 Current Population Survey; calculations from several tables.

programs—from cash assistance to social insurance to earned income credits—in reducing the gap. From 1979 to 1996, the number of people in poverty based on reported cash income before government transfers fluctuated between 42.8 million and 60.4 million. The poverty gap during the same years fluctuated between about $140 million and $205 million (in constant 1996 dollars), meaning it would have taken additional transfers of $140–205 million per year to bring all poor households up to the poverty line. The amount of money *per poor person* needed to eliminate the poverty gap varied between about $3,300 and $3,450 during the same years (U.S. House of Representatives, Committee on Ways and Means 1998, Appendix H, Table H-23).

Poverty gap analysis has been used to understand program impacts when the simple indicator of having income above or below the poverty line is insensitive to important changes. For instance, Porter and Dupree (2001) used poverty gap analysis to assess the impact on household income of movement into the labor force before and after welfare reform and the parallel loss of public benefits for single mothers with children. They conclude that though single mothers with children moved into the labor force and off of cash welfare assistance in unprecedented numbers in the years following welfare reform, they did not materially increase their economic situation. And the Department of Health and Human Services, Office of Family Assistance, used several alternative measures of the poverty gap to show the amount of money it would have taken to raise all poor families with children out of poverty each year from 1991 through 2003 in its seventh annual report to Congress on the Temporary Assistance to Needy Families program (Office of Family Assistance 2007).

How Little Is Too Little?

The concept of *poverty* suggests that those in a poor household do not have enough resources to provide themselves with basic necessities. So far, this chapter has reviewed the derivation of the U.S. poverty standard, its income base, and its invariance in the face of diverse local conditions or changes in the composition of household expenditures over time; has proposed alternative definitions of absolute and relative poverty; and has presented the concept of a poverty gap. Another way to look at poverty is to ask where to draw the poverty line from a consumption perspective—that is, are basic needs being met? How much money do people need for food and shelter? The National Survey of America's Families provides evidence for addressing that question (Nelson 2004, and special data runs for single-parent households with incomes below 100 percent of poverty).

Among single-parent households with incomes below 100 percent of poverty, 61 percent reported food hardship in 2002, and 39 percent reported housing hardship. Food hardship was measured by questions about running out of food or cutting the size of meals because the household did not have enough money to buy food; housing hardship was measured by questions about ability to pay the rent, mortgage, or utilities. Households indicating those problems in the 12 months before being surveyed were considered to be in a hardship situation. Low-income single-parent households—those with incomes up to 200 percent of poverty—reported basically the same hardship levels as households that had below-poverty income. With 59 percent of those low-income single-parent families reporting food hardship and 35 percent reporting housing hardship, problems in acquiring basic necessities clearly affect not only officially poor households but also those households with incomes up to twice the poverty level. Low-income (up to 200 percent of poverty) married-parent households fared only slightly better, with 46 percent reporting food hardship and 23 percent reporting housing hardship in 2002. From a consumption perspective, then, the "poverty" line should be drawn considerably higher, possibly as much as twice as high as it now is.

Poverty Duration and Distribution

Other than the sheer amount of poverty at any given time in the United States, several other aspects of poverty have concerned policymakers interested in reducing poverty (Blank 2008; Cellini et al. 2008; Mincy 1994). These aspects include, first, transitions in and out of poverty, duration of poverty spells, persistent poverty, and poverty across generations; and, second, geography-related issues, such as areas of concentrated poverty (e.g., locales where 40 percent or more of households are poor) and concentrations of negative or problem behaviors.

Length of Poverty Spells

If poverty is only a short-term situation for a household, it may be able to move out of poverty on its own, without assistance from government programs. But if poverty is a long-term condition, intervention and support by government programs may be able to break the pattern and help families leave poverty. If poverty is multigenerational, with children most likely to experience the same very low income levels as their parents and grandparents, even greater thought must be given to the types of interventions that could break that cycle.

Spell Length

Many people assume that poverty is a *trait* of those who are poor—a long-lasting condition that reflects something basic about the people who are in it. The evidence for length of poverty spells, however, shows otherwise. Most spells of poverty are quite short, lasting considerably less than a year, and only a very few people remain poor for very long periods of time. Iceland (2003) provides the basic data on the length of poverty spells for the last half of the 1990s, based on the longitudinal Survey of Income and Program Participation (SIPP). Ruggles and Williams (n.d.), analyzing data from the same survey a decade earlier, find similar patterns, although the absolute proportion of people with various spell lengths differs.

Figure 2.3 shows how long the average spell of poverty lasted for American households from January 1996 through December 1999, a period of four complete years.[3] It is obvious from figure 2.3 that most spells of

Figure 2.3. Duration of Poverty Spells

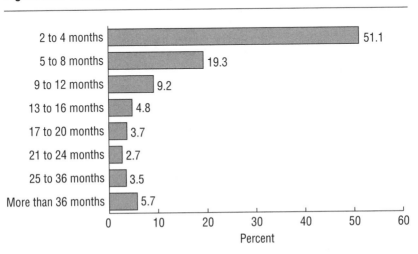

Source: Iceland (2003), figure 8.

Note: Excludes spells underway during the first interview month.

poverty are short—slightly more than half lasted four months or less, and only one in five lasted more than a year. Figure 2.4 shows the median length of a poverty spell in the years 1996 through 1999, for all households and broken out by various household characteristics. Spells for black and Hispanic households tended to be longer than spells for white non-Hispanic households, as did spells experienced by female householders.

The proportion of people in persistent poverty (poor during all months of the four-year study period) was very much smaller than the proportion experiencing at least one poverty spell during the same four years (2.0 versus 34.2 percent). Figure 2.5 shows that even among the subgroups most likely to experience persistent poverty, less than 6 percent of households were poor at all times during the four-year period 1996 through 1999.

Nevertheless, among people who *were* poor in 1996, about half (50.5 percent) were still poor in 1999 (Iceland 2003, figure 11). White

Figure 2.4. Median Length of Poverty Spells, 1996–1999

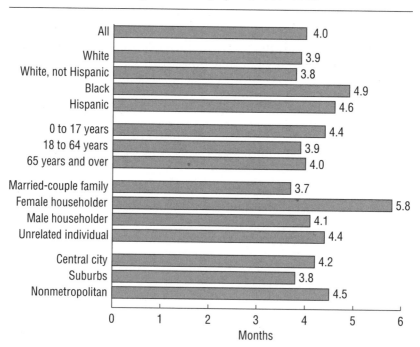

Source: Iceland (2003), figure 9.

Note: Excludes spells under way during the first interview month.

Figure 2.5. Chronic Poverty Rates: 1996–1999

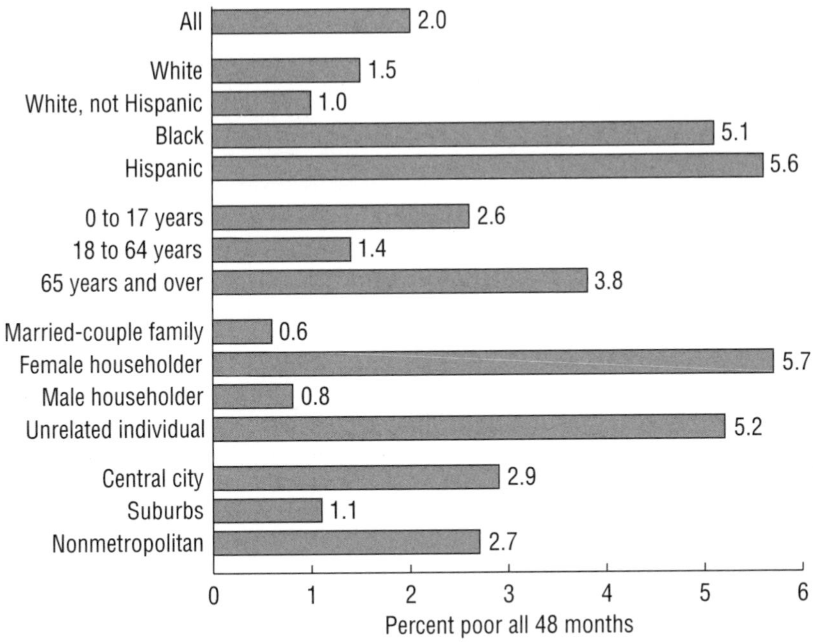

Source: Iceland (2003), figure 7.

non-Hispanic households were least likely to be poor during the entire four years (42.9 percent), while about 58 percent of black and Hispanic households were likely to be poor for the whole period.

Because the 1996–99 period saw unprecedented economic growth and reduction in the overall poverty rate, one might think that these favorable economic circumstances would affect spell length. But the basic patterns are remarkably stable. For example, Ruggles and Williams (n.d.) used SIPP data to estimate spell lengths from September 1983 through April 1986—a 32-month period during which the economy was not especially dynamic. For this period, more than a decade earlier than the Iceland (2003) analysis, median spell length was about four months when the same poverty definition as Iceland (income below poverty level for at least two months, then above poverty for at least two months) was used—essentially the same median length that Iceland (2003) reported. In addition, the same 80 percent of households with a poverty spell had left poverty within two years. That pattern held, even with alternative definitions, including one in which income had to either increase by one-half or reach a level of 125 percent of poverty and be sustained for at least two months before counting as an exit from poverty.

Cellini at al. (2008) review and summarize the results of more than 30 analyses covering more than 30 years that use longitudinal datasets to address three questions, including, what is the duration of poverty? That seemingly simple question has multiple meanings, many of which researchers have explored. In answer to the related question—how long does a spell of poverty last?—results of those studies are remarkably consistent in showing that most people who enter a spell of poverty leave it very quickly. When monthly data are used, median spell lengths are between four and five months, as we saw above with Iceland's analysis of SIPP data. Furthermore, how long an individual stays poor is related to how long he or she has already been poor; if a person has been poor only a short while, he or she is much more likely to leave poverty quickly (making the entire spell short) than the person who has been poor for a long time.

In answer to the question, how long are people poor?—which takes account of the fact that some people move in and out of poverty multiple times over a span of years—analyses show that about 30 percent are poor less than one year and about twice as many are poor less than four years. A final question explored by several analyses reviewed by Cellini et al. (2008) is, what are the odds that a person will have experienced poverty as an adult (starting at age 25) by the time he or she is 30 or 50 years old? Studies by Rank and Hirschl (2001) indicate that about 27 percent will have done so by age 30 and 42 percent by age 50. Between the ages of 25 and 75, 51 percent of adults will have experienced at least one year below the poverty line.

Concentrated Poverty and Concentrated Social Problems

Another important poverty trend relates to changes in the number of persons living in blocks or neighborhoods that have high concentrations of poverty. When first introduced as a domain of study, such neighborhoods were designated as *underclass.* This term has since gone out of favor, but we sometimes use it in this discussion because the literature of the time used it extensively and avoiding it is awkward. One policy concern is that families living in these neighborhoods remain in poverty for generations, often relying on welfare because they have little opportunity for upward mobility.

Although the two concepts of *concentrated* poverty and *underclass* have sometimes been used interchangeably, they are defined and operationalized quite differently. The 2000 census dramatically shows why they should not be equated. *Concentrated poverty* refers to census tracts in which at least 40 percent of the households have incomes below the federal poverty line for their size and household composition. The Census Bureau identifies such tracts as "extreme poverty areas," another term in common use.

In contrast, high levels of "destructive or antisocial behaviors" are the defining criteria for what Ricketts and Sawhill (1988) termed "underclass" neighborhoods. The four variables they chose were failure to complete high school, nonmarital childbearing, not working or seeking work, and criminal behavior. Because those researchers had to rely on decennial census data to operationalize their definition of these neighborhoods, they had to use variables the census collected, which did not include criminal behavior or marital status at childbirth. Ricketts and Sawhill ultimately used the proportions of teens dropping out of high school, women heading a family, households on public assistance, and prime-age and able-bodied men not in the labor force. Census tracts that were one standard deviation or more above the national mean on all four variables used to measure the extent of social problems were considered underclass. In practice, they selected tracts in which more than a quarter of adults had less than a high school education, more than a third lived in female-headed families, more than a sixth were on welfare, and more than half the men were out of the labor force. Because "the underclass" was a geographically based concept, everyone living there was considered part of the category, whether or not they personally met any of the criteria.

The term *underclass* has been used by some sociologists to convey the idea that areas with high concentrations of persistent poverty also have high rates of related problems, including those analyzed by Ricketts and Sawhill as well as decaying housing and infrastructure, low employment growth, and reduced opportunities for upward mobility. The identification of some neighborhoods as underclass was also meant to convey that children growing up in these neighborhoods are exposed to, and likely to adapt as their own, norms that run counter to basic American expectations for earning a living, getting married before having children, and being law-abiding.

The dramatic changes in the past 30 years in areas with concentrated poverty and concentrated social problems can be seen in figures 2.6 and 2.7. Both figures show the increases from 1970 to 1980 and from 1980 to 1990 that prompted such concern among policymakers in the decades that followed. Both also show substantial declines between 1990 and 2000 (Jargowsky 2003; Jargowsky and Sawhill 2006).

It is important to note two points regarding the different measures and the overlap in people living in areas of concentrated poverty and people living in areas with concentrated social problems. First, as comparing the two figures makes clear, the number of people in high-poverty census tracts is three to four times greater than the number living in tracts with high concentrations of social problems, even when one considers only the concentrated poverty population in metropolitan areas.[4] For instance, in 2000, the figures show about 2.2 million people in concentrated poverty areas (shown in figure 2.7) but about 7 million people living in metropolitan areas with concentrated social problems (shown in figure 2.6) (7.9 million if one includes high-poverty nonmetropolitan areas). Second, some tracts with considerable social problems do not

Figure 2.6. High-Poverty Neighborhoods and High-Poverty Neighborhood Population, U.S. Metropolitan Areas, 1970–2000

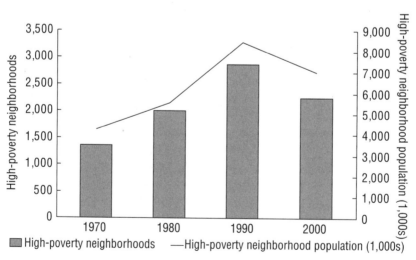

Source: Jargowsky (2003), figure 1.

Note: Based on metropolitan areas as defined in year of census.

Figure 2.7. The Underclass

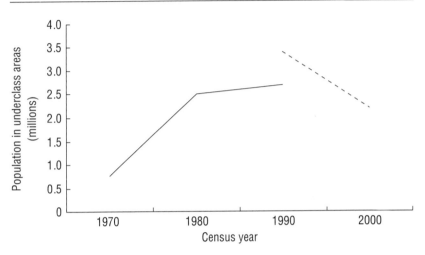

Source: Jargowsky and Sawhill 2006, figure 1.

Note: 1970 figure from Ricketts and Mincy (1990); 1980 figure from Ricketts and Sawhill (1988); bottom 1990 figure from Mincy and Wiener (1993). These three measures of the underclass population were determined using 1980 means and standard deviations. Top 1990 and 2000 figures from Jargowsky and Yang (2006), based on 1990 means and standard deviations.

qualify as high poverty and vice versa. In 2000, only 57 percent of neighborhoods with high levels of social problems also met the criteria for concentrated poverty.

The rates of severe poverty concentrations, using either definition, declined between 1990 and 2000. Jargowsky and Sawhill (2006) summarize the most likely explanations for the decline in both indicators, though firm evidence is scant as yet. The boom economy of the second half of the 1990s is likely to have played some role since the poverty *rate* was lower in 2000 than it had been in 1990 (11.3 versus 13.5 percent), even though the *number* of people in poverty actually increased by slightly more than 2 million people during the same period. Social policy changes are also likely to have affected one or both indicators. For example, with respect to concentrated poverty, housing policy changes have had the effect of dispersing some occupants of highly concentrated public housing, thus changing the income mix of households in numerous census tracts that previously had very high poverty concentrations. Similarly, using the indicator based on areas with high rates of social problems, changes in

nonmarital births and welfare policy changes both likely made a difference. As the welfare rolls dropped by half during the later 1990s and fewer
teenagers and young women had babies, fewer neighborhoods would
have met the underclass criteria for welfare dependency and female
household headship.

Changes in Household Composition and Their Effects on Poverty

The changes in children's poverty rates described above (figure 2.2 and
accompanying text) stem largely from changes in household composition. Many changes in family structure have occurred during the 45 years
covered by figures 2.1 and 2.2. Among the more important poverty trends
are those related to women, children, and minorities. In all recent years,
poverty rates for children and for ethnic minorities have been higher than
for adults and whites. Changes over the years in the participation of men
with only a high school education or less in the labor force and their ability to earn enough to support a family and in childbearing outside of marriage, especially to adolescent girls, contribute substantially to the upward
trend in single-parent households. The poverty rate for children in female-
headed families has been particularly high since the early 1980s, giving rise
to what is often referred to as the "feminization of poverty." In the sections
that follow, we examine each of these trends.

Employment and Earnings Trends for Young Men

In the 1950s and even the 1960s, a young man who had just finished high
school, or even one who had dropped out, could follow his father into the
factory and be reasonably sure that he could earn enough to support a
family. That assumption became increasingly less valid after 1973, the
peak year for the earning power of individuals with only a high school
education or less. Statistics that reflect the extent of that trend are hard to
find because census data tend to report incomes and associated characteristics only for full-time, year-round workers. A good part of the problem for the young people of greatest concern, however, is that they are not
firmly attached to the labor force, and they are certainly not "full-time,
year-round" workers. According to Mincy, Lewis, and Han (2006, 1),

half of our youth and young adults are having great difficulty transitioning into adulthood. . . . These young people are distinguished by the absence of postsecondary schooling. Dropouts . . . have the most difficulty. However, many 18- to 24-year-olds who graduated from high school but are not enrolled in any form of postsecondary schooling remain out of work or have jobs paying too little to sustain themselves and their families.

Earnings difficulties affect less-educated young men of all races. For example, Blackburn, Bloom, and Freeman (1990) detail the declining fortunes of white men without postsecondary education, which parallel those for young men of other races. But young men with a high school education or less are increasingly not white. In 1979, 78 percent of less-educated men ages 16 to 24 were white; by 2001, that proportion had fallen to about 58 percent. The higher likelihood that young nonwhite men will fall into the less-educated group compounds the vulnerability of nonwhite families to living in poverty.

Holtzer and Offner (2006) analyze the trends in employment outcomes for "nonenrolled" young men and women for the period 1979 through 2000. Nonenrolled young people are ages 16 to 24, with a high school education or less, and not enrolled in school. Employment rates for all groups (white, black, and Hispanic men and women) respond to economic cycles, increasing during boom times and declining during recessions. On top of these trends, the patterns for less-educated men show constant or declining employment over time, while those for women show rising employment. For less-educated black men, employment rates are significantly lower than those for white and Hispanic men, while the rates for black and Hispanic women are similar, and both are significantly lower than rates for white women. The data also show that labor force participation rates for all less-educated men declined between 1979 and 2000, most sharply for young black men.

To make matters worse for family formation and the likelihood that children will grow up in households with above-poverty income, the same young men who are least likely to work, or to work at well-paying jobs, are very likely to father children at a young age and to do so with women who themselves have relatively low earnings potential. These families face great difficulty in escaping poverty for a number of reasons, one of which is that they have only one potential worker—the mother. Two-parent families facing poverty often decide that both parents will work, but when there is no possibility of a second income, the family may be trapped in or near poverty.

Adolescent Pregnancy and Parenting

During the decades of the 1970s, 1980s, and 1990s, when young men without a college education were losing their earning power and with it their ability to support a family and therefore their desirability as husbands, young women were increasingly having babies outside marriage. Both men and women were delaying marriage until their mid- to late 20s. In combination, the two trends increased the number of female-headed families without sufficient income to raise a family out of poverty.

In the 1950s, more than half of all women married by age 20. Age of marriage for both men and women has been increasing steadily since the 1960s, and the proportion marrying by age 20 has been decreasing. For men and women born in 1940 to 1944, who would have been 20 in 1960 to 1964, 24.1 percent of men and 46.2 percent of women married by age 20. Table 2.2 shows the proportion of men and women marrying by age 20 during the next 30 years, dropping to only 8.1 percent of men and 17.5 percent of women during 1995–99. Thus, about two of every three men and women who in 1955 would have married by age 20 do not marry until later. In 2003, the median age at marriage was 27 for men and 25 for women (Kreider 2005).

While age at first marriage was increasing during the last half of the 1900s, births to teens were not decreasing proportionally. Births to women age 15 to 19 were high in the 1950s (81.6 per 1,000) compared to later decades, but the nonmarital birth rate (15 per 1,000) was only 2.8 percent

Table 2.2. Percentage of Men and Women Marrying by Age 20, 1955–99

Birth cohort	Year when age 20	Men	Women
1935–39	1955–59	20.9	51.3
1940–44	1960–64	24.1	46.2
1945–49	1965–69	20.4	44.8
1950–54	1970–74	23.0	40.5
1955–59	1975–79	17.6	36.6
1960–64	1980–84	15.8	30.2
1965–69	1985–89	13.0	24.6
1970–74	1990–94	11.0	21.9
1975–79	1995–99	8.1	17.5

Source: Kreider (2005), table 1.

of the marital birth rate (531 per 1,000). By 2003, when fewer than one in five women married by age 20, births to women age 15 to 19 had declined to 41.7 per 1,000 women. But the nonmarital birth rate stood at 11.0 percent of the marital birth rate (35 versus 284 per 1,000). In sheer numbers, births to women under age 20 did not decline as rapidly as the birth rate because the number of women in their teens increased over the years (Facts at a Glance 2005; Kreider 2005). As a result, more families were begun by a teen birth to an unmarried woman, and more children were living in families headed by women—23.6 percent of all children in 2004, compared to 16.2 percent in 1975 and only 9 percent in 1960.

The proportion of people living in families headed by women has been increasing over the past three decades for all racial and ethnic groups, going from 12.4 percent in 1975 to 17.4 percent in 2004. The proportion among whites went from 8.9 percent in 1975 to 11.9 percent in 2004; comparable figures are 35.4 to 43.9 percent for African Americans and 17.6 to 21.4 percent for Hispanics.

Families headed by women tend disproportionately to be members of minority groups. Whites made up 65.1 percent of people in families in 2006, but only 44.8 percent of people in female-headed families (table 2.3). Conversely, blacks and Hispanics constituted 28.5 percent of people in families but 50 percent of people in female-headed families. While relevant statistics by race and Hispanic origin go back only to the mid-1970s, they are sufficient to show that the white proportion of female-headed families has been shrinking in the past three decades. This change is due largely to the increase in the Hispanic population, which approximately doubled between 1975 and 1990 and doubled again between 1990 and 2006. In 1975, only 5.5 percent of people in families were Hispanic, compared to 9.0 percent in 1990 and 16 percent in 2006.

Female-headed families are also more likely to be poor than other households, and those who are also members of racial or ethnic minorities are more likely to be poor than their white female-headed counterparts. After the major changes in social programs in 1965, the overall poverty rate dropped into the range of 11 to 14 percent. Large differences by race and ethnicity are clear, however: the poverty rate for non-Hispanic whites has stayed below 10 percent while the rates for non-Hispanic blacks have been below 30 percent only since 1995, and rates for Hispanics are only slightly lower.

The right panel of table 2.4 shows the substantially higher poverty rates in all years for families with a female head and no husband present—

Table 2.3. Racial and Ethnic Distribution of All People in Families and for People in Female-Headed Families, Selected Years, 1975–2006

	Distribution by Race and Ethnicity of All People in Families			Distribution by Race and Ethnicity of People in Families with Female Head, No Husband Present		
Year	White, non-Hispanic	Black, non-Hispanic	Hispanic	White, non-Hispanic	Black, non-Hispanic	Hispanic
2006	65.1	12.5	16	44.8	30.6	20.0
1990	75.1	12.5	9.0	50.8	35.1	11.8
1975	81.6	11.4	5.5	58.6	32.6	7.8

Source: U.S. Bureau of the Census, Historic Poverty Tables; calculations made from data in table 2. http://www.census.gov/hhes/www/poverty/histpov/hstpov2.html.

Note: Rows do not sum to 100 because members of other races are omitted.

Table 2.4. Poverty Rates, by Family Status and by Race and Ethnicity, Selected Years, 1960–2006

Year	Poverty Rates for All People				Poverty Rates for People in Families with Female Head, No Husband Present			
	All races	White, non-Hispanic	Black, non-Hispanic	Hispanic	All races	White, non-Hispanic	Black, non-Hispanic	Hispanic
2006	12.3	8.2	24.3	20.6	30.5	22.5	39.1	36.9
2000	11.3	7.4	22.5	21.5	28.5	18.8	38.6	37.8
1995	13.8	8.5	29.3	30.3	36.5	22.8	48.2	52.8
1990	13.5	8.8	31.9	28.1	37.2	25.0	50.6	53.0
1985	14.0	9.7	31.3	29.0	37.6	24.7	53.2	55.7
1980	13.0	9.1	32.5	25.7	36.5	24.1	53.4	54.5
1975	12.3	8.6	31.3	26.9	37.5	25.9	54.3	57.2
1970	12.6	NA	NA	NA	38.1	NA	NA	NA
1965	17.3	NA	NA	NA	46.0	NA	NA	NA
1960	22.2	NA	NA	NA	48.9	NA	NA	NA

Source: U.S. Bureau of the Census, Historic Poverty Tables, table 2. http://www.census.gov/hhes/www/poverty/histpov/hstpov2.html.

Note: NA = not available.

the core target population for AFDC and later TANF. Poverty rates for African American and Hispanic female-headed families are approximately the same—around double the poverty rate for whites in female-headed families. Rates for people in white female-headed families are two to three times as high as rates for all whites; rates for people in female-headed African American and Hispanic families are about one and a half to two times as high as rates for all African Americans or all Hispanics. Fewer whites than African Americans or Hispanics live in female-headed families, but those who do are more likely to be poor than those who do not.

Immigrants

Immigration to the United States reached levels in the 1980s unseen since the turn of the last century, with the years 1985 through 1990 seeing the biggest influx. The pace continued in the 1990s. In 1970, just 4.7 percent of the U.S. population was foreign-born (Lapham, Montgomery, and Niner 1993). By 1990, the proportion was 7.9 percent, up by two-thirds in 20 years. By 2000, the proportion of foreign-born was more than double (11.1 percent) what it had been in 1970.[4]

While many immigrants enter the United States with job skills and educational credentials that allow them to move into jobs above the low-wage level, many do not. Lower educational and skills levels, often coupled with limited English proficiency, confine many immigrants to the low-wage sector, contributing to the number of U.S. households whose incomes are at poverty or near-poverty levels despite considerable work effort.

During the 1990s, half of all new workers were immigrants, and immigrants were more likely than the native-born population to work. While immigrants in 2000 were 11 percent of all U.S. residents, they made up 14 percent of all workers and 20 percent of low-wage workers—those whose jobs pay less than twice the prevailing federal or state minimum wage (Capps et al. 2003). Nearly half of all immigrant workers are low wage, compared to a third of native workers. Undocumented status—being in the United States illegally—is a factor in wage rates and consequent poverty. About two-thirds (65 percent) of undocumented workers earn low wages, and this group comprises 40 percent of all low-wage immigrant workers.

Working Poor

Another important poverty trend relates to employment and the "working poor." In each recent year, an estimated 2 million individuals in the United States lived in poverty even though someone in the household worked full-time and year-round. In addition, millions more are underemployed, either working part time even though they would prefer full-time work or working at a job considerably below their skill level. Several factors explain the increasing difficulty of supporting a family above poverty even with substantial work effort, including changes in the value of the federal minimum wage; changes in type of available employment, particularly the loss of well-paying manufacturing jobs and the shift to a service economy; and the effects of immigration. That said, one federal program, the earned income tax credit, has in recent years helped *reduce* poverty, encouraging work by supplementing the incomes of poor working families to raise them closer to or above the poverty level.

Minimum Wage

Congress first established a federal minimum wage in 1938. That floor has never been automatically adjusted, as would have happened had it been indexed to inflation. Rather, it requires an act of Congress to change the federal minimum wage. During the 1950s and 1960s, the federal minimum wage fluctuated at about 50 percent of the average private nonsupervisory wage, with Congress deliberately making reference to prevailing wages on the principle that minimum-wage workers should not fall too far behind other workers. Fairly frequent adjustments occurred to ensure that the federal minimum wage adhered to this principle (Bernstein and Shapiro 2005). From the 1950s through the early 1980s, one full-time year-round worker making minimum wage could have raised a family of three just above the poverty level.

Starting in 1970, however, the value of the federal minimum wage as a proportion of average wages began to drop, from around 50 percent in the 1950s and 1960s and over 45 percent in the 1970s to just 32 percent in 2005—a level lower than in any year since 1948. Except for one year (1998), the federal minimum wage has been below 40 percent of the average wage since 1985. The drop in the purchasing power of a minimum-wage worker has been equally precipitous. Between 1980 and 1989, the minimum wage lost about 27 percent of its purchasing power, instead of experiencing the slight rise it took between 1970 and 1979, thanks to frequent adjustments. In 2005, the real purchasing power of the minimum wage was lower than at any time since the 1950s, with one exception (1989). Now it takes almost two full-time, year-round workers at minimum wage to raise a family of three out of poverty.

By early 2008, 22 states had reacted to the stagnation of the federal minimum wage by setting their own minimum wage higher.[5] These include the most populous states of California, Florida, Illinois, and New York, bringing at least half the country's low-wage workers under a higher standard than Congress had set. The higher state minimum levels ranged from $6.15 to $8.07, compared to the federal $5.85 that took effect in July 2007. The most common state standards, applicable in the most populous states, were 30 to 45 percent higher than the federal minimum wage in early 2008. Some states with their own minimum wage set their level at $1.00 above the federal minimum wage, others index their level to inflation, and others rely on new legislation to change the rate.

After the longest period without adjustment in the history of the minimum wage, Congress finally took action in the Fair Minimum Wage Act of 2007, establishing $0.70 increases over three years—to $5.85 in July 2007, $6.55 in July 2008, and $7.25 in July 2009. These changes meant minimum wage increases in 26 states in 2008 that were at or below the federal minimum, and further increases following the 2009 change. Federal law still does not provide an index to inflation or any other standard, so future increases in the federal minimum wage will still be dependent on congressional action.

Changes in Available Jobs

Much research has focused on the relationship between the economy and poverty, especially by geographic area and for particular population subgroups. The relationship between poverty levels and changes in economic activity is obvious from figures 2.1 and 2.2, which show poverty increasing in recessions (the gray lines in the figures) and decreasing during periods of economic growth and prosperity.

Other, longer-term economic changes have had more systematic effects on particular population groups. The post–World War II era saw extensive migration from rural areas and states, especially in the South, to urban industrial areas, mainly in the Northeast and Midwest. The migration of

African Americans to industrialized urban areas was particularly heavy, prompted largely by the prospect of fairly well paying, and often unionized, jobs for noncollege educated workers. As the share of the U.S. economy in goods production (manufacturing) has shrunk and the share in services has grown, many of the former well-paying opportunities for workers without postsecondary education or training began to disappear. Inner-city urban areas were particularly affected. Policy books published in the 1980s and 1990s—with titles such as *The Great U-Turn* (Harrison and Bluestone 1988), *A Future of Lousy Jobs* (Burtless 1990), *The Truly Disadvantaged* (Wilson 1987), and *When Work Disappears* (Wilson 1996)—reflect the problems raised by those trends.

For the first half of the 20th century and a little beyond, the manufacturing sector drove U.S. economic growth and improvements in the well-being of individuals and households. Workers with only a high school education, or even without one, could earn enough to support a middle-class lifestyle, and one worker's paycheck—the husband's—was enough. Since the 1960s, the economy has increasingly shifted away from manufacturing and toward services employment. The trend has been called *deindustrialization* (Harrison and Bluestone 1988), *postindustrialism* (Berman, Bound, and Griliches 1994), and *economic restructuring* (Chevan and Stokes 2000). Manufacturing employment peaked in the early 1940s at 32 percent of the workforce; by 2000, it had declined to just below 13 percent (Forbes 2004). And the loss continues—the Congressional Budget Office (2004) estimated that the 14.3 million manufacturing jobs as of January 2004 were down 3.0 million, or 17.5 percent, since July 2000, and stood at the lowest level experienced in the United States since July 1950.

Instead of manufacturing jobs, the U.S. economy today is dominated by jobs in services. Not all service jobs are alike, of course. They can be divided into three major categories: professional services, business services, and trade and personal services. The latter, consisting of jobs in the retail, wholesale, entertainment, and recreation industries, has seen the highest growth and the lowest wages. Looking at census data for 1990, Chevan and Stokes (2000) describe the distribution of earnings within income quintiles by job type. Half (50.2 percent) of U.S. households with a full-time worker in manufacturing were in the two top income quintiles, whereas only 24.3 percent of households relying on trade and personal service jobs were in those quintiles. In 1990, census data show the mean family income for the fourth and fifth income quintiles as $69,325 and $128,838, respectively. Conversely, 33.5 percent of households with trade and personal services jobs were in the lowest income quintile, compared to 10.6 percent of households relying on manufacturing jobs. In 1990, census data show the mean family income for the lowest quintile as about $13,400, or about equal to the poverty level ($13,359) for a family of four. Clearly, job growth in this service sector does little to raise families out of poverty even if they work very hard.

Earned Income Tax Credit

People who earn income but are still poor and file a federal income tax return can qualify for a refundable federal income tax credit known as the earned income tax credit (EITC). The credit reduces the amount of tax households owe. If they are poor enough and have worked enough, households may receive a refund that is more than the amount of tax they owe. Only people who work are eligible for the EITC, and for workers with very low earnings the size of the credit increases with each additional dollar of earnings, providing an incentive to work more.

The EITC is the nation's largest cash assistance program for working families. In 2006, families with two or more children were eligible for a credit worth up to $4,536; the average credit for the 23.0 million households that received EITC payments in that year was $1,926.

Congress originally approved EITC legislation in 1975, in part to offset the burden of increased Social Security payroll taxes and to provide an incentive to work. After three expansions, the refundable tax credit is doing more to reduce poverty than any program other than Social Security. The Tax Reform Act of 1986 increased the amount a household could earn and still receive the credit and provided a larger credit for families with two or more children. With these changes, significantly more families found it worthwhile to file a tax return.

After 1991, legislation removed EITC income as a factor in determining eligibility for most means-tested programs, making more families eligible for welfare or food stamps, since EITC returns no longer put them over the maximum income-eligibility levels. Other provisions also enabled taxpayers with children living with them for more than half the year to receive a credit, regardless of who provided child support. Legislation in 1993 raised the amount the EITC would pay, and changes in 1994 expanded the EITC to provide a small credit to childless low-income families and individuals. About 13.7 million households received some level of EITC credit for their 1990 income tax return (received in 1991); the number increased to about 19.3 million households for 1994 tax returns and stayed at about that level or slightly higher through 2001 (for 2000 tax returns). Then it increased gradually to about 23 million households in 2006 for their 2005 tax returns (the latest year available). Higher returns for those who file, better publicity, and wider knowledge of the EITC explain the increase in households receiving these credits.

A good deal of research, summarized by Greenstein (2005), shows that the EITC increases employment among single parents, reduces poverty, and accounts for a significant amount of the reduction in welfare rolls that followed the major welfare reforms of 1996 (see chapter 3). More than half the large increase in employment among single mothers during that period ties back to the EITC expansions instituted between 1984 and 1996, with the most significant gains shown by mothers with young children or low educational levels. Census data show that in 2004 the EITC lifted about 5 million people out of poverty, including about 2.7 million children. Without the EITC, the poverty rate among children would have been nearly one-fourth higher—about 22 percent rather than the current 17.8 percent.

According to census data, the EITC lifts more children out of poverty than any other single program or category of programs. With respect to reducing the number of households in poverty, the EITC is more effective than raising the minimum wage would be, because all the households receiving EITC payments would be poor without it, whereas many people working at minimum-wage jobs live in households whose income is already above the poverty line. Other studies have found that because of the EITC's success in increasing employment among single mothers, expansions of the EITC produced large declines in receipt of cash welfare assistance—moving perhaps as many as half a million families from AFDC cash assistance to work annually, at least during TANF's early years. In fact, the EITC may be the single most important factor in recent increases in work and earnings and declines in receipt of cash welfare assistance among female-headed families—much more significant than the effects of welfare time limits and other policy changes on labor supply, welfare receipt, and income. The EITC fits so well with the general prowork norms and beliefs of American politicians that for the 2007 tax year, 23 states offered their own earned income tax credit to supplement the federal program—up from 16 states for 2005.

The EITC has one drawback as an antipoverty measure, however, because it is pro- rather than countercyclical. That is, in good economic times, when people can get jobs but still do not earn much, the EITC supplements their income, making good times better. But in times of high unemployment when many households have no earned income or much less than they do in good times, the EITC does not help families who have lost jobs because a person must have earned income to qualify for the EITC. Thus, when the economy worsens, the EITC becomes *less* effective at reducing poverty at the very time when more families need help.

Conclusions

How do public officials or politicians think about poverty? Is more poverty bad, or is it good? Do they respond to need or only to statistics and how the numbers make them look? And on broader fronts, do they or don't they have a commitment to reducing or ending poverty? Do they perceive a connection between continuing to have a large proportion of our population living in poverty—with inadequate nutrition, served by inadequate schools, getting inadequate health care, and acquiring inadequate skills—and American competitiveness abroad?

At several critical decision points, public officials opted to define poverty in a way that minimized the number of people and households that could be considered poor. The Social Security Administration made the first such decision when it chose to multiply the low-income and economy food plans by three rather than by four to establish the Orshansky poverty thresholds. The Office of Economic Opportunity made a second such decision when it chose to adopt the lower poverty thresholds based on the more stringent economy food plan rather than on the somewhat more generous low-cost food plan. The major consequence of having fewer officially poor households is that safety net programs whose eligibility is keyed to poverty status do not serve most of the people in need—indeed, they do not serve even many of the people who are technically eligible.

Resistance to modifying poverty definitions and poverty thresholds, which can be seen in repeated failures to act on the recommendations of the commissions and task forces that have addressed the issue, stems from many reasonable bases, including the value of having consistent measures across time. But also at stake is that virtually any change in the poverty definition, which considers only a household's cash income before government transfers, would result in defining more people as poor. No administrator wants to be responsible for, and no politician wants to vote for, something that will make it look as if poverty has increased—even when they could explain that the basic reality of people's lives has not changed. Nor do they want to vote for something that would greatly increase the cost of safety net programs because more people would become eligible for them. Thus, despite the documented effects of safety net and social insurance programs on reducing the poverty gap, raising families out of poverty, and improving the health of poor people, predicting what politicians will do when faced with undeniable need in combination with financial and public image issues is a tricky business (Blank 2008).

The area of social psychology known as attribution theory uses two dimensions to characterize how people's actions or failures to act will be perceived. Those two dimensions are ability (*could* they do it?) and motivation (do they *want* to do it?). Although the want to/able to concepts are not often applied to public policy, it occasionally happens with respect to understanding and characterizing different policy decisions. As part of a major Urban Institute research agenda called "Changing Domestic Priorities," Burt and Pittman (1985) used this scheme to summarize the responses of four communities to major changes in safety net programs established in the early years of the Reagan administration that affected three vulnerable populations—children in the child welfare system, the low-income elderly, and people with serious mental illness. These populations clearly fall in the category of "people who are not able to look after their own welfare"; they are the vulnerable "deserving" poor, the ones who should have been considered "truly needy," in the Reagan administration's phrase for those whom the government *should* help.

Burt and Pittman used state and local funding availability to indicate *ability* to compensate for federal cuts and whether the community did compensate to indicate *willingness*. The four communities arrayed themselves all along the spectrum of the want to/able to dimensions. In Michigan, both the local community and the state *did* use their own funding to compensate for cuts, despite being the most hard-hit by the major recession of the early 1980s and having very little in government coffers. They had the *will* and therefore found a way even under conditions of very scarce resources. Massachusetts was in better financial circumstances and used its resources to compensate for most of the federal cuts. It wanted to and was able to, so it did. Virginia, and Richmond in particular, was not completely strapped for resources but nevertheless chose not to compensate for cuts. It was able to but did not want to. Finally, although the state of California provided resources to compensate for almost all cuts, the local community being studied, San Diego, chose not to take those state resources or withdrew resources of its own when new state resources were available, in accord with local motivation that differed considerably from that prevailing in the state as a whole. San Diego did not want to and so it did not, even though resources were available.

As a nation, we—and therefore our politicians—get tangled up in the "want to" dimension much more than in the "able to" dimension. It would be hard to argue that, in a country as rich as this one, we are unable to ensure an income floor for all families, or at least for all children and all senior citizens, if we wanted to. We could ensure everyone a home by providing the resources to subsidize housing costs for everyone with worst-case housing needs. We could ensure that everyone gets enough to eat by increasing the eligibility for and benefits of the Food Stamp Program. We could take a deep breath and raise the poverty threshold until it indicates a level of income that could meet basic needs for food and shelter—somewhere between 150 and 200 percent of the current poverty line—and then adapt programs to provide the resources to cover those needs. The list could go on. But the value conundrums identified and analyzed in chapter 1 have historically made us pull our punches. Politicians take some action because they recognize problems and want to address them, but they are also afraid that if they do too much it will inhibit individual responsibility and initiative. As a result of the ambivalence, our safety net programs have many holes that reflect vacillation of will, not ability.

Sometimes not knowing what will work complicates the want to/able to analysis, since all approaches to cash welfare involve trying to figure out what interventions actually help disadvantaged families increase their income from earnings. But the same cannot be said about housing and food—if we help people pay for housing, they will have housing; and if we give them the resources to acquire more food, they and their children will eat better and their children will do better in school. We *could* do these things, but thus far in our history we keep going through decade-long pendulum swings of expanding and contracting programs without ever reaching the point of actual solutions to specific problems. Nor, except during the Great Depression and the mid-1960s, have we launched and sustained an overarching approach to ending poverty and enabling poor people—one that transcends particular congressional committees and government departments and deals with the issue comprehensively.

This chapter and the preceding one have shown poverty to be very complex; the nation's struggle to address its causes and consequences has produced an extensive but uncoordinated set of policies and programs. In chapter 3, we discuss the specifics of reforms to welfare and other major safety net programs from 1996 to 2006. Thereafter, we describe the policy and practice of applying for and becoming a beneficiary of safety net programs before and after welfare reform (chapter 4), including eligibility criteria, caseloads, and intake practices. We return to the issue of an integrated approach to helping people in chapter 5, where we examine system responses to assisting individuals and households with complex issues.

3

Recent Changes to U.S. Social Safety Net Policies

Much has happened to social safety net programs since the mid-1990s. The Personal Responsibility and Work Opportunity Reconciliation Act of 1996 (PRWORA) ended Aid to Families with Dependent Children and replaced it with Temporary Assistance for Needy Families. It also changed the Food Stamp Program in a number of ways, some of which are still in effect and some of which were further altered in subsequent years. With the Workforce Investment Act of 1998 (WIA), programs that provide help with employment shifted their emphasis from job training for individuals to meeting the needs of businesses. Health insurance coverage for children in low-income families expanded when the State Children's Health Insurance Program (SCHIP) was created in 1997. Federal programs offering housing assistance to low-income households also changed; while some were cut back, the most recent change, passed in July 2008, established a national housing trust fund to help pay for developing more affordable housing.

In addition to describing these changes, this chapter discusses issues that surrounded major policy shifts and their consequences. All the programs just mentioned are covered, but a more detailed discussion of legislation affecting housing is provided. This approach establishes the pattern for subsequent chapters. While every chapter that follows contains material pertinent to an array of safety net programs, each gives more weight to some programs than to others. This chapter offers greater detail on housing and legislation related to homelessness, while chapter 4 focuses on TANF, Food Stamps, Medicaid, SCHIP, and the EITC; chapter 5 concentrates mostly on TANF and welfare-to-work programs and also provides extended examples related to youth programming; chapter 7 examines Medicaid and public policy shifts related to homelessness. Together, chapters 3 through 7 provide balanced coverage of the major American safety net programs.

Changing Times, Changing Policies

The steady economic growth that the nation enjoyed after World War II slowed considerably around 1973. As a result, less tax revenue flowed into government coffers, forcing policymakers to make hard choices about their spending priorities. Welfare and antipoverty programs became a lightning rod of sorts, attracting public and political controversy and revealing the nation's underlying general economic frustration. The hope of the 1960s that expanded social policies would greatly reduce poverty appeared unfulfilled, as welfare caseloads rose continuously and poverty barely declined. Wages stagnated, adding to anxiety in middle-class families struggling to make ends meet even with two workers (Steuerle et al. 1998).

The values conundrums articulated by Ellwood (1989) and described in chapter 1 became especially evident in challenges in social safety net policies after the mid-1970s. Core policy questions included the following: If we are to make a national commitment to eliminate or alleviate poverty, then whom should we help out of poverty, and who decides? Should government provide an income floor that will sustain some basic standard of living? If so, where should the floor be set? Should we provide that floor for everyone, and if not, then who gets it and who does not? If we provide a basic standard of living, will it discourage individual effort and employment? How do we keep such help from rewarding inappropriate behaviors that could negatively affect children or weaken family structures? What is the responsibility of governments, businesses, communities, and individuals to reach such a standard? Who should bear the cost of attacking poverty and maintaining a social safety net?

Policymakers have continued to search for the "correct" (that is, politically acceptable) balance between government provision of services and benefits and individual initiative and responsibility—in other words, the appropriate social contract. Many programs have been added to the nation's safety net, while others have been eliminated. Policy changes and reforms have been particularly extensive since 1980, partly in response to growing discouragement about the persistence of poverty, as discussed in chapter 2, and partly in response to increasing federal and state fiscal constraints. None, though, attempted to create a comprehensive social safety net, some programs actually conflicted with others, and rarely did any public dialogue address how the changes, separately and together, were going to help eliminate poverty.

The nation is still far from consensus on the many questions raised by the idea of a safety net, most of which are values questions rather than issues that can be resolved by policy analysis. Experimentation with different approaches has continued, providing opportunities to learn about effective strategies and programs by analyzing results. With or without data-based answers, federal policies to address poverty and hardship adopted a new mantra in the mid-1990s—*work*. In many different policy areas, programs transitioned from simply providing income transfers, benefits, and social services to minimizing disincentives to working in the regular labor market, in keeping with one side of Ellwood's first value conundrum.

Program structures were compatible with the idea that people who can work, should work and that social safety net policies should not discourage work in the regular labor market. Although the role of employment and the balance between publicly provided support services and cash benefits and individual work effort vary across programs, the interaction among these three dimensions—services, benefits, and work—is apparent in the ways welfare, workforce development, food stamps, and (somewhat less directly) health assistance programs were changed during the final years of the 20th century. They were also designed with the expectation that they would reduce long-term public dependency and some of its repercussions, such as nonmarital childbearing. Emerging policy issues included, Who can work? What precisely should be considered "work"? Should the government help working families more directly and if so, which ones and how?

In contrast to the work-based social safety net policies that were the subject of major policy reforms in recent years, safety net programs that provide mainly direct benefits or subsidies, such as housing subsidies, and those that are more services focused, such as child care, have continued with minimal reforms, often beleaguered by an increase in the needy population and sometimes beset by funding cuts. These safety net policies include last-resort programs targeted to the most vulnerable persons and families in dire situations, usually unable to work—children at risk of abuse or neglect, persons in crisis needing emergency services, individuals with severe disabilities, and those who are homeless. The important exceptions to the generalization about work orientation are the Food Stamp Program and health insurance for children. Although it is true that welfare reform legislation imposed a work requirement on single able-bodied adults who receive food stamps for more than a month or two, other significant changes to the Food Stamp Program between 2002 and 2008 have further reinforced its critical role in the social safety net, particularly for low-income working families.

In work- and services-based programs and in last-resort programs, regardless of whether they have been the focus of major reforms, the federal government has devolved more responsibility to states and localities. This shift, in turn, has led to more privatization of service delivery as states and localities contract with nonprofit and for-profit agencies to do the actual work with program clients. The roles of different levels of government and of nongovernmental entities have been redefined, along with their shared responsibilities for alleviating poverty and ameliorating risk and hardship. We mention these administrative changes here and discuss them at length in chapter 6.

Work-Based Policy Reforms

During the transition from the 20th to the 21st century, major changes came about in some of the largest U.S. income and benefit programs, reflecting the swing of the pendulum away from social support and back to work. While cash welfare assistance, food assistance, and health care programs serve employable as well as unemployable persons, such as the elderly, the disabled, and children, work was central to the national policy reforms of the 1990s. Cash assistance became a limited option, as the objective shifted from providing income to poor children and their families to actively moving people from public assistance to work. Food stamps and health care continued to serve as key federal safety nets, but, along with views on child care, such benefits began to be perceived as "work supports" rather than as assistance valuable in itself. That shift aligns with the federal policy priority of employment and its interpretation as being the main social safety net for families (i.e., the individual, not the government, is his or her own safety net).

Consistent with the work focus, the nation's employment and training system was also revamped during this time. Reforms to the welfare and the employment systems, however, occurred separately and were not always complementary. Without intention—and somewhat ironically—the restructured employment services system was not specifically charged with improving the employability of the poor or those on public assistance. In fact, with much less federal funding than in previous years, federal workforce policies gradually refocused on business needs and higher-skilled workers rather than on the poor and less-skilled workers who had been the target in the 1970s. Training through the main federal employment programs, therefore, was actually less available to help parents on TANF than it had been for AFDC parents.

Cash Welfare for Families with Children

Of all the U.S. safety net programs, cash welfare assistance to needy families with children changed most dramatically in the 1980s and 1990s. What had begun as an entitlement program for all children and their families below a certain income level—with the federal government committed to covering most of the cost and establishing fairly stringent regulations on the design of the program—became a temporary assistance program for which states receive a fixed sum of federal funds as a block grant and families are limited to just five years of federally funded assistance in their lifetime.

The Personal Responsibility and Work Opportunity Reconciliation Act of 1996 replaced the former cash assistance program AFDC and its Job Opportunities and Basic Skills Training Program with the Temporary Assistance for Needy Families program. This federal change came after about 15 years of reform experiments and demonstrations, most designed by various states with encouragement and support from the federal government. Special provisions allow states to request waivers from federal laws and regulations to experiment with new strategies in a number of social programs, including AFDC, the Food Stamp Program, Child Welfare, Child Support Enforcement, and Medicaid. So-called waiver demonstrations resulted in extensive research on a range of practices and policies, such as work requirements, income eligibility rules, child care, and cashing-out food stamps (Harvey, Camasso, and Jagannathan 2000; Williamson, Jackson, and Klerman 1997; Winston 2002). States were increasingly prominent in welfare reform, with some adopting program requirements more stringent than federal law and some, instead, instituting more service- and client-oriented approaches. State experience had an important influence on the character of national decisions on welfare reform.

The new law enacted in 1996 placed a five-year lifetime limit on cash assistance provided with federal funds (some states have set even shorter time limits) and imposed work participation goals on states. The new law also increased the flexibility of the states in designing their welfare programs without having to request federal waivers, including how much of the federal funding is used for cash benefits, employment services, supportive services, and other activities.

Employment is a critical objective of national welfare reform.[1] Underlying the emphasis on work is the assumption that through employment, individuals and families can become economically self-sufficient and thus break the cycle and culture of public dependency. In addition to compelling states to ensure that specific percentages of TANF parents participate in work activities (defined in federal regulations), the 1996 law also obliges states to establish work requirements for individual recipients to make sure the work objective is maintained.

More specifically, the federal law includes work-related program goals that all states must meet. All adults on TANF must be "engaged" in work or work-related activities by the time they have received 24 months of cash assistance. States decide what types of activities are acceptable for meeting the individual work requirements, which might include education and training, searching for a job, or working in the regular labor market. States also decide whether to impose work requirements sooner than 24 months after enrollment.

While states determine what work requirements to impose on welfare families, all states must also meet specific program goals related to work participation, and the federal government specifies what counts toward meeting those goals. Since 2001, states have had to show that adults in 50 percent of all TANF cases with one adult and 90 percent of two-parent cases are working or participating in federally defined work-related activities. The federal government allows states to count recipients who are actively engaged in a job or are involved in 1 of 12 legislatively specified work activities for at least 35 hours a week (or 20 hours a week for parents with a child under the age of 6). Many states apply these same rules to the work requirements that they impose on individual recipients, while some states have broader or narrower rules.

As a result of federal welfare reform, more variation now exists in TANF programs across states than had been the case for welfare programs under AFDC. Operationally, all states have work programs for TANF recipients, often continuing or modifying the more federally directed programs they administered before 1996 (Holcomb and Nightingale 1997). Most typically, TANF agencies shifted their focus to immediate employment, sometimes referred to as "work first," to move individuals as quickly as possible from welfare to regular employment. Both the work requirements and the five-year lifetime limit on receipt of benefits reinforce the focus on immediate employment to prepare families for the postwelfare reality in which they must depend on their earnings rather than on public assistance. Some states go further and impose work requirements even before families formally apply for benefits, attempting to divert them from public assistance by helping them find jobs or by providing other services that will allow them to avoid welfare altogether.

Probably no single TANF program uses any one work strategy alone. Instead, many variations exist, and mixed models combine strategies. Most states have adopted a stronger work-first objective than they had used under AFDC. Several states have more balanced policies, however, that use work-first but also allow some recipients to participate in longer-term education or job training to enhance long-term employability and potential for earning a wage. For instance, some programs combine vocational training with basic skills education, either in the workplace or in instructional centers or schools. Others integrate preemployment preparation with jobs in the public or nonprofit sector, personal counseling, treatment, education, and peer support. In many states, all of these strategies operate at once, depending on the circumstances of individual families (Holcomb and Martinson 2002).

As the number of families receiving cash assistance declined after welfare reform, state administrators recognized that the observable characteristics (e.g., age, number of children, and ethnicity) of TANF recipients were similar to those of households on welfare before the reforms (Acs and Loprest 2007a); but they also noted that many of those who remain on the rolls for long periods have a multiplicity of barriers to employment that make it difficult or even impossible for them to make the transition to work. Such barriers may include mental health and substance abuse problems, domestic violence, parenting problems, skills deficits, and learning disabilities, among others. States have developed programs and strategies to promote work among these hard-to-employ parents. Case workers in some states arrange for services to treat health and mental health problems, workshops in life-skills, parenting and household management, remedial education, occupational training, job development, postemployment supports to help people retain jobs, and the like. Some states have also established programs for households that have not made significant progress toward achieving self-sufficiency but have reached or are nearing their five-year time limit for federally funded assistance (Holcomb and Martinson 2002).

In February 2006, Congress reauthorized the TANF legislation but did not substantially change the work-first focus of the 1996 law, despite the operational evidence that those remaining on assistance often face very serious barriers to employment. In fact, the major change in 2006 relates to the definitions of work-participation rates that states must meet, actually increasing the emphasis on work-related activities with little allowance for parents with serious barriers to work. The emphasis on employment, work-related activities, and work requirements remains a critically important aspect of TANF. In 2008, states were grappling with how to raise their rates of work participation since their caseload increasingly consists of less employable persons.

Despite continued controversy and disagreement about the substantive focus of welfare reform, there is broad agreement on the general results. Caseloads have declined by over 50 percent nationwide, and most of those who leave the welfare rolls work at some point in the year or two following welfare exit. The culture of cash welfare has changed, and more low-income parents are working. The wages of former recipients, however, tend to be low (about $7–8 an hour); few have jobs that provide employee benefits, such as health insurance, sick leave, or vacation allowances; there is little evidence of upward job mobility; and poverty rates remain above 50 percent (Acs and Loprest 2007a). That is, former welfare recipients are generally entering the low-wage job market.

Food Assistance

The vast movement of persons off the welfare rolls and their limited ability to move out of poverty and remain economically self-sufficient raise new policy questions about the safety net for employable poor adults with children. Should work be the centerpiece of the safety net for able-bodied poor adults? If so, what, if any, government policies should be in place to ensure that workers are not poor? What should a work-based safety net look like: guaranteed wages or guaranteed jobs? Access to better jobs? Social supports for workers? What should happen when the economy is weak or in a recession?

Some of these questions have been the subject of policy discussions for many years, although through the end of 2008, little movement occurred at the federal level to address their implications in the current era, aside from recognizing the importance of what have come to be referred to as "work supports." These are services and policies expected to help working parents better balance work and family roles. Perhaps the most critical work support—and one of the largest and broadest components of the U.S. social safety net for the poor, working or not—is the Food Stamp Program.

The Food Stamp Program is the largest of the federal food assistance efforts, with expenditures for 2008 of around $38 billion (U.S. Department of Agriculture 2009b).[2] Even before the 1996 welfare reform, food assistance was a major part of the social safety net for the poor. For example, at a time when about 14 million persons (in 5 million families) received AFDC welfare benefits in its peak year of 1994, about 21 million people received food stamps. In 2008, over 28 million people received food stamps each month.

The U.S. safety net also includes more than a dozen other programs that provide food assistance to low-income individuals and families, representing an additional $25 billion in federal funds in 2008 (U.S. Department of Agriculture 2009a). Some programs target specific low-income populations, such as school children (the School Breakfast Program, the National School Lunch Program), Native Americans (Food Distribution on Indian Reservations), young and old people in day care programs (the Child and Adult Care Food Program), and low-income women with infants and children up to age 5 (the Special Supplemental Nutrition Program for Women, Infants, and Children). The Food Stamp Program, though, is the only major means-tested program in the United States that covers nearly all types of low-income persons and households and the only one that does so as an entitlement and with standard criteria nationwide. Its food security and antihunger purposes are central to its mission.

The Food Stamp Program also fills income gaps—the poorer the household, the higher the benefit—and national standards for eligibility help equalize income regardless of the state in which a household resides. For these reasons, the Food Stamp Program has been and remains the preeminent safety net program in the United States, even though legislation over the years has periodically adjusted eligibility and benefit levels to constrain program scale. In the 1980s, for example, many administrative requirements were added that discouraged households with earnings from maintaining their enrollment, required work registration for adults without dependent children, and excluded many categories of immigrants from eligibility. Changes restricting eligibility, however, have typically been only marginal or have eventually been rescinded by Congress when their effects on the poor became evident. This tendency to restore benefits was especially evident in the early 2000s.

After welfare reform, as the cash assistance caseload declined, food programs took on an even more important role. The special connection between cash welfare and food stamps, which became more prominent after welfare reform, spurred recent administrative and legislative reform. With few exceptions, families receiving welfare are eligible for food stamps. When families apply for welfare, an integrated intake process also determines their eligibility for food stamps (and Medicaid). Families leaving welfare retain their eligibility for food stamps as long as their incomes are low enough and they comply with program rules, including reporting their income regularly and providing acceptable verification of assets, citizenship, and legal immigration status.

Analysis of food stamp participation in the late 1990s revealed what were probably some unintended effects of welfare reform. As welfare cases declined, so did the number of food stamps cases, despite the fact that former welfare recipients, while usually working, nevertheless had below-poverty earnings and thus retained their eligibility for food stamps. Families leaving welfare apparently did not know that they were still eligible for food stamps, prompting concerns that administrative procedures did not do enough to help them retain their enrollment in the Food Stamp Program. Federal and state governments took significant actions to inform those eligible households, through public information campaigns, increased outreach, and improved intake procedures and office operations (see chapter 4).

In the farm bills of 2002, 2007, and especially 2008, Congress simplified the administrative requirements of the Food Stamp Program to promote participation among the eligible population, liberalized benefits for working families, and strengthened the safety net value of food assistance. The 2002 law restored benefits for many legal immigrants after they have been in the country for five years, for whom eligibility had been terminated as part of PRWORA. In the 2008 law, Congress raised the minimum amount of the benefit, indexed the benefit and standard eligibility provisions to inflation, and eliminated the cost of dependent child care and more of the amount in people's savings and education accounts from calculations of income eligibility (Dean, Pawling, and Rosenbaum 2008; U.S. House of Representatives, Committee on Agriculture 2008). In addition, the program acquired a new name, the Supplemental Nutrition Assistance Program (SNAP), as of October 2008, in keeping with the electronic issuance of benefits required by the 2007 bill. Given that electronic transfer of benefits has increasingly been the practice during the past decade at least, it has been a long time since the program issued any physical "stamps" or coupons as it did in its early days.

Analyses indicate that changes in eligibility and benefits made in 2008 will qualify over 100,000 more persons for food assistance and that the average monthly benefit will rise as well. For working families, these changes reinforce the work-centered policies of welfare reform by increasing the supportiveness of the Food Stamp Program. In addition, many more elderly and disabled people are likely to apply for food stamps under the new rules and liberalizations because the value of the benefit is higher than in previous years. Clearly, food assistance remains one of the most significant pieces of the U.S. safety net.

Workforce Development and Employment Services

Work has always been at the center of the American dream. For example, health insurance became a common employment-related benefit in the 1950s as unions negotiated with industry to cover member needs and businesses competed for workers. Given the importance of the work ethic in the national character, it is not surprising that work has become such a key part of the social and economic safety net, primarily through welfare reform. The main premise is that those who work hard can get ahead economically in the United States and support themselves and their children. The self-sufficiency and family-strengthening dimensions of welfare reform reflect these values.

Somewhat ironically, at the same time that welfare was being revised on the assumption that work was the route to self-sufficiency, the labor market became more volatile for those without college degrees. To live comfortably, more families required the incomes of two workers. Welfare reform emphasized work and expected that through work, families would become self-sufficient. But welfare reform was encouraging more low-income parents, most single parents with relatively low skills and limited education, to enter the labor market, where there was an increasing gap in wages paid, based on education and skills.

National programs that fund employment and training services also have changed in the past three decades, but less dramatically and more gradually than welfare reform. One obvious change regards terminology. The term *workforce development* has replaced the older term *employment and training*. The shift in labeling reflects in part the emphasis on improving the skills of the U.S. workforce to meet the growing demand of business for skilled workers and to enable the nation to compete globally. During the 1960s and 1970s, employment services and job training were part of the broad War on Poverty, and many federally funded programs targeted low-income, economically disadvantaged adults and youth. Public service employment that provided federally subsidized jobs to low-income unemployed workers complemented direct job training and employment services, particularly for those unemployed for a long time. At its peak, the national public service employment program subsidized over 600,000 workers.

As noted earlier, by the late 1970s, the purpose of federal employment and training programs shifted toward meeting the needs of businesses, with the advisory boards that plan and oversee local programs now drawn mostly from the business community. Nearly 100 federal programs offer employment services and job training of one type or another, for one group or another. While the largest programs are administered by the U.S. Department of Labor, seven other federal departments also have employment programs, including the Department of Health and Human Services, the Department of Education, and the Department of Veterans Affairs. Despite the plethora of programs, however, the federal funding for employment and training activities has continuously declined since around 1980. The current law authorizing employment and training programs is the Workforce Investment Act of 1998. Funding for programs under WIA, for example, decreased from nearly $14 billion in fiscal year 1977 to $7.3 billion in fiscal year 2007 (Office of Management and Budget 2008). In addition, programs were reoriented to focus on general job search services and short-term training, particularly training needed by businesses, rather than on the public jobs that were common in the 1970s (U.S. House, Committee on Ways and Means 2002).

Unlike welfare, federal funding for employment and training programs has always been discretionary and capped, not open ended, meaning that program size depends on funds appropriated annually by Congress. After

1980, as a result of limited funding and an increased business focus, fewer people were able to obtain job training through these programs—a shift that especially affected those with low skills. Workforce development services under the current WIA were also consolidated to encourage closer coordination among various vocational training, social services, education, and employment programs. One-stop career centers—locally designed and overseen by the business-dominated workforce investment boards—now oversee the services (Barnow and Nightingale 2007).

While WIA specifies that intensive training should be targeted toward those with employment barriers (including welfare recipients), the federal priority in the first decade of the 21st century was clearly on meeting the needs of businesses for skilled workers in occupations experiencing growth. State and local programs vary, though, in how much they focus on businesses and economic development. Some states and local agencies have maintained their historical emphasis on serving economically disadvantaged workers, while also trying to address the demands of businesses. Many local employment agencies, for example, offered welfare-to-work services, administering the work programs under the old AFDC program and the new TANF program. Yet because federal funding for employment and training declined considerably, fewer low-income workers (and fewer workers altogether) are able to receive employment services or job training. At a time when welfare policy developed a major emphasis on employment, Congress cut back and refocused the nation's employment system.

The Earned Income Tax Credit

The earned income tax credit directly rewards work through the federal tax system. Chapter 2 has already described the EITC, which was first established in 1975, and chapter 4 provides more detail, so we mention it only briefly here. The EITC is available only to households with at least one worker but whose income still remains below the poverty line. For such households that file federal taxes, the EITC returns any taxes they paid *plus* tax credits. The EITC operates to fill a household's poverty gap, with households getting more credits the lower their income is in relation to the official poverty line. At first, relatively few eligible households filed for the EITC, either because they did not know about it, they did not file tax returns, or its restrictions made them ineligible. Legislative changes in eligibility caused significant increases in households filing and credits paid in 1994, and the number of beneficiaries has been rising slowly since then (figure 4.3 in chapter 4 shows the growth in households with children receiving EITC payments). Most states with a state income tax have also enacted their own tax credits for working poor families—23 states in 2007.

Health Care for Families and Children

In addition to ensuring adequate nutrition, many consider the provision of adequate health care as a critical work support as well as a way to guarantee that children get the care they need to grow into healthy adults and gain the most from their education. Yet access to health care is very uneven in the United States—sufficiently so that the idea of universal health care is no longer a completely unacceptable concept in American public policy. A major issue in the 2008 presidential campaign, it will likely be fiercely debated, and possibly resolved, in coming years.

Since health care in the United States is also expensive, the issue is how Americans pay for it. In 2008, they did so in four major ways: (1) private insurance offered through their employment, usually with both employers and employees paying a share; (2) government health insurance programs, which include federal Medicare and Medicaid, CHAMPUS (for members of the military), the veterans' health care system, and various state and local health insurance systems with structures similar to Medicaid; (3) private insurance individuals pay for entirely on their own; and (4) by individuals paying out of pocket each time they need care or forgoing health care entirely because they cannot afford either insurance or payment.

Health Insurance through Employers

Most working-age individuals and their families who have health insurance receive it through their employment, participating in employer-sponsored health insurance plans that usually cover the worker and any dependents but typically require employees to contribute toward the cost of coverage. Many retirees, whether 65 years old or somewhat younger, have work-related health insurance coverage as part of their retirement or pension plans. In recent years, however, many employers who offer health insurance have cut back coverage and have raised the copayments required of employees. In addition, workers face loss of benefits if hours are reduced, part-time workers may get no benefits at all, retirement coverage for future retirees is being reduced or eliminated, and even people already retired and covered by retiree health plans risk losing benefits. An increasing number of employers, especially small firms that employ a large proportion of low-wage workers, do not offer health insurance at all (DeNavas-Walt, Proctor, and Smith 2007; National Coalition on Health Care 2007).

Federal and Federal-State Programs

Although the federal government offers a number of health insurance programs, all serve specific populations only; none is universal.

Medicare

Medicare is available to most persons age 65 and older, some family members and survivors of such people, and anyone who worked long enough to qualify for the program but became disabled enough to qualify for Social Security Disability Insurance before reaching retirement. Medicare is a federal government program, with no state contribution to funding, and beneficiaries also must pay a monthly premium for coverage. In 2007, Congress added a Medicare prescription drug benefit—a benefit that has widespread public support but is very expensive. The compromises needed to pass the benefit produced an extremely complex structure that is difficult for the public to understand and still leaves many recipients vulnerable to charges for prescription drugs that they cannot afford to pay. There is great pressure to constrain the rising costs of the program due to increasing numbers of beneficiaries and rising health care costs. In 2008, Congress defeated proposals to significantly reduce payments to doctors, in part out of fear that more and more doctors would refuse to serve Medicare patients because payments were so low.

Medicaid

Medicaid covers low-income people, mainly those who qualify because they are in a particular program. Families that receive TANF or would have been eligible for AFDC under rules applying in 1995 are eligible for Medicaid, as are people who qualify because they receive Supplemental Security Income (SSI), usually because they are permanently and completely disabled. All children in Medicaid qualify for periodic pediatric examinations under the Early and Periodic Screening, Diagnosis, and Treatment Program to detect, prevent, and treat physical and mental conditions as early as possible. Like Medicare, Medicaid is under constant pressure to contain costs, at the same time that many states are using waivers of Medicaid rules to expand coverage of people and services. Federal and state governments (and local governments in some states) share the costs of Medicaid. Because of that payment structure, states find it more beneficial to expand Medicaid rather than to launch or enlarge their own health insurance programs, since the federal government will cover part of the cost of expansion whereas they would have to pay the entire cost of state-only plans.

SCHIP

The State Children's Health Insurance Program was enacted in 1997 to expand medical coverage to children in low-income families whose income was nevertheless too high to qualify for Medicaid and for whom private insurance was either unavailable or unaffordable. States have considerable discretion over the program; about one-third designed SCHIP by expanding Medicaid, one-third established separate child health insurance programs, and one-third used a combination of the two. SCHIP substantially broadened publicly funded health insurance for low-income children to the point that over half of all children in the country are eligible for SCHIP. About 4 million participate at any given time, with about 6.7 million (and about 700,000 adults) participating at some time during the course of a year (Dubay, Holahan, and Cook 2007; Kenney 2008). Under SCHIP, the federal government has encouraged states to expand coverage to include older children (from 5 or younger up to 12 and even 17 or younger) and those in households with higher (but still not high) incomes (from about one-third of the poverty level, on average, in 1996, up to several times the poverty level more recently). Many states have also invested their own resources, taking advantage of federal waivers to expand health coverage to parents in households with covered children and to childless adults. Even with SCHIP, however, about 9.4 million low-income children remain uninsured, two-thirds of whom are eligible for either Medicaid or SCHIP but have not enrolled (Kaiser Commission on Medicaid and the Uninsured 2008).

Under the federal-state Medicaid partnership, SCHIP has in many ways become the basis for state expansion of public health coverage. Many states increased coverage to parents, and some used the SCHIP framework to consider more universal coverage policies. While most experts agree that SCHIP has been a success because millions more children have coverage, some funding and regulatory concerns make implementation and coverage difficult (Kenney 2008). In addition, during periods of economic distress and high unemployment, applications for health insurance rise as more workers lose their jobs.

That increase in demand adds to financial pressures at the state and federal level because the federal contribution to some optional SCHIP provisions in some states is uncertain. Coverage for adults is one area vulnerable to federal funding reductions. Unlike Medicaid, an entitlement with open-ended federal funding available to states to cover all who qualify, the federal share of SCHIP is in the form of a block grant. Because federal funding is capped, states may restrict or narrow eligibility during periods of serious economic stress.

The SCHIP programs have begun to reduce the number of uninsured children, and Congress passed two versions of legislation reauthorizing SCHIP in 2007 with bipartisan support, both of which would have expanded coverage. President Bush vetoed both and neither veto was overridden by Congress. Stopgap funding for SCHIP did pass and was signed into law in fall 2007. Major controversial issues included income eligibility limits; treatment of immigrants, parents, and childless adults; and concerns that expanding coverage would reduce the health insurance offered by employers (known as "crowd out"). As one of their first legislative actions, the new Congress and the Obama administration that took office in January 2009 finally reauthorized SCHIP for five years, extending coverage to about 4 million more children or about 40 percent of those who remained uninsured.

State and Local Programs

Many states have added their own health insurance structures onto their Medicaid (and SCHIP) programs, as have some localities as well. For example, in Texas, the city of Houston and Harris County's Gold Card gives indigents access to health care. While many of such programs cover health care for indigents only, some states have committed themselves to offering significantly broader coverage to low- and moderate-income families. Among the first states to do so were Massachusetts (MassHealth), Minnesota (MinnesotaCare), and Oregon (Oregon Health Plan). In addition, several states—including Hawaii, Rhode Island, and Tennessee—took advantage of waivers available under the Medicaid program to greatly expand their health care coverage during the 1990s. Still, not all states, though, have a medically indigent program; in those states, adults without children have no health insurance options unless they are disabled enough to qualify for federal SSI and through SSI gain automatic eligibility for Medicaid.

States continue to move forward with health insurance reform, although fiscal constraints have caused some to curtail the programs they started in the 1990s, sometimes severely. But Massachusetts passed measures in 2007 designed to ensure that every state resident would have access to health care. Within one year, these measures had reduced the uninsured population in that state by half, from 13 to 7 percent; by the end of the second year (2008), about two-thirds of the remaining uninsured were covered, and only 2.6 percent were still without insurance (Long, Cook, and Stockley 2008). The District of Columbia is also planning to ensure health care to everyone. Chapter 7 provides more examples of ways that states are leading the push toward health care reform and, eventually, universal health care. If health insurance reform follows the pattern of welfare reform a decade earlier, the policies adopted by states and their experiences may serve as models for national reforms.

People without Health Insurance

While publicly supported health insurance programs in the United States are very large in financial terms, they nevertheless leave many groups without coverage. Chief among such groups are workers without access to employer coverage, nonelderly adults without children, and families with children whose incomes are too high to qualify for Medicaid or SCHIP. About 20 percent of nonelderly persons in the United States are without health insurance coverage from an employer or from public programs such as Medicaid. By 1999, the number of uninsured people had risen to about 40 million, and it has continued to grow, reaching about 46 million in 2006 (Graves and Long 2006; McLaughlin et al. 2004). The rise in the uninsured population is particularly striking since it occurred during a time when SCHIP was increasingly providing coverage to children in low-income families. Without SCHIP, the number of uninsured people would have been at least 4 million higher in 2006, around 50 million.

Economic changes in the nation explain some of the increase in the uninsured population. Over the past 20 years, the percentage of employees with employer-sponsored health insurance has been declining as businesses face the rising costs of health insurance premiums. A third of U.S. firms did not offer coverage in 2006 (National Coalition on Health Care 2007). The lack of insurance is especially serious for lower-income workers. While nearly 90 percent of working families with incomes four times the poverty threshold have employer-sponsored health insurance, fewer than half of lower-income working families—those below 200 percent of the poverty income level—have access to that benefit (Graves and Long 2006). Health insurance coverage is also vulnerable to economic downturns. When the economy worsens, employers reduce benefits, including health insurance; and when people lose jobs, they lose not only income but often their health insurance as well. As of 2009, the nation had no policies in place to deal with that situation.

Because the application process for Medicaid had been so closely connected with that of applying for AFDC, Medicaid enrollment dropped off sharply when that program changed to TANF in 1996, similar to what happened in the Food Stamp Program. Efforts to increase enrollment in Medicaid and SCHIP in recent years have partially reversed this trend (Holahan and Weil 2002; Kenney, Haley, and Tebay 2003). Chapter 4 provides more detail on these enrollment patterns and the policies and practices responsible for both the decline and the response.

Since 1997, expansions in medical coverage through SCHIP have substantially increased coverage for poor children and have had an important influence on the debate on universal health insurance policies in the nation. As discussed, some states have taken the next step and are also using the SCHIP framework to provide coverage for low-income parents. Still, the total number of uninsured people in the United States rises each year, prompting grave concerns about the large numbers of persons, including low-and moderate-income childless adults and workers, who lack access to regular and preventive health care.

Housing Assistance

In 1949, Congress set a national goal to provide "a decent home in a suitable living environment for every American family." We are not close to meeting that goal yet. Paying for housing, including the cost of the rent or mortgage and utilities, is the biggest part of most families' budget, especially for low-income families. During the period of economic expansion in the late 1990s, incomes rose for even the poorest households, making housing somewhat more affordable. But since 2001, affordability has been declining. At the same time that the poorest households are having an increasingly difficult time paying for housing, federal policy has *reduced* the availability of housing subsidies.

Decreasing Affordability

Before describing changes in the affordability of housing for low-income households, some attention to terminology will be helpful, because the housing world uses different concepts and measures than other social programs to talk about poor people. In chapter 2, we explained that the Department of Housing and Urban Development uses a relative measure—"household income as a percent of the median income in the area where you live" (AMI)—to identify households in need of assistance with housing, rather than the more common federal poverty line that is applied throughout the country. HUD divides households as follows:

- Extremely low income (ELI) households have incomes at 0–30 percent of AMI.
- Very low income (VLI) households have incomes at 0–50 percent of AMI and include ELI households.
- Low-income (LI) households have incomes at 0–80 percent of AMI and include VLI households.

As a rough comparison at the national level, the federal poverty line would be equivalent to about 30 percent of AMI, although that can vary greatly from community to community.

HUD uses two approaches to examining housing affordability for low-income households. One is called "worst-case housing needs." Since 1990, HUD has reported to Congress every two years on the number of households with severe rent burden (those paying 50 percent or more of their income for housing costs plus utilities) and those in severely inadequate housing (housing with major structural defects or malfunctioning systems). Two factors can affect this measure—rent levels and income levels. If rents are steady and household incomes rise, fewer households will have a severe rent burden. If household incomes rise but rents rise faster, more households will have a severe rent burden. And since severe rent burden is a far greater problem for households with extremely low incomes than for any others, changes in either rents or incomes among that group of households will have the greatest effect on worst-case housing needs. Even if the incomes of the richest 20 percent of households increase substantially, that change will have no effect on worst-case housing needs.

From 1989 through 1997, rents rose faster than incomes, and the proportion of ELI and VLI households with worst-case housing needs rose proportionally. For a brief period between 1997 and 1999, while the nation was enjoying an unusually long period of job growth and prosperity that reached even extremely low income families, worst-case housing needs dipped for the first time in a decade (HUD 2001).

Worst-Case Housing Needs

- 1997—5.4 million households
- 1999—4.9 million households
- 2001—5.0 million households
- 2003—5.2 million households
- 2005—6.0 million households

But that happy news was short-lived. By 2001, rates were climbing again, the number of households with worst-case housing needs reaching the highest reported level ever in 2005, the latest year available (see text box). In that year, about 6 million households had worst-case housing needs, more than three-quarters of whom had incomes at the ELI level (i.e., they were poor by federal poverty line standards).

The second approach used by HUD to measure affordability is an index of the number of rental units that are "affordable and available." Affordable, as defined by HUD, means that housing costs are equal to or less than 30 percent of the household's income. Available is defined as on the market and available to rent. This second criterion is an important addition to the affordability criterion because many units with low rents are occupied by households with relatively high incomes and thus are not available to poor households looking for a place to live.

The affordability index is expressed as units per 100 renters. From 1991 to 1997, this index was expressed for all renters (i.e., not just ELI or VLI renters). During that period, the number of units affordable and available to renters went from 47 to 36 per 100 renter households—a 23 percent decline (HUD 1999). In recent years, the concern about affordability has focused on poor households, so the index has been expressed in terms of VLI or ELI renters. In 2003, there were 81 units affordable and available for every 100 VLI households. This 20 percent shortfall worsened by 2005 to 77 units for every VLI household—a 5 percent decrease. Extremely low income households are the hardest pressed to find affordable housing; in 2005, there were only 44 affordable and available units for every 100 ELI households (HUD 2007).

Explanations for the increasing scarcity of housing affordable and available to low-income renters are numerous. Among the more common factors are gentrification, decreasing financial attractiveness of rental housing compared to other investment options, and policies that favor subsidizing existing units over producing new affordable housing. The growing appeal of city living to many people with resources changed the usual progression of neighborhood occupancy. Throughout most of the 20th century, urban housing built for middle-class households gradually shifted to occupancy by poorer households as the better-off moved to the suburbs. In the past several decades, that trend has reversed, with better-off people reclaiming inner-city neighborhoods and displacing the low-income households who lived there. Since the better-off households usually have fewer members than the low-income households—and sometimes acquire more than one unit to convert for their own use—the trend also meant that fewer households and fewer household members now occupy much available housing, leaving the displaced households to compete for the remaining affordable units.

Since the mid-1980s, many landlords have followed their own financial interests and converted their buildings to ownership housing as condominiums or cooperatives, attracting higher-income residents. Again, this trend removed units affordable to low-income renters from the market. Finally, as described next, starting in the mid-1970s and accelerating in the 1990s, the emphasis of federal housing policies shifted from building new affordable housing to depending on the availability of existing housing. But as we just saw, without new affordable housing coming into the market, the cost of renting increased beyond what many poor households could pay.

Federal Housing Programs and Recent Changes

At the federal level, HUD manages the major federal programs dedicated to rental assistance, including public housing, the Section 202 and Section 811 programs, and the Section 8/Housing Choice Voucher Program.

The Housing Act of 1937 was the first federal foray into publicly provided housing. A significant part of the motivation for this legislation was to create jobs by building housing for millions of out-of-work Americans as part of the New Deal, not to provide housing per se, although people certainly needed it. The result was public housing buildings built and maintained by about 3,300 public housing authorities nationwide. The federal government allocates funding to the housing authorities every year to maintain and operate these public housing structures.

After World War II, the nation renewed its commitment to housing, as noted at the beginning of this section. But rental housing was not the focus. Rather, investment mostly took the form of low-interest, low-down-payment loans to support home ownership among veterans and lower-income Americans through the Veterans Affairs (VA) guaranteed home loan and the Federal Housing Administration.

Public housing authorities also run two specialized programs that provide rent-subsidized housing for low-income elderly people and households with disabilities—Section 202 and Section 811, respectively. Section 202, authorized in 1959, originally covered both elderly and disabled households, but the two functions were divided in 1990, with the Section 811 program created to cover the disabled population. As with public housing, Section 202 and Section 811 housing is usually offered in buildings owned and operated by the public housing authority.

In 1974, the focus of housing assistance began to change from housing authority–owned buildings to rental assistance for units in the private market through the program long known as Section 8 but recently renamed the Housing Choice Voucher Program. These resources are attached either to particular projects developed by private landlords (project-based assistance) or to particular households that may use them in any qualifying unit (tenant-based assistance). The project-based approach, which came first, still created new affordable housing units by paying for capital development as well as for long-term operating costs. Although a household living in a unit subsidized by project-based assistance may move, the subsidy stays with the unit and assists the next tenant. As the project-based approach came to be perceived as too expensive, the program switched to tenant-based assistance, which does not create new housing. A household with a tenant-based voucher "owns" that voucher and takes it to the private rental market to find a qualifying unit. If the household moves, the voucher moves with it.

HUD will pay the difference between what housing costs and the amount affordable to a household—30 percent of its income—up to a level that HUD defines as the "fair market rent" for an apartment of the size the household needs. Thus, if a household's income is $10,000 and the household lives in HUD-assisted housing, it would pay $3,000 a year ($250 a month) toward the rent of its dwelling, and HUD would pay the rest.[3] How far HUD's housing assistance dollar stretches is thus highly dependent on rent levels *and* household incomes—the higher the rent and the lower the incomes, the fewer households can be accommodated.

Housing assistance is not an entitlement in the United States. HUD receives annual appropriations for its various housing assistance programs and distributes it to housing authorities. When that federal money is gone, the housing authorities cannot help anyone else, regardless of need or qualifications, unless they are able to use state or local resources. In 2008, more than 1.2 million households lived in public housing, and another 2 million households received rent subsidies through the Housing Choice Voucher Program.

Proposed Cuts to Housing Assistance Programs

During the Bush administration, federal authorities made persistent attempts to reduce the national government's involvement in housing assistance. Administrative changes in 2004 and 2005 to the Housing Choice Voucher Program squeezed out funding for about 75,000 vouchers in use, with the result that 75,000 households with vouchers lost that benefit unless housing authorities used local funds to reinstate the assistance. President Bush's budget proposals for subsequent years would have eliminated subsidies for about 600,000 households in five years (a 30 percent cut), but as with some other Bush administration proposals for cuts to federal housing assistance programs, these never were enacted by Congress.

Meanwhile, the Section 202 Program, which had had mostly consistent federal funding during the early 2000s, experienced cuts in later years, although these were a small fraction of the reductions requested by the administration. The same thing happened to the Section 811 Program, which in the 2000s had been funded at only about two-thirds of its funding level in the 1990s, with even deeper cuts proposed by the Bush White House but rejected by Congress.

Low Income Housing Tax Credits

The Low Income Housing Tax Credits program (LIHTC) was created as part of the Tax Reform Act of 1986 to provide an incentive to private housing developers to build housing affordable to low-income renters. Between 1987 and 2006, the LIHTC program distributed more than $8.3 billion in tax credits used to create about 1.6 million affordable housing units. Developers must commit to renting either 20 percent of the units to households with incomes at or below 50 percent of AMI or 40 percent of the units to households at or below 60 percent of AMI. While not *required* to house poor households (those with incomes at or below 30 percent of AMI), many developments using LIHTC funding do include low-income renters in their mix. In addition, nothing prevents a developer from targeting some or all units to lower-income households. In many LIHTC properties, tenants are likely to have a range of incomes, but some projects are specifically for extremely low income households. The original law required that landlords keep the housing affordable for 15 years, but that time frame has since been increased to 30 years.

The following explanation presents a simplified idea of the LIHTC structure. Every year, HUD uses a formula to distribute tax credits among state housing finance agencies. Developers who propose projects to these agencies and get approval receive an allocation of a certain amount in tax credit. The developers then recruit investors to the project. Once the project is built and occupied, investors receive a dollar-for-dollar tax credit against their own tax liability every year for 10 years, as long as the project complies with LIHTC rules to maintain unit affordability. Thus, the federal tax system helps subsidize affordable housing. Because the cost of building the housing is underwritten by public money, developers can charge lower rents and still make a profit.

The LIHTC has been an interesting and successful experiment in several ways. First, it operates completely in the private market. No public housing authority builds, rents, or controls the units, although state housing finance agencies are the point of application for obtaining the tax credit allocation. Second, it creates many mixed-income developments, which is a tenant pattern believed to foster the most supportive environment for low-income households (see the description of HOPE VI below). This approach contrasts with that used for Section 8 project-based vouchers, which also relied on private developers to create housing but in which low-income households occupy all units in a project. Third, it uses the tax system rather than program appropriations as a funding source and investors' self-interest as the motivation for creating affordable housing. Although some questioned the proportion of units that go to the neediest households rather than to somewhat better-off families, even people at 60 percent of AMI are having a hard time affording housing these days, so many people benefit.

Housing Opportunities for People Everywhere

Many of the nation's 3,300 public housing authorities do a good job of managing and maintaining their properties. But some are so badly managed that they end up in receivership; and some, but not all, structures owned by other authorities end up in very bad shape. The potential inadequacy of public housing prompted Congress in 1989 to appoint a National Commission on Severely Distressed Public Housing. This commission issued a report in 1992 recommending that HUD "eliminate and replace" about 86,000 units—about 6 percent of the approximately 1.3 million housing authority units existing at that time.

What became the Housing Opportunities for People Everywhere (HOPE VI) program in 1999 through an amendment adding a new section to the Housing Act of 1937 began as an annual congressional appropriation in 1993, immediately following the commission's report. Program goals included improving the living environment of residents of severely distressed public housing; making available to them resources, services, and supports that could help them move toward self-sufficiency; decreasing concentrated poverty; and building sustainable communities. Housing authorities could apply for grants from HUD to replace severely inadequate units. Over the years, HUD has made about 450 grants to 166 cities under HOPE VI, which totaled $6.25 billion from 1993 through 2006. These billions of federal dollars have leveraged at least as much in local public, private, and foundation funding.

HOPE VI is a very controversial program. Using its resources, housing authorities are not just replacing units but are changing both the structure of housing and the income mix of tenants that will occupy it. Destroyed housing is being replaced by fewer units, and less than half the tenant households that had to move during demolition and new construction eventually move back into units in the new buildings. Much of HOPE VI funding goes for housing choice vouchers to help former tenants rent units in surrounding neighborhoods, in the expectation that they will stay there. This strategy aims to reduce the concentrated poverty that existed in large high-rise public housing structures, spreading former tenants out into other neighborhoods, and also inviting mixed-income households to occupy the new construction. In addition, the new developments are supposed to create "defensible spaces" by using low-rise, less concentrated structures; by being organized to provide good sight lines of public spaces; and by encouraging community building and similar objectives. These different structures are expected to reduce crime and bring people together.

Another aspect of HOPE VI is the expectation that public housing authorities will enter into partnerships with many stakeholders in their community, such as local governments, nonprofit service providers, and the business community, to bring resources into the new developments and help residents move toward self-sufficiency if they are not already there. As described in chapter 2, changed residential patterns associated with HOPE VI contributed to the reduction in concentrated poverty that occurred between the 1990 and 2000 censuses. But because no systematic national evaluations of its impact have been attempted (although there are many case studies), the impact of the program is subject to interpretation. In 2004, after a decade of HOPE VI, a conference of many stakeholders was convened to assess HOPE VI (Popkin et al. 2004). A summary of the results follows, which we quote at length because it so ably presents the difficulties inherent in setting, implementing, and assessing a major public policy (Popkin et al. 2004, 3–4):

> In part because of the absence of definitive data and evaluation results, perceptions about the impacts of HOPE VI vary widely. Some people characterize it as a dramatic success, while others view it as a profound failure. There is no question that the program has had some notable accomplishments. Hundreds of profoundly distressed developments have been targeted for demolition, and many of them are now replaced with well-designed, high-quality housing serving a mix of income levels. HOPE VI has been an incubator for innovations in project financing, management, and service delivery. Some projects have helped turn around conditions in the surrounding neighborhoods and have contributed to the revitalization of whole inner-city communities. However, HOPE VI implementation has also encountered significant challenges. Some HOPE VI projects have been stalled by ineffective implementation on the part of the housing authority or conflict with city government. In others, developments were simply rehabilitated or rebuilt in the same distressed communities, with little thought to innovative design, effective services, or neighborhood revitalization.
>
> Most seriously, there is substantial evidence that the original residents of HOPE VI projects have not always benefited from redevelopment, even in some sites that were otherwise successful. This can be partly attributed to a lack of meaningful resident participation in planning and insufficient attention to relocation strategies and services. As a consequence, some of the original residents of these developments may live in equally or even more precarious circumstances today.

So how people value HOPE VI depends on what they value on other fronts. If they place highest priority on the well-being of poor people, they will see HOPE VI as a failure, and one that could have been avoided with more emphasis on ensuring that at the very least no one would be worse off as a consequence of HOPE VI. If their highest priority is less crime and better-organized housing and neighborhoods, they will see HOPE VI as a success. The problem is, it is extremely difficult to design and carry out a public policy that will satisfy all of the people all of the time. The challenge is, we should probably try.

National Housing Trust Fund

Advocates have long sought a national housing trust fund that would provide resources for developing more affordable housing. Some states and localities have such funds, which are more or less helpful depending on the reliability of their funding sources and the amount of money those sources generate. In 2008, faced with a very weak housing market and widespread foreclosures because of a crisis in the markets that lend to low-income households, Congress established a national housing trust fund as part of the Housing and Economic Recovery Act of 2008. This is the first new federal housing production program since the HOME program was created in 1990 and the first new production program specifically targeted to extremely low income households since the Section 8 Program was created in 1974.

The National Housing Trust Fund is a permanent program with a dedicated source of funding. It is not subject to the annual appropriations process and is therefore not vulnerable to changing priorities and potential cuts. Resources for the Housing Trust Fund will come from annual contributions made by Fannie Mae and Freddie Mac based on a percentage of each company's annual new business. If the Housing Trust Fund had been operating in 2008, it would have received about $300 million from these sources. Funding at that level or above is expected for future years. President Obama has requested $1 billion in the FY 2010 budget to capitalize this fund.

At least 90 percent of the Housing Trust Fund's resources must be used for the production, preservation, rehabilitation, or operation of rental housing, thus targeting the low-income population (the other 10 percent may be used to promote home ownership). Furthermore, at least 75 percent of the rental housing funds must benefit ELI households (those at or below 30 percent of AMI). All must benefit VLI households (those at or below 50 percent of AMI).

Emergency and Crisis Services

Throughout this chapter, we have described some of the complexities of the U.S. safety net and the types of reforms or changes made or attempted in the past decade, since the primary vehicle of welfare reform, PRWORA, passed in 1996. Many of the reforms had elements that emphasized employment, including TANF, food assistance expansions, and workforce development. Health care is a major issue on which the focus of reforms has been to provide coverage for low-income children. State forays into the universal health insurance arena, as noted above, have attempted to expand health coverage to adults and working parents—but with little forward motion for the nation as a whole, since we continue to disagree on how to pay for such expansions and who should be covered. The unemployable elderly and disabled are generally provided income assistance through Social Security and Supplemental Security Income but for the disabled at an income level that generally tops off at 75 percent of the federal poverty line—not exactly a lavish income. Those who are neither elderly nor totally disabled, though—particularly if they also are childless—face a much more fragmented safety net.

When all else fails and people face crises they cannot handle, protective and emergency services are the last resort. We briefly look at one such emergency service: homeless assistance.

During the Great Depression in the 1930s, the plight of the homeless was very visible. But homelessness was not again a publicly recognized problem until the early 1980s, when the 1981–82 recession brought more and different people to the streets. At that time, virtually all response to homelessness was private, concentrated in missions and feeding programs serving single men in run-down areas of major cities. In the early 1980s, the problem was first attributed to jobs lost during the recession, which helped explain why women and whole families with children were showing up in shelters and soup kitchens that were ill-equipped to handle the influx. The assumption was that the problem would end when the recession was over or shortly thereafter, but that did not happen.

As the problem of homelessness grew, from arguably no more than 100,000 people nationwide at the start of the 1980s to an estimated 500,000 to 600,000 people on any given day in 1987 (Burt 1992), first local government and then federal attention turned to what to do. Emergency shelters were the first answer, and the first level of response came from local governments and nonprofit agencies. In 1983, Congress passed a jobs bill that also included emergency relief to affected families in the form of the Emergency Food and Shelter Program (EFSP), which was and still is run by the Federal Emergency Management Administration. The EFSP was set up to make temporary funding available, but five additional waves were provided between 1983 and 1986 as the "emergency" did not disappear.

Major federal legislation investing in the development of homeless assistance services began in 1987 with the Stewart B. McKinney Homeless Assistance Act, incorporating the EFSP and making it a permanent program as well as providing additional assistance to emergency shelters (Emergency Shelter Grants); new program types, such as transitional housing Health Care for the Homeless (now offering programs in hundreds of locations throughout the nation and serving more than 800,000 homeless people in 2006); and several demonstration programs for permanent supportive housing for people with disabilities (Permanent Housing for Homeless People with Disabilities).

Important additions to homeless assistance came in the form of Housing Opportunities for People with AIDS (HOPWA, first authorized in 1992), Shelter Plus Care (begun in 1995 and now providing rent subsidies for formerly homeless disabled adults and families in tens of thousands of units in most communities in the nation), and set-asides beginning in the late 1990s for permanent supportive housing to end the homelessness of more than 100,000 chronically homeless people with disabilities severe enough to make self-sufficiency an unrealistic goal. Federal funds through the McKinney Act, as amended, also go to programs to help homeless children attend school, to help homeless people connect to employment, to help homeless veterans deal with their health issues and return to housing, and to help people with serious mental illness find services and housing, among other activities.

In 1987, federal homeless assistance was authorized at over $1 billion, but actual appropriations totaled at most a third of that amount. The Clinton administration began increasing funding in 1992, and the second Bush administration continued the upward trend. FY 2008 appropriations totaled about $2.5 billion. State, local, and private funding accounts for at least that much again, and probably much more.

In part because the crisis in affordable housing has only worsened since the early 1980s and in part because homeless assistance programs were the only growth area for poverty-related public funding during the 1990s and early 2000s, homeless assistance programs have proliferated. Even mainstream public agencies have applied for and received "homeless" dollars from HUD, often to do what might be considered their basic job that should be done with their own resources. For instance, public health agencies have received HUD homeless dollars to create respite care programs for homeless people too sick to be released from hospitals on their own, public mental health agencies have received HUD homeless dollars to create community-based housing for their own clients, publicly funded substance abuse treatment agencies have received HUD homeless dollars to create transitional housing programs for people recovering from addictions, and child welfare agencies have received HUD dollars to provide housing for youth aging out of foster care.

Since 2000, in recognition that such investment had not slowed movement into homelessness despite the numbers of households assisted, public policy efforts have undergone a paradigm shift. They have gone from "managing homelessness" to developing complex plans to end it, either just for people with long histories of homelessness or for all people who are or who might experience homelessness. Example 12 in chapter 7 provides a detailed description of what happened and what the change has meant for chronically homeless people.

Conclusions

With the American social safety net made up of hundreds of different programs, an almost continuous stream of proposals for new laws, new programs, and reforms flows onto the desks of decisionmakers. Our federalist structure means that across the country, states and some local governments are making changes to various programs, sometimes leading the way for what may eventually become federal policies. Recent developments in welfare reform, food assistance, workforce development, health care coverage through insurance, housing, and emergency services for homeless people provide a small glimpse into the complexity of the safety net and the magnitude of changes that are often occurring simultaneously at any given moment.

Some changes are congruent, reflecting similar objectives; but some conflict with others. Not infrequently it seems that the right hand does not know what the left hand is doing. Some of the inconsistencies reflect the complexity of government structure, as discussed in chapter 6, but some exemplify the difficulty the nation has had in grappling with problems of poverty and the role of government in alleviating it.

Since the early 1980s, the social safety net has undergone major changes, in part reflecting the dramatic transformations in the nation as the post–World War II economic growth slowed and workers' earnings stagnated. Pressures on the federal budget also mounted to continue to fund both the expanded social programs instituted in better times and the growing costs of entitlement programs for the elderly. One result of that pressure was the major welfare reform legislation in 1996 that restructured AFDC, the former entitlement program for poor families with children, and replaced it with a short-term work-based program that provides families just temporary cash assistance and help finding a job.

Many supports for working families, including those leaving welfare, expanded in the 1990s and early 2000s. Food assistance programs were liberalized and SCHIP provided health insurance to millions of formerly uninsured children, many of whom were in families with at least one worker. These work supports, along with the major expansions of the largest work-based antipoverty policy, the earned income tax credit, place clear emphasis on the importance of work in the nation's social safety net. As a result, the number of low-income parents who work, especially mothers, has increased markedly, even though their work often does little to raise household income above the poverty line. As the welfare rolls have shrunk, more people are working, but more workers are poor than before the reforms in welfare and work.

Meanwhile, the employment and training system, which one might expect could help achieve the types of welfare reforms envisioned, has been going in a somewhat different direction. The revamped—and renamed—workforce development system is focused more on the needs of businesses (which often means high-skilled workers) and less on employment and training for the disadvantaged than earlier program incarnations going back to the 1960s. In addition, federal support for housing assistance went backwards, with vital rent subsidies that made housing affordable for millions of households either eliminated or under threat.

Certainly programs, such as Food Stamps and SCHIP, that function as work supports (as well as serving other purposes) make life easier for poor families in which at least one parent can and does work. The situation for those who cannot work, or cannot always work, is bleaker. Housing supports have been curtailed at the same time that housing costs, housing insecurity, and other economic hardships have risen.

The reforms introduced to welfare have placed new attention on families with the most serious problems. Those remaining on the welfare rolls tend to have serious and multiple barriers that make it difficult for them to work or prepare to work. These are typically the very families that may appear in more than one public program—they are on welfare, their children are at higher risk of abuse and neglect, they and their children are likely to have limited education, they have an unstable work history, and they have medical and mental health problems that limit their ability to work. Problems finding stable housing and legal and other hardships further complicate the picture. Maneuvering through the complex system of social supports is a major undertaking for those families seeking help and for the agencies attempting to help them. The next chapter examines caseloads and the mechanisms involved in gaining access to the social safety net, while chapter 5 describes approaches to serving individuals and families with the most serious barriers.

4

Getting onto the Rolls
Caseloads, Eligibility Processes, Targeting, and Outreach

The whole point of a safety net is that it "be there" for people when they get into serious trouble, such as when they lose their income, get very sick, or lack the money to feed and house themselves. Since general hard times will put more households in serious jeopardy, the number of people who participate in safety net programs will naturally fluctuate in relation to the state of the economy. In addition, program policies, eligibility criteria, and administrative practices will influence caseload levels to varying degrees. This chapter examines participation in the three biggest safety net programs—Aid to Families with Dependent Children, which became Temporary Assistance for Needy Families; Food Stamps; and Medicaid and the State Children's Health Insurance Program—as well as some reasons why participation levels may have changed.

The chapter begins with an overview of caseloads—that is, the number of people served by the three major U.S. safety net programs from the early 1990s, before federal welfare reform, to the most recent year for which data are available, usually 2006 or 2007. It will be obvious from the caseload data that legislation enacted in the mid-1990s and reviewed in chapter 3 had a dramatic effect on the number of households participating in these programs. In addition to documenting simple caseload changes for each safety net program, we also examine other critical aspects: (1) the program's "coverage," that is, the extent to which households that might be eligible for a program are actually enrolled; and (2) systematic differences in participation rates for eligible households, with a focus on how particular household characteristics, the level of benefits, and the policies and operations of programs could affect a household's willingness or ability to apply.

After presenting the basic caseload information for the three major programs, we look at the evidence for the number of safety net programs in which households participate simultaneously and how long people continue to receive benefits from those programs—whether their spells are short or long, recurring or one-time.

The balance of the chapter discusses how people enroll in safety net programs and the ever-changing policy environment that makes enrollment easier or harder. As will become clear, the differences between policy as codified in law and policy as practiced in myriad local public offices are sometimes striking. "Implementation" refers to that conversion of law into practice. More and more, policymakers are recognizing how important it is to examine the way programs actually run. Without a sound knowledge of how a program is implemented and how it runs day to day, we cannot tell whether the program is effective. If nothing changes for participants, it could be that the program does not work, but it could also be that the program was not correctly run—it may never have gotten off the ground. Even if things do change for participants, we cannot tell without knowledge of implementation whether the program itself should get the credit for any observed changes in the lives of program participants or whether changes should be attributed to other causes. Because this is such an important issue, the chapter concludes with a look at the research that tries to explain *why* caseloads changed so much and weighs the role of program changes, the changing economy, and other factors including policy changes not directly related to the safety net programs in question.

Caseloads and Caseload Changes—AFDC/TANF

AFDC and, after 1996, TANF serve needy households with children, including one-parent households, two-parent households, and households in which only the children receive benefits (referred to as "child-only" cases). From the early to the late 1990s, AFDC/TANF caseloads fell dramatically. Declines began early in the decade, even before states started

Figure 4.1. Average Monthly AFDC/TANF Caseload of Families and Recipients, 1980–2007 (in millions)

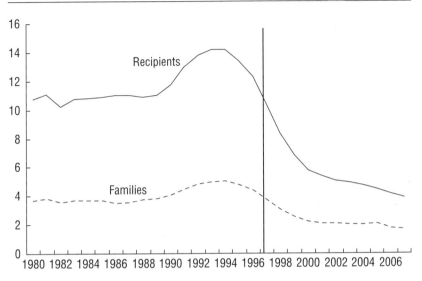

Source: ACF/HHS/OFA TANF caseload data. http://www.acf.hhs.gov/programs/ofa/datareports/caseload/2007/2007_recipient_tan.htm.

to implement TANF in 1997. Figure 4.1 shows the pattern from 1980 through 2007, with 1997, the first year of TANF implementation, marked by a vertical line. The peak years of AFDC enrollment were 1993 and 1994, when over 5 million families with 14 million recipients were on the rolls during an average month. Between the highs of 1993 and 1994 and the last full year of AFDC, the rolls had already decreased by about 12 percent, to 4.4 million families and 12.3 million recipients. Between 1996 and 1999, these caseloads fell by 44 or 45 percent, with continued declines in families (down 20 percent) and recipients (down 26 percent) between 1999 and 2002. Caseloads did not increase even in the leaner economic times of the mid-2000s—family cases declined another 19 per-cent, and individual recipients were down by 23 percent between 2002 and 2007. Altogether, there were about two-thirds *fewer* families on the TANF caseload in 2007 than had received AFDC in 1993 and 1994. Toward the end of this chapter, we examine some of the reasons for these dramatic caseload declines.

The TANF caseload consists of several different family types—single-parent, two-parent, and child-only. Two-parent families were, and remain, a very small proportion (about 2 percent) of all TANF families. Child-only cases are those in which no parent is receiving any cash benefits. Sometimes, for example, a child is being cared for by relatives without a parent present in the household, or perhaps the parent in the household is not eligible for cash benefits, is beyond the TANF time limit, receives Supplemental Security Income, has been sanctioned by TANF, or is not in this country legally.

Single-parent households are the predominant TANF household type but also the type that has experienced the greatest decline. In the peak AFDC caseload year of 1994, single-parent families constituted about 81 percent of all households receiving benefits. Child-only cases were just 17 percent of all cases in that year—869,000 such cases. By 2007, the number of child-only cases had shrunk to about 772,000, down 11 percent from 1994. But in 2007 these cases made up 46 percent of all TANF cases, largely because there were so many fewer TANF cases overall. As child-only cases are not subject to time limits and are not likely to be resolved by a parent going to work, they did not decrease much.

Dramatic declines in TANF caseloads raise the question of "coverage"—did the underlying need for welfare change during the years of caseload decline, or did the TANF program not "cover" as high a proportion of eligible or needy people as AFDC did? The answer to this question appears to be that coverage of needy families and children is significantly lower under TANF than it was under AFDC. In the early 1990s, about 80 percent of eligible families received AFDC; in 2001, that proportion had declined to 48 percent (Center on Budget and Policy Priorities 2006, citing DHHS data). Focusing just on poor children, who cannot realistically do anything personally about increasing family income, coverage under TANF has declined by half. In 1995, 61.5 percent of poor children lived in households receiving AFDC; in 2005, the latest year for which data are available, only 28.9 percent lived in households receiving TANF, including child-only cases (Child Trends 2007).

Caseloads and Caseload Changes—Food Stamps

As chapter 1 explains, the Food Stamp Program (after October 1, 2008, the Supplemental Nutrition Assistance Program, or SNAP) is the nation's only "all-purpose" safety net program, since anyone poor enough is eligible. A person does not have to be elderly or disabled or live in a household with children—single adults, couples, and families with children are all potentially eligible, regardless of age or disability status. More than any other program, one would expect the Food Stamp Program to be countercyclical; that is, its caseload should increase in hard economic times and shrink in times of prosperity (McKernan and Ratcliffe 2003). And that is essentially what happens, as figure 4.2 reveals. Food stamp caseloads increase toward the end of recessions and stay high for a while as the effects of recession wear off. The recessions of July 1990–March 1991 and of March–November 2001 show up in figure 4.2 as substantial increases in unemployment, poverty, and food stamp receipt in following years. Conversely, the good economic times of the second half of the 1990s show up as a decline in all three measures of economic stress.

Of all U.S. safety net programs, the Food Stamp Program is the most sensitive barometer of changes in the economy. It is not surprising, therefore, that food stamp rolls have been rising as the economy worsens and

Figure 4.2. Number of People in Poverty, Participants in the Food Stamp Program, and the Unemployed, 1985–2007

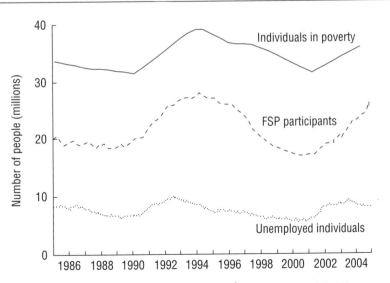

Source: Center on Budget and Policy Priorities, http://www.cbpp.org/3-15-05fa-f4.jpg.

more families face financial hard times. The food stamp rolls stood at 26.5 million monthly in 2007, on average, but are expected to average 27.8 million monthly for 2008 and 28 million or more for 2009.[1]

Comparing Changes in TANF and the Food Stamp Program

When AFDC was the nation's primary cash welfare program for needy families, it played a role similar to food stamps in helping to counter the effects of economic downturns and increases in poverty. Caseload evidence suggests, however, that TANF is not continuing to play that role, or at least is not playing it as strongly. Figure 4.3 shows both AFDC and food stamp enrollments increasing during and after the recession of July 1990 to March 1991. In the recession from March to November 2001, however, TANF enrollment continued to drop despite the increasing economic hardship affecting families with children. That trend still continues. Participation by families with children in the earned income

Figure 4.3. Number of AFDC/TANF Beneficiaries, Food Stamp Enrollees, and Families with Children Receiving EITC (in millions)

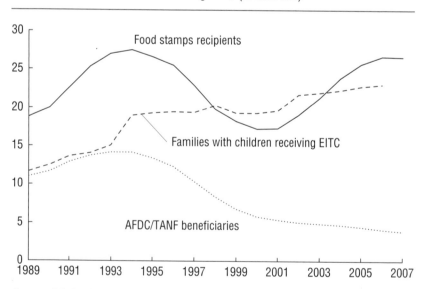

Sources: U.S. DHHS 2007 for AFDC/TANF beneficiaries; Statistical Abstracts 2008 for food stamp recipients; Internal Revenue Service Statistical Division for families with children receiving EITC (2007 not available).

tax credit, though, shows a small but reasonably steady rise throughout the period 1994–2006.

Caseloads and Caseload Changes—Medicaid and SCHIP

Before welfare reform, receiving AFDC made a family eligible for Medicaid (referred to as *categorical eligibility* because anyone in the AFDC "category" was eligible) and almost certainly eligible for food stamps by reason of low income. Before TANF, most states and localities had simplified the process for AFDC recipients to apply for Medicaid and food stamps, with most jurisdictions operating an integrated application process to save both themselves and their clients extra paperwork. This integrated application process, which still exists, works to help households applying for TANF obtain the related "package" of food stamps and health insurance.

The 1996 welfare reform legislation that changed cash welfare from an entitlement (AFDC) to a capped, work-oriented program (TANF) explicitly maintained Medicaid as an entitlement program. Further, eligibility for Medicaid was kept the same as it was before TANF—that is, if a family would have qualified for AFDC in 1995, it qualifies for Medicaid, even if it does *not* qualify for TANF at the time of application. In theory, then, Medicaid enrollment need not have declined following passage of the Personal Responsibility and Work Opportunity Reconciliation Act of 1996 (PRWORA).

At least initially, however, changes in TANF caseloads had fairly devastating effects on participation in Medicaid, just as we saw occurring with food stamps. During the first half of the 1990s, Medicaid enrollment had been increasing, from 28.9 million in 1990 to 41.7 million in 1995, with a slight drop to 41.3 million in 1996 (Holahan, Bruen, and Liska 1998). A large part of this growth stemmed from federal and state expansions of coverage for low-income children and pregnant women, increases in enrollment in Supplemental Security Income (which also makes one categorically eligible for Medicaid), and expansions in eligibility for both Medicare and Medicaid.

In response to congressional concerns about potential reductions in health care coverage following welfare reform, the General Accounting Office (now the Government Accountability Office) examined Medicaid enrollment for families and children for 1995 and 1997, bracketing the year that welfare reform was enacted (GAO 1999). GAO found that

Medicaid receipt for families and children had indeed declined by about 7 percent or 1.7 million people during this transition period—not as much as the 23 percent change from AFDC to TANF enrollment, but still substantial. Most states registered declines, with 12 states showing declines of 10 percent or more.

Medicaid caseloads continued to decline through 1998, after which they began to rebound, slowly at first but then fairly substantially in 2001 and 2002, as shown in figure 4.4.[2] Increased outreach, a strong focus on enrolling children in SCHIP, accompanied by relaxed application and eligibility determination processes, and state interest in having the federal government share the burden of health care costs, as it does under Medicaid and SCHIP, are the likely explanations for the turnaround.

Enrollment decreased slightly between December 2005 and December 2006, showing the first decline in eight years. Enrollment for federal fiscal years 2007 and 2008 and projections for 2009 come from annual surveys of state and District of Columbia Medicaid directors conducted for

Figure 4.4. Total Medicaid Enrollment in the 50 States and the District of Columbia

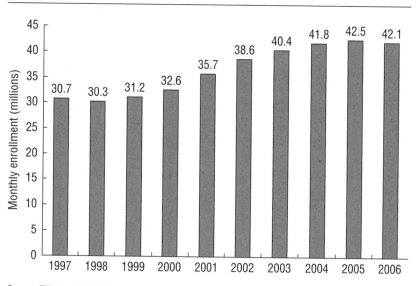

Source: Ellis et al. (2008).

the Kaiser Commission on Medicaid and the Uninsured. Smith, Cooke, et al. (2007) reported that FY 2007 showed the first enrollment decline since 1998, a drop of 0.5 percent. Medicaid directors attributed this decline to the strength of the economy at that time and also to change in some eligibility procedures. One year later, the same all-state survey of Medicaid directors (Smith et al. 2008) reported an increase across all states of 2.1 percent in Medicaid enrollment for 2008 as well as a projected further increase of 3.6 percent for 2009. Medicaid directors attributed this substantial shift largely to the worsening economy.

Concern with children's health, and clear evidence over many years that having health insurance increases access to health care and better health outcomes, prompted Congress to create SCHIP in 1997. SCHIP extended the already strong trend in the states to expand health insurance coverage for poor and low-income children. As figure 4.5 indicates, enrollment in SCHIP quickly increased to 2.4 million children within the program's first three years, to 3.94 million in 2004, and to 4.41 million in 2007.

Figure 4.5. U.S. SCHIP Enrollment of Children, December of Each Year, 1997 to 2007

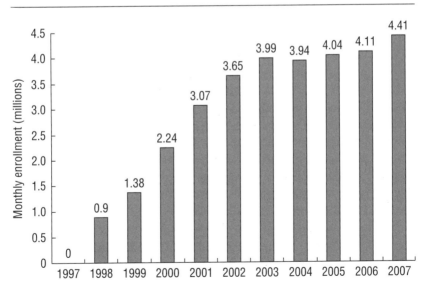

Source: Smith, Cooke, et al. (2007).

Overlapping Program Eligibility and Receipt

Families who are eligible for TANF are automatically eligible for Medicaid, and the large majority is also eligible for food stamps. These overlapping eligibilities reflect program rules that incorporate legislative intent to meet the most basic needs of households that have little or no independent income. In addition, many poor households are eligible for Medicaid and food stamps after they no longer receive TANF or even if they never were TANF beneficiaries. As just noted, PRWORA left Medicaid eligibility for families with children unchanged from what it was under AFDC rules, and food stamps have always been available to poor households that did not receive AFDC or TANF. But because eligibility does not necessarily mean enrollment and continued participation, it is a matter of some interest to see how program enrollments overlap. We look at this question in two ways—for families that received TANF at some time and for working poor families that do not receive TANF.

For TANF Families

The first analysis focuses on female-headed families in W2, Wisconsin's TANF program, who entered during W2's first year, from September 1997 through August 1998. Cancian, Meyer, and Wu (2006) used administrative records to examine program participation in cash welfare, food stamps, Medicaid, and SCHIP each month after enrollment for a total follow-up period of 36 months. At enrollment, about 85 percent of families received cash assistance, virtually all received Medicaid, and about 80 percent received food stamps. Receipt of cash assistance declined fairly rapidly, with fewer than a third of families still receiving cash payments at 12 months, and only 12 percent receiving them at 36 months. This pattern reflects the very strong push that W2 gives participants to get a job; once a household has earned income, the amount of cash welfare offered by W2 drops significantly. Since other states phase out cash benefits more slowly than Wisconsin, in those states a somewhat higher share of welfare families might still be receiving benefits after a year; but the W2 evidence is informative because it helps clarify the cross-program interactions after welfare reform. In Wisconsin, Medicaid participation declined much more slowly than cash benefits, as it did elsewhere, so that by the end of the three-year follow-up period almost three-quarters of the families still had at least one person enrolled in Medicaid. The pattern of participation in the Food Stamp Program was closer to the Medicaid than to the TANF pattern, leveling out at about 50 percent of families still receiving this assistance after two years and remaining at that level.

Equally interesting is the pattern of multiple program use reported by Cancian and colleagues (2006). As early as three months after enrollment, only about half the families were still participating in all three programs, another 20 percent or so were receiving only food stamps and Medicaid, and 5 or 6 percent were enrolled only in Medicaid. The proportion participating in all three programs dropped sharply in each three-month period, reaching only about one-fourth of all families by the 12-month mark. At 36 months, only 10 percent were still enrolled in all three programs, with another 37 or 38 percent receiving both food stamps and Medicaid and 22 or 23 percent receiving only Medicaid. Thirty percent were not participating in any of the three programs by three years after initial enrollment in W2. While Wisconsin's program differs from that of any other state, the W2 research provides useful insight into how programs relate to each other.

A major reason why welfare reform legislation in 1996 left eligibility for Medicaid and food stamps essentially unchanged was policymakers' belief that these supports may help a family that leaves welfare remain off the rolls.[3] And so it has proved to be. Former welfare recipients who have taken advantage of Medicaid, SCHIP, and food stamps are less likely to return to welfare than those who had fewer, or none, of these benefits. Other factors may also help people stay off welfare, such as labor market conditions, personal abilities, and family supports. But work supports seem to be important, and the pattern held true even in the harder economic times of the 2001–2002 period (Acs and Loprest 2007b; Golden 2005).

For Working Poor Families

Any policymaker who really believes the rationale for welfare reform—that is, that welfare should be a program to support families in employment and productive activity rather than being just a handout—should be a strong supporter of programs that make it easier for poor people to work. These include Medicaid and SCHIP (because most low-wage jobs do not come with health insurance), food stamps (because a poverty-level income does not leave much for other essentials after paying for housing), and child care (to ensure that children are safe and cared for while parents work). In addition, if it is possible to use the tax code to encourage work rather than welfare, the same policymaker should be eager to do so.

In fact, federal and state government spending on Medicaid, food stamps, and child care increased significantly after 1996. In addition, Congress created SCHIP to provide health insurance for children in low-income families that were not TANF-eligible, and the earned income tax credit was expanded to almost triple the amount a poor working family could receive if its income were low enough and if it filed taxes. Taken together, spending for these work support programs increased between 1996 and 2002 by 28 percent, after controlling for inflation (Zedlewski et al. 2006). Even so, many families do not participate in these programs, except for the EITC. Thirty-five percent of low-income families (those with incomes below 200 percent of poverty) do not receive food stamps or child care or participate in Medicaid/SCHIP, and another third receive only one of the three (usually Medicaid/SCHIP). Only 5 percent of all low-income families receive all three benefits.

The EITC is used more broadly. Eighty-six percent of working poor families receive some EITC payment. Furthermore, many families are able to combine receipt of EITC with participation in one or more other programs that support work. While about one in four (23 percent) gets only the EITC, 25 percent get the EITC with Medicaid and about a third (31 percent) get EITC plus Medicaid and food stamps. Only 7 percent participate in all four programs that support working families (Zedlewski et al. 2006).

Explaining Caseload Changes

"Welfare reform" often gets credit in the popular media for the reductions in the welfare rolls described earlier in this chapter. But such a view is greatly oversimplified, as often happens when public interest is high but the topic is very complex. A good deal of research has been done to explain the caseload changes that safety net programs have experienced since 1996. Some of the credit certainly goes to welfare reform, but a good deal goes to the strong economy during the late 1990s, other policy changes such as the increased value of the EITC, and factors related to welfare that have little to do with recent programmatic changes. Even "welfare reform" is not a simple concept. Researchers have tried, with some success, to differentiate the effects of various enrollment procedures from the effects of basic program characteristics that, for TANF, include time limits and sanction severity. For Food Stamps and Medicaid, the most basic characteristic of all—how much a person would receive if enrolled—shares some of the responsibility. In addition, the basic welfare reform legislation, PRWORA, made one entire group of legal immigrants ineligible for welfare benefits, with obvious consequences for caseload reductions that had little to do with encouraging work effort.

In this section, we look first at welfare reform factors, starting with those related to the enrollment process and continuing on to program characteristics. We then look at the effects of restrictions on legal immigrants and end the discussion with the effects of stigma on the likelihood that eligible households will apply for benefits. Thereafter, we consider the effects of the economy and the EITC on caseload changes.

Eligibility Determination—The *Process* of Getting and Keeping Benefits

Any family needing assistance from social safety net programs must go through an application process, which may involve more or fewer hoops to jump through and hurdles to get over. The more hoops and hurdles, the fewer people will persist long enough to participate; with fewer hoops and hurdles, more people will complete the process. This equation is perfectly plain to program administrators and legislators. For instance, when food stamp rolls dropped precipitously following welfare reform, program administrators appealed to Congress to relax some of the strictures governing states, which were expected in turn to be passed on to applicants in the form of relaxed enrollment requirements. Congress took the recommended steps, many states followed suit, and the changes in application requirements contributed to a turnaround in food stamp participation (Hanratty 2006). These administrative changes contributed as much to increased food stamp participation as the worsening economic situation—each contributed an increase of one or two percentage points between 2001 and 2003 (Hanratty 2006).

General Application Procedures and Their Effects

The process of applying for any safety net benefit in the United States is rarely short or simple. It usually involves at least one in-person office visit and sometimes more. Under TANF, for instance, before potential enrollees can formally apply, most states require them to attend an orientation session that explains program rules and the obligations of participants. TANF offices must also request an applicant's cooperation with child support enforcement, including naming the father of each child and how to locate him. Applicants who do not comply are not eligible for TANF, unless there is good reason to believe that approaching the father for money to support his child or children would create a danger to the mother or children. Some states require that an applicant immediately begin a job search, and some require that the applicant be able to prove that she has already made a specific number of contacts about potential jobs before they accept her application. Some states will take a family's application and enroll it immediately in Food Stamps and Medicaid but not begin to provide cash benefits until after a period of time during which the applicant must search for jobs. Finally, states vary in their approach to applicants with substantial barriers to employment. Some require people to seek jobs and offer special assistance to reduce barriers only if the recipient fails to get a job. Others do an up-front assessment of an applicant's job prospects, and if the applicant has substantial barriers to employment, these states may defer the job search and offer the family help in reducing some of the barriers before requiring the applicant to seek employment.

In addition to the time involved, applying for public benefits always requires assembling documents to show income and assets and may also involve documentation of citizenship, age, or disability. Each safety net program has its own requirements and forms, but in the 1980s and early 1990s, most states had moved toward a "universal" application form that collected all the information needed for AFDC, Food Stamps, and Medicaid applications. This single combined application simplified the enrollment process for families before welfare reform. But the change of cash welfare from an entitlement to a block grant under TANF has to some extent decoupled the three programs. Although universal application procedures still exist in most states, people eligible for food stamps and Medicaid often do not apply because they do not understand that they are still eligible, even if they are not likely to get cash welfare.

In general, practices and requirements that make it easier to apply for public benefits result in higher program participation by eligible households, while those that make it harder to apply have the opposite effect. We list application procedures that might apply to any public benefit program, after which we discuss some procedures specific to particular programs:

- Is there a telephone hotline for interested households to call to see if they might be eligible or that applicants may call to get answers to questions they have about the application? Is there a user-friendly web site with the same information?
- Where is the application office? How accessible is it to public transportation? What hours is it open? Does it have any evening or weekend hours? Does the application have to be made in person or can it be made, or at least initiated, over the phone or on the Internet? If in person, how many visits are required to complete the application?
- How much documentation must be submitted, and for what? How hard is it for applicants to get?
- How many programs can one apply for at once, with a consolidated or universal application?
- How long is the period between application and enrollment? Between application and receipt of benefits?
- Are there any actions that applicants are required to perform before application or between application and enrollment? If yes, how much effort do they require?
- Are there any outreach procedures, or efforts to reach potentially eligible people in venues other than the program office?
- Is anyone other than the applicants interested in seeing them qualify for benefits (e.g., health care providers who may help people apply for Medicaid because they want to be reimbursed for care)?
- Are "presumptive eligibility" procedures in place—procedures by which an agency is allowed to assume that the applicant is qualified and therefore starts benefits while the application is being processed?
- Are materials available in several languages? Are translators available when needed?

A good deal of research has shown that these factors, alone and in combination, influence participation rates. For families leaving welfare, efforts to educate them about their continuing eligibility for food stamps and to help them complete applications to prevent disruption of benefits have increased the proportion of very poor recent welfare leavers who receive food stamps from 50 percent in 1997 to 64 percent in 2002 (Zedlewski 2004). Hanratty (2006) reports that increased food stamp receipt following relaxation of requirements for documentation can be attributed to that procedural change. Stuber and Kronebusch (2004) report that simplified Medicaid enrollment procedures increased enrollment among eligible people by 13 percentage points, from 42 to 55 percent.

Outreach and Other Specific Efforts to Enroll Participants

Administrators of the programs that remained entitlements under the 1996 welfare reform legislation—Food Stamps and Medicaid—reacted to declining caseloads with a number of measures designed specifically to bring people back to the rolls. In addition, those administering SCHIP, a new program, had to take steps to ensure that eligible families knew about its benefits and enrolled their children. One of the most effective approaches to increasing enrollment in these programs has been to conduct outreach—that is, to make arrangements to meet and enroll people at locations other than the welfare office. Locations might be public health clinics, schools with high proportions of low-income children, health fairs, and other venues where potentially eligible people congregate. The USDA Food and Nutrition Service, which runs the Food Stamp Program, took further steps to attract eligible households. It developed advertising materials and distributed them widely; food stamp posters, often in several languages, began to appear in the windows of grocery stores and pharmacies, on the sides of buses and in subway cars, and in other places where they might attract attention. A national telephone hotline was established, a web site was developed that included an online eligibility and benefits calculator so people could see what they might receive in benefits if they applied, and several outreach approaches were pilot tested in different communities.

States developed another effective approach to increasing enrollment in the Food Stamp Program, which essentially was to reverse policies and actions that had contributed to disenrollment. Coming into the TANF years, many states continued their earlier practices of using a combined application for cash welfare, Food Stamps, and Medicaid, so that people signing up for TANF were also signed up for the other two programs. Then, when families left TANF, many states automatically disenrolled them from Food Stamps even though they continued to be eligible. Many families did not reapply or even know they could. Once the sharp drop in Food Stamp participation became clear, along with the contributory role played by the 1996 welfare reforms (GAO 1999; Zedlewski and Brauner 1999; Zedlewski and Gruber 2001), states changed their behavior. They developed several ways to help families leaving TANF continue to receive food stamps, including better information about eligibility and ready access to continuing applications. These efforts clearly paid off, as already noted, for very poor welfare leavers (those with incomes at or below 50 percent of the federal poverty level). Even for welfare leavers with incomes between 50 and 100 percent of poverty, changes in program behavior helped increase their participation from about one-third in 1999 to about one-half in 2002 (Zedlewski 2004).

Program-Specific Application Requirements and Procedures

Under AFDC, an applicant was screened for eligibility, then went through intake for cash assistance, and then, for those required to work, attended an orientation that described work-related program rules and services. The application process also covered food stamps and Medicaid, for which AFDC recipients were (almost always) categorically eligible. Under TANF, the applicant first gets informational materials and participates in an individual or group orientation addressing eligibility requirements, time limits, work requirements, and the (usually limited) criteria for being exempted from work requirements.

Under AFDC, cash assistance was guaranteed as an entitlement without time limit for those who qualified. TANF, however, focuses on what people need to do for themselves, with some prodding and some help from the TANF agency. States and localities vary in their emphasis on the prodding or the help, but all TANF agencies do some of both.

States vary considerably in their use of some TANF-specific application procedures, including having a formal or informal diversion strategy, requiring a job search up front, and having a waiting period between enrollment and the beginning of a family's cash payments. According to the most recent compilation of welfare rules available (Rowe and Giannarelli 2006), 28 states have a formal diversion strategy, which pays a family a fixed amount to meet a current emergency and prohibits the family from reapplying for TANF for one year. Arkansas offers the lowest diversion payment ($612 as of July 2003), Alaska offers the highest ($2,769), and neither state has a fixed maximum. As of July 2003, 16 states required an up-front job search, so that applicants have to prove that they have made a certain number of contacts with prospective employers just before or immediately after applying for TANF. Several states enroll people during this job search effort but do not give them cash payments until it is clear that the job search has not resulted in employment. Both a formal cash diversion program and up-front job-search requirements have been shown to reduce TANF participation among eligible people in states that have those features (Stuber and Kronebusch 2004).

Food stamps. The Food Stamp Program has had a reputation for many years of having a burdensome application procedure as well as cumbersome procedures for maintaining eligibility. As the nation's sole "universal" safety net program—the only basic qualification being a low enough income—one would hope that people in need could access and use it quite easily. But since the amount of aid a household receives depends on the number of adults and children in the household, the household's assets, and the household's income (which may change), the program requires extensive initial documentation from which the appropriate benefit level is calculated. And because recipients must also recertify their eligibility and provide income records periodically, benefits may be adjusted if income or household characteristics change. Some states have made the recertification period quite short for at least some recipients (e.g., every two months), while others have extended the length of time between recertifications (again, at least for some recipients). More frequent recertification periods reduce Food Stamp Program enrollment (Currie and Grogger 2001; Kabbani and Wilde 2003). Paperwork burden definitely discourages households from applying for food stamps, and frequent recertifications probably do the same.

When food stamp caseloads dropped by 40 percent between 1994 and 2000 (Zedlewski 2004), Congress took steps to remedy the situation during program reauthorization in the Farm Security and Rural Investment Act of 2002. This act, more commonly known as the 2002 Farm Bill, added almost $7 billion in resources to the Food Stamp Program and significantly strengthened it in a variety of ways designed to improve access and continuing enrollment. Several relevant provisions were included:

- restoring benefits to many (although not all) legal immigrants who were made ineligible for food stamps under the 1996 welfare law
- improving benefit levels by raising the standard deduction for larger households and adjusting benefit amounts annually to reflect inflation
- simplifying the program and streamlining benefit delivery to make the program much less burdensome and stressful for families to use
- reforming the quality control system

Food stamp caseloads are currently on the rise, having increased 55 percent between 2000 and 2006. Not until 2005, however, did they reach the level attained before enactment of federal welfare reform in 1996 (U.S. Bureau of the Census 2008b, table 551).

Medicaid. Compared to the degree of need for health care and the ability to pay for it, relatively few people are eligible for Medicaid coverage. In 2006, about 47 million people in the United States were without health insurance (Kaiser Commission on Medicaid and the Uninsured 2008). That number, which has grown steadily in the past two decades, now represents 16 percent of the total U.S. population, people in households in the lower third of the income distribution who cannot afford health care and do not qualify for any public program. In comparison, public health insurance programs (Medicaid, SCHIP, programs linked to Medicaid but paid for entirely with state dollars, and military-related health care) cover 12 percent of the population.[4]

Access to Medicaid is controlled by categorical eligibility, which means that one has to be in a relevant category to be eligible. Relevant categories are families that would have been eligible to receive AFDC under the rules prevailing in 1995 (that is, before PRWORA) and those who receive SSI (poor aged, blind, and disabled people).

If one is categorically eligible for Medicaid, getting on the rolls is relatively easy in theory. Most states still use a universal application that collects everything programs need to know to determine eligibility for TANF, food stamps, and Medicaid. As discussed earlier in this chapter, however, even categorical eligibility is no guarantee when the whole structure of applying for welfare has changed. Medicaid enrollment went down at the same time and in the same ways as food stamp enrollment, and local agencies had to take specific, directed measures to bring it back up.

Because eligibility for the basic Medicaid program, with its federal-state shared funding, does not begin to meet the need for health care insurance, many states have expanded eligibility in a number of ways that they pay for entirely themselves. At least 35 states and the District of Columbia have "medically needy" programs through which they pay health care costs for people whose incomes exceed Medicaid eligibility limits but whose health care costs are far beyond their ability to pay. A number of states provide health care coverage for indigents—people whose incomes are extremely low but who are not categorically eligible for Medicaid or who are eligible but have not been able to enroll on their own. In addition to these sources of coverage for people who are very poor, a few states provide public health insurance coverage for working poor and near-poor families. States with an interest in and willingness to provide health care to more of their needy residents have used a variety of waivers and other strategies to expand both coverage (who gets care) and services (what can be paid for), some of which we describe in chapter 7. At least one state, Massachusetts, and the District of Columbia have committed to providing health care coverage to all residents. Holahan and Pohl (2003) summarize and explain the substantial policy differences across states and their consequences for poor people's access to health care.

States with the mind-set and motivation to increase health care coverage have used many outreach and recruitment techniques to bring eligible people into their programs, as described elsewhere in this chapter. Health care *providers* are major allies in the effort to increase enrollment of eligible children and adults, because their income is directly affected. Eligible non-participants are likely to be using publicly supported health care facilities, which are obliged to serve them even if they cannot pay for care. Helping these patients establish eligibility for Medicaid and any type of state supplemental coverage is decidedly in the best interests of such providers.

SCHIP. States vary on a number of procedures or practices that affect the proportion of SCHIP-eligible households that actually enroll in the program (the SCHIP take-up rate). Practices shown to affect the take-up rate include presumptive eligibility, the existence and length of a period without insurance before a child is allowed to enroll, and whether the family has to pay part of the premium for the insurance. Presumptive eligibility increases the proportion of eligible people who enroll, while having any requirement for a period without insurance and having a longer period reduces take-up, as does having to pay a premium (Wolfe and Scrivner 2005).

Program Characteristics

Even under AFDC, states had considerable flexibility in setting their own initial eligibility threshold (how low a person's income has to be to qualify), maximum benefit level, income level to retain eligibility, and policies related to work. TANF gave states a great deal more flexibility, with the result that hardly anything about TANF is the same across all states. Medicaid is much the same, except that federal rules still specify certain minimum requirements for covered services and that pre-TANF eligibility rules apply. Food stamp practices are the most consistent across states because they are set entirely by federal policy. But because local welfare offices administer food stamps, application practices still vary considerably. These variations give researchers a lot to work with when they try to identify specific program characteristics that encourage or discourage enrollment among eligible households.

One of the most obvious differences in TANF and Medicaid programs across states is their benefit levels. TANF, for instance, pays only 15 percent of the federal poverty level in Mississippi and Alabama, while Alaska, the highest-benefit state, pays about 82 percent of the federal poverty level. The remaining states array themselves fairly evenly across the spectrum of payment levels between these two extremes. State Medicaid programs vary widely in the types of care they provide beyond the minimum required, as do state SCHIP programs. Most studies that look at factors affecting caseload levels include the benefits a program provides, and all find that higher benefits are associated with higher program participation.

TANF policies differ among states in quite a few ways that likely influence the decision of eligible households to participate in the program. In general, the more stringent or demanding the policies, the more they might be expected to discourage enrollment. Research findings generally bear out this expectation, although not always for every aspect of every policy. Policies include

- *Work requirement:* Work requirements may apply, such as whether recipients have any time on the rolls before they are required to participate in work activities; the number of hours a week participants are required to work (a few states are as low as 20, most require 30, and a few require 40); the timing of job search requirements (before application, at application, later); and grounds for exemptions (depending on the age of the youngest child in the household, illness or incapacity, caring for an ill or incapacitated relative, being elderly, and sometimes being in danger due to domestic violence).
- *The severity of sanction:* Sanctions can be imposed for the first and subsequent failures to comply with work requirements. TANF sanctions dock money from the household's cash assistance. The amount of money different states dock in a first sanction range from none to 100 percent of a family's grant. Sanctions may also have a time limit or be absolute. Some states keep the sanction in place for some months or until the family "cures" the sanction by complying with work requirements. States with the most extreme sanctions cut

a family off from cash benefits completely at the first instance of noncompliance. At the most extreme, at least one state extends such a full-family sanction to cover the entire childhood of all the children in the family.

- *Time limits:* According to federal time limits imposed by PRWORA, a family may receive no more than 60 months (five years) of TANF support in a lifetime. Most states have adopted this time limit, but some have shorter time limits, and some have a shorter time for an initial spell of welfare receipt but will allow a later return to welfare as long as the total time does not exceed 60 months.

- *Work encouragements:* TANF recipients are allowed to stay on TANF and continue to receive cash payments even after they begin working and have some earned income, although in some states it does not take very many hours of work a week, even at minimum wage, to raise family income above the eligibility cutoff. States may choose to "disregard" a certain amount of earned income for a period of time, allowing a family to retain benefits while accumulating some resources. States vary in the amount of income they disregard in this way, and for how long. Some states allow recipients to keep all or almost all their earnings for at least a few months while still receiving cash payments, and a few states set their policies to allow families to come close to earning above the poverty level before losing all cash benefits. Most states expanded their disregards under TANF, albeit to different degrees. Another work encouragement that varies across states is the value of a car that one may have and still retain benefits, recognizing that transportation may be necessary if recipients are to work.

- *Work supports:* Child care is a primary support offered to working TANF recipients by all states, but as with all else in TANF, accessibility and support vary across states and localities within states. Other supports may be offered to recipients with barriers to employment, including assistance to resolve mental health and substance abuse issues, educational gaps (e.g., by earning a general equivalency diploma, or GED), and threats from domestic violence.

Other Influences

Policy analysts have included many factors other than program implementation in their examination of caseload changes following PRWORA, including restrictions new with PRWORA on eligibility for certain groups, which in some cases have been amended by later legislation. The factors also include those associated with individuals who might be eligible for benefits, including fear of stigma (not wanting to be known to receive welfare), lack of knowledge about eligibility, limited English proficiency, low cognitive ability, and the value of the benefit they might receive. We look briefly at many of these influences.

Exclusion from Eligibility—Legal Immigrants

PRWORA provisions that excluded certain groups from many safety net programs affected caseload levels. Noncitizens legally residing in the United States are chief among these, especially those arriving after August 22, 1996.[5] TANF and Food Stamps were the chief programs affected. Food stamp participation received the most research attention because so many initially lost benefits and also many got them back quickly. Benefits were restored after only two years for children, the elderly, and disabled legal residents. In 2002, most other people who had been eligible for food stamps before PRWORA were made eligible again. These multiple changes in a short time frame prompted research to determine whether the restorations had succeeded in bringing participation back up to pre-PRWORA levels.

Hispanics and other immigrants have low food stamp participation rates even when they are eligible. Between 1994 and 1998, however, owing to PRWORA's restrictions on eligibility, the number of *eligible* legal immigrants dropped by 85 percent, from 4.25 million to 629,000, and the number of legal immigrants who were actually beneficiaries of food stamps dropped from 1.45 million to 356,000. Even "citizen children," meaning children born in the United States to legal immigrants, were less likely to receive food stamps after PRWORA, although PRWORA had not changed their eligibility. In 1994, 2.34 million citizen children were eligible for food stamps, a number that actually increased to 2.79 million by 1998. Actual participation, however, had dropped from 1.78 million in 1994 to 1.07 million in 1998 (Castner 2000, table III.6). By 2001, legal immigrants and their children were participating at rates far lower than those for the general eligible population. Only about 40 percent of eligible noncitizens and 34 percent of citizen children received food stamps, compared with 62 percent for the general population (Cunnyngham 2003).

The drop in food stamp participation following PRWORA, generally and for legal immigrants in particular, prompted advocates to pressure

Congress to restore legal immigrants to eligibility and also to reduce the burden of the application process (Capps et al. 2004). Advocates felt that the time and amount of documentation required were preventing many families from receiving the benefits that the Food Stamp Program was intended to provide. As already noted, the Farm Bill of 2002 did restore most legal immigrants to eligibility. The USDA Food and Nutrition Service estimated that these changes would bring about 400,000 more legal immigrants onto the rolls by 2006. Urban Institute simulations indicate that had the legal immigrant restrictions not been in place, 1.3 million more individuals would have been eligible for food stamps in 2001–2002 and that close to 1 million more individuals would have been receiving food stamps (Capps, Henderson, and Finegold 2006).

Stigma

Stigma is an easy concept to grasp intellectually but a hard one to capture in research. If people feel that it is shameful or degrading to be on welfare and that they do not want anyone to know that they receive or need welfare, they view welfare as stigmatizing. As people generally tend to avoid putting themselves in situations they consider shameful or degrading—that is, in stigmatized situations—they will avoid applying for welfare.

Recent research by Stuber and Kronebusch (2004) examined several aspects of stigma and their effects on participation in safety net programs. These researchers asked low-income people using public health centers in 10 states and the District of Columbia about two types of stigma—*identity stigma* and *treatment stigma*. Identity stigma refers to what people think about those on welfare or Medicaid, while treatment stigma refers to how applicants expect they would be treated by these programs, including whether they would be humiliated by the application process.

Identity stigma was stronger in relation to TANF than Medicaid—66 percent thought "many people on welfare do not want other people to know they are on welfare," but only 33 percent thought the same about people on Medicaid. Furthermore, identity stigma affected the likelihood of participation in TANF. In states where respondents reported high TANF identity stigma, actual TANF participation among study respondents was much lower than in states with less identity stigma. Conversely, low TANF identity stigma was associated with higher enrollment rates. Perceptions that they would be poorly treated or humiliated during TANF application (TANF treatment stigma) did not affect enrollment. Medicaid identity stigma (i.e., expecting to feel shame if known to be receiving Medicaid) did not reduce Medicaid enrollment. *TANF-related* identity stigma, though, reduced not only TANF enrollment but also Medicaid enrollment. Medicaid enrollment was also affected by how people thought Medicaid eligibility staff would treat them. Because the effects of stigma were comparable to the effects of Medicaid enrollment barriers and the effects of knowing less about Medicaid program rules, we can conclude that something as intangible as stigma can have significant effects on enrollment rates.

Stigma surrounding the use of food stamps, because of the visibility of paying with stamps at grocery stores, has long been known to discourage eligible households from applying for food stamps. One way to reduce that stigma, though, is through electronic benefits transfer (EBT); with EBT the recipient receives a card that closely resembles a credit card and pays with that. Both TANF and food stamp benefit amounts can be transferred electronically to a recipient's bank account, which the recipient accesses by using the EBT card. Electronic benefits transfer systems have been shown to increase participation in general (Kornfeld 2002) as well as that of some groups not wishing to appear to need food stamps (Currie and Grogger 2001).

Individual Characteristics Influencing Participation

Household income is the biggest determinant of participation in safety net programs. Although it is obvious that a high income makes a household ineligible for most safety net programs, the amount of income matters even among people whose incomes are low enough to qualify. For TANF and food stamps, the higher the income, the less cash or food stamp benefits a household receives. All other things equal, people who would receive only a little tend not to apply. Ignorance of the program or inaccurate knowledge, such as a belief that one is not eligible, is associated with lower enrollment, as is ignorance of where or how to apply. All the outreach and education mechanisms that the Food Stamp Program undertook to raise enrollment, described earlier in this chapter, paid off with increased participation by people for whom ignorance was a major reason for failure to apply. Language barriers may also reduce enrollment and contribute to low participation rates among eligible immigrants.

The Economy, the EITC, and the Minimum Wage

Finally, we come to the economy—the factor that makes the most difference of all in enrollment in safety net programs. During the first years of welfare reform, the U.S. economy was performing extremely well. Unemployment was the lowest it had been in decades—annual unemployment rates dropped below 5 percent for the first time since 1973 and stayed low through 2001. In addition, the country was recession free for a decade, from March 1991 to March 2001. With more people working, more people had incomes that raised them above thresholds for safety net eligibility, and fewer people needed help from such programs. Interest was keen in learning whether the strong economy alone had produced the caseload declines.

Many studies aimed to assess the effects of the economy and compare them to the effects of policy and program changes; all agree that the burgeoning economy of the mid- and late 1990s gets a good deal of the credit. These studies used different data sources, different units of analysis (e.g., some used states, while others used individuals or households), and different populations (all people or eligibles only). They also differed in the years they included in their analyses, the ways they represented safety net program characteristics, welfare reform in general (e.g., including a "before or after 1997" variable, year-to-year variations, or both), and what they took as their dependent variable (e.g., caseload levels, participation rates among eligibles). Finally, their analytic techniques varied. They were probably most consistent in the way they represented "the economy"—they all used unemployment as the key indicator.

For all the differences in the ways the studies were conducted, they all found that the economy was a powerful influence on participation in the safety net program. Kornfeld (2002) summarizes nine studies that looked at participation in TANF or the Food Stamp Program and found that the economy explained from 20 to 56 percent of caseload or participation changes, with the higher proportions tending to be found in studies that spanned more of the 1990s (i.e., 1993 or 1994 through 1999, rather than 1994–96). Results are more mixed with respect to the effects of welfare policy changes, but studies that include TANF changes as well as the pre-

TANF changes under waivers indicate that changes in policy and practice also contributed to caseload declines. These effects are not, however, as consistent as the effects of the economy.

Two mechanisms that might be expected to affect enrollment in safety net programs through their influence on household income are the EITC and the minimum wage. The EITC uses the tax system to reward employment for households that remain poor despite substantial work effort. Not only do poor households get back what they pay in federal taxes under the EITC, but many receive up to several thousand dollars more. The minimum wage is also intended to raise household income by paying low-wage workers more for the same work. It is less efficient at reducing poverty than the EITC, however, because many minimum wage workers are third and fourth earners in households with incomes that are already above the poverty level (e.g., teenagers). Another problem with relying on the minimum wage to raise household income is that an increase in the minimum wage may have the perverse effect of reducing opportunities for employment, as employers hire fewer people to keep their labor costs steady. The EITC—because the tax system rather than employers is responsible for enhancing household income—is less likely to produce a restricted labor market. Researchers have examined both of these mechanisms to see if they can identify an effect of changes on welfare caseloads.

Of all the policy changes made during the 1990s, increasing the amount a poor working family could receive through the earned income tax credit was the one most directly supportive of employment and most appropriately considered in this chapter along with economic effects. Chapter 2 described the EITC and its antipoverty impact, second only to Social Security at raising households out of poverty. It is reasonable to assume, therefore, that the EITC may have played a role in reducing the caseloads of safety net programs, since its impact would be to raise household income to a point above eligibility thresholds. Not surprisingly, research has shown that the EITC, by rewarding employment, also accounts for a significant amount of the reduction in welfare rolls that followed the major welfare reforms of 1996 (see Greenstein 2005 for a summary of numerous studies). Families receiving EITC payments were less likely to be on welfare. The EITC is less effective at reducing poverty in periods of high unemployment, however, because it is not available to people with no earnings in a given year.

Effects of variations in the minimum wage on welfare rolls have not received the same level of scrutiny as the EITC. A recent study (Page,

Spetz, and Millar 2006) using data from AFDC average monthly caseloads between 1983 and 1996, suggests that in the period before PRWORA, a higher minimum wage actually *increased* welfare rolls. These years cover changes in the federal minimum wage from $3.35 (1981–90) to $3.80 (1991) to $4.25 (1992–96) and substantial variation in state minimum wages that began after 1985. Findings indicate that a 10 percent increase in the minimum wage is likely to increase welfare caseloads by 1 or 2 percent. Thus, if reducing poverty is the goal, with the secondary benefit of reducing welfare rolls, it appears that the EITC is the more effective mechanism to use. The policy choice probably comes down to the difference in "who pays" and the likelihood that a policy will actually increase the amount paid. For the EITC, employers establish jobs and hire and pay employees for the work they do, while federal and state governments (through state EITCs) forgo taxes and supplement wages. With the minimum wage, employers control both elements and appear to make the choice to keep their costs as close to unchanged as possible, with the result that people with jobs earn more, but fewer jobs are available overall and fewer people are working.

Conclusions

In describing changes in enrollment patterns in the major safety net programs and the great array of factors that affect participation levels, we have described those factors that policymakers might have to make decisions about. Should they keep policies as they are, change them in the direction of expanding participation, or change them in the direction of shrinking program rolls? What do they care about? Are they trying to reduce poverty or just have fewer people on welfare? Is the emphasis on work in safety net programs since 1996 really helping people reach the level of income that makes them self-sufficient (i.e., able to afford the things they need, including housing, food, health care, and other basics) or just pushing them into jobs in the low-wage labor market that have no benefits and no future?

In chapter 1, we talked about the value conundrums that sometimes pull U.S. safety net policy in different directions. We might also pose the possibility that money trumps them all. Time and again, we see policymakers expand eligibility for safety net programs or increase benefits in response to demonstrable need among poor people, and time and again the same expansions are curtailed because the increased costs of the expansions reduce political support. The Food Stamp Program goes through frequent swings of this sort, with Congress routinely asking itself what it can do to increase enrollment and why various eligible groups do not enroll (Eisinger 1998). Then, when rolls increase in response to outreach and recruitment efforts, Congress reacts by cutting back benefits or restricting eligibility. Supplemental Security Income goes through the same fluctuations—periods when local offices are encouraged to help more eligible people get on the rolls and periods when rising costs provoke cutbacks and stricter procedures. Even the earned income tax credit—the darling of everyone who applauds an approach structured to reward work and with the resources sufficient to raise many families out of poverty—has its detractors and has been called by some "the runaway program."

Service Delivery Mechanisms and Innovations

This chapter focuses on a very pragmatic issue—how safety net programs *actually work* to get services to the people who need them. All the legislative and regulatory changes in the world often come down to one front-line staff person sitting with one person in need, figuring out what would help the person, and doing what is possible—and sometimes even what is impossible—to connect that person to appropriate services and resources. Many things can happen between the legislation and that personal interaction; some of those will help needy people and promote program goals, but others will stymie the best intentions of policymakers, program planners, and staff. This chapter explores the things that help and the things that hinder, looking primarily at situations in which success is likely to hinge on the ability of two or more agencies to work together. Most of the examples come from the interactions of employment and training TANF agencies, but some describe supports for young people and approaches to reaching and serving homeless people. Many of the challenges and lessons are similar regardless of program.

The First Challenge: People with Complex Needs

For people with single, simple problems, service delivery may be relatively straightforward. One or more staff in a single agency will be able to handle the case, working only on the single issue they know how to handle, such as employment, substance abuse, mental health, or basic educational skills. For people with a particular need, it is most efficient to let the single-focus agencies do the work they are good at, without adding layers of unneeded coordination with other agencies.

Even in the single-issue, single-agency case, however, some agencies or offices may be more or less effective at processing applications, keeping track of caseloads, or achieving program goals. For example, an early study of local offices administering the Work Incentive Program (WIN) (Mitchell, Chadwin, and Nightingale 1979) for the U.S. Department of Labor explored the reasons why some offices did very well and others did quite poorly at achieving the program's goal, which was to reduce the cycle of poverty of welfare recipients by helping them move into employment.[1] Later in this chapter, we will look at the factors that characterized the more successful offices.

The true challenge for service delivery is meeting the needs of those who approach safety net programs with a complex array of problems or who depend on them for long-term support. Single-focus agencies may try to address their single issue with such clients, but they often fail to help them with that one issue because the clients' other problems interfere. For instance, TANF agencies try to get clients into jobs as quickly as possible, but a client's educational level, learning disabilities, mental health conditions, or addictions might make that goal impossible to achieve, at least in the short term. Nor is it usually possible to send those with multiple problems to other agencies to get those problems out of the way first, because the other agencies are equally unprepared to address complex needs simultaneously.

Thus, people with complex problems often fall through the cracks. Many probably never receive the full range of services they need and often fail to receive even the things that agencies *can* deliver because they have a hard time getting to, or through, the application process. Those who enroll in safety net programs that are basically set up to maintain them on the rolls, such as SSI, the old AFDC program, and Medicaid, may continue to receive a specific benefit for years but never receive assistance that actually helps them pull their lives together. Other people operate outside the system, sometimes not even approaching it and other times never getting past the front door. Often a single barrier prevents an individual in need from getting assistance because that barrier is a big one—for example, she may not speak English, or he may have a serious disability. An individual may have many other skills, talents, and motivations, but service systems are not set up to help him or her successfully navigate the intake and application process. Later in this chapter, we look at examples that show how some communities have addressed and eliminated some of these barriers to helping clients with complex needs.

Sometimes a population group may be defined as "the problem" rather than as people who also need help. Poor fathers who do not live with their children, for example, may be expected to pay child support but may lack the necessary education, employment skills, and earning to do so. In fact, these fathers—largely ignored by the safety net system—often see that system as an entity that wants something *from* them rather than as one prepared to engage them in ways that may bring positive outcomes for both them and their children. The service innovations described below focus specifically on strategies for including and assisting groups often excluded from safety net programs, such as those with disabilities, poor noncustodial fathers, and people with limited English language skills.

Approaches to Categorizing Households with Complex Needs

It has become commonplace in recent years to hear people with complex problems described as "hard to serve." As the foregoing discussion suggests, this term covers a multitude of individual circumstances. We might further infer that no single approach is likely to work with all "hard-to-serve" households and that we need to think clearly about the barriers that households face if we are to develop successful approaches to helping them. With respect to TANF recipients, thinking about this issue has become increasingly important because, as welfare rolls have shrunk, many of the families who meet or exceed time limits may be harder to employ. That is, they may face many barriers to employment and self-sufficiency that have prevented them from benefiting from the easy, fast, and simple approaches most TANF agencies use. So if these agencies are to make significant progress in the future, they must find ways to work with multiple-barrier households. They are not only hard to employ but also hard to serve.

Because such issues are important to practitioners, they become important to policymakers and thereafter to researchers. Analysts have developed different ways of thinking about and characterizing the hard-to-serve population, which is quite heterogeneous even though discussions often proceed as if that population comprised individuals and households with similar characteristics. The heterogeneity of people considered hard to serve means that some may respond well to one set of interventions, while the same set of interventions will have no effect on a different subgroup. Thus, in shaping programs for maximum effect, we must understand the nature and co-occurrence of barriers that may make a person or household hard to serve or we will not be able to offer appropriate interventions. We briefly describe two examples of research studies conducted to understand better the characteristics of people considered hard to serve—one that tries to define barriers to employment and the effects of various barriers on employment and one that tries to group barriers according to the types of interventions or services that might alleviate them.

Articulating the Most Common Barriers to Employment

As part of their work on the Women's Employment Study, which followed a cohort of welfare recipients in one urban county starting in 1997, Danziger and Seefeldt (2002) identify barriers to employment for "hard to serve" women and describe how sanctions, time limits, and other welfare policies may affect them. According to their study, research that finds little difference between households on welfare before TANF and those still on welfare after TANF's first few years may have mismeasured the most serious barriers to employment or not measured them at all. Data collected for the Women's Employment Study obtained good measures of the following types of barriers:

- work skills, training, and experience (e.g., not having a high school diploma, low work experience, few job skills, learning disability, low literacy)
- recent behavioral health issues (e.g., alcohol and drug dependence, anxiety disorder, major depressive episode, trauma-related stress)
- physical health problems (self or child)
- other barriers (e.g., severe domestic violence, criminal record, having transportation or child care problems)

Danziger and Seefeldt report that, over time, the women who worked the most (at least 75 percent of the time) had significantly fewer barriers than women who worked less than 75 percent of the time. Women who worked less were less likely to have a high school diploma and had fewer job skills, more mental health problems, and transportation and other problems in all three years of the study. In contrast, members of the consistently employed group had fewer barriers and were quite unlikely to report the persistence of barriers over time.

Conversely, women who remained on TANF at least 75 percent of the time (i.e., 45 months or longer) were significantly more likely to have six of the nine barriers assessed than women who were not on the welfare rolls as long. Further, their health, domestic violence, and transportation problems were more persistent, occurring in two or more follow-up years. The researchers' conclusion—women who spend more time on the welfare rolls in the post-TANF, work-first environment appear to have significantly more barriers to employment than women who are able to leave quickly and stay consistently employed.

A Typology of Hard-to-Serve People

Burt (2002) recently made an attempt to sort out the different things that hard-to-serve might mean, by grouping a household's barriers to self-sufficiency into three categories—those that can be overcome quickly with appropriate resources; those that are treatable, controllable, or reversible; and those that are permanent.

Barriers in the first group—those that are readily removed with sufficient resources—include lack of child care, job search skills, and transportation. TANF agencies and their community partners have had considerable success in removing these barriers, as they have had resources under the TANF block grant and related state funding to provide child care, repair or even buy cars, increase the asset limits so a more valuable family car will still fall within eligibility guidelines, provide tokens or vouchers for public transportation, organize van pools to get recipients to work, and offer classes in job search and job readiness skills and job clubs to encourage persistence until jobs are found. Clients are most likely to succeed in getting and keeping employment if they face only one of the barriers in this group, but even clients with all three barriers have been able to move into employment once they receive the appropriate resources. The relative ease of resolving these barriers once resources are available, and the ability of a single type of agency to remove the barriers with resources under its control, distinguishes the barriers in this group from those in the next.

Barriers in the second group—those that are treatable, controllable, or reversible—include a parent's physical and mental illnesses or disabilities, addictions, illiteracy, lack of basic and work-related skills, inability to speak or understand English, lack of work experience, and recent release from a correctional institution. In addition, situations such as domestic violence, homelessness, or being involved with child welfare may complicate a parent's situation and need to be resolved before a recipient can realistically be expected to obtain and retain a job.

As the time frame for reducing these barriers or resolving these situations may be months long, a TANF or other agency wanting to move the parent into employment has some choices to make with respect to what to offer and also when to offer it. Treatment for physical and mental health conditions and addictions takes some time, and success is not guaranteed. Similarly, learning a new language or acquiring basic reading and arithmetic skills or earning a general equivalency diploma takes time. TANF agencies may ignore these barriers and insist that people try to find work immediately, but the failure rate is likely to be very high. Or the agencies may conduct assessments to identify the families with significant barriers of this type and provide the necessary treatments and supports to help remove them. While most TANF agencies started out in 1997 with the first approach, as their caseloads dwindled and more of their remaining recipients had multiple barriers, many gradually switched to the latter strategy (Martinson and Holcomb 2002). For households in this second group, the primary agency is likely to need to coordinate with other agencies to help clients get the full array of services that will address their issues.

Barriers in the third group—those that are permanent—include some physical disabilities, mental illnesses, and learning or developmental disabilities that are permanent and may pose insurmountable barriers to work at a level that could sustain a family without cash assistance. If the condition is serious enough, TANF agencies may help recipients apply and qualify for Supplemental Security Income, the federal program that offers cash assistance to disabled people, along with Medicaid eligibility. But many such conditions are not that severe, although they still leave the recipient unable to sustain work or to earn enough to be self-sufficient. Helping people with permanent conditions engage in work-related activities and eventually get and keep a job requires both greater attention to matching recipients with work environments and more sophisticated, ongoing relationships with potential employers to create more workplace accommodations. To do this, some TANF agencies partner with vocational rehabilitation, mental health, and other agencies that specialize in helping people with disabilities.

The more barriers to self-sufficiency a household has, the more it needs safety net programs. In addition, the more interacting barriers it has (for instance, substance abuse and physical or mental disabilities), the more it needs the various safety net programs to work together. That brings us to the second challenge to appropriate service delivery—structural barriers to interagency cooperation or collaboration.

The Second Challenge: Structural Barriers

For as long as safety net programs have tried to serve people with complex needs, program staff have complained about the many structural barriers that get in their way. By "structural," we mean characteristics that are built into laws and regulations controlling and limiting what can be done with a particular funding stream, who can be served and for how long, what information can be revealed to other agencies, and similar issues. We also mean the actual organizational structures of public agencies and their subsidiary programs as well as the self-defined purposes and boundaries of nonprofit service providers.

In recent years, the image of the "silo" has been used as a metaphor for the sum total of these barriers, conveying the idea that separate programs operate within tall, isolating, windowless structures that keep them apart and are virtually impossible to climb out of. Each program's silo starts in Congress, continues through federal and state bureaucracies, and eventually comes down to a struggling local welfare office or nonprofit service provider faced with clients with many problems. Different congressional committees and subcommittees have responsibility for different safety net programs. Each committee hears from its own specialized set of lobbyists, and members pursue their own interests in creating and modifying laws that govern the programs. Decisions are almost always made without regard for how they may affect the functioning of other programs or the ultimate ability of programs to meet participant needs.

From Congress, programs go to a federal agency for administration. Federal agencies and their subparts function mostly in isolation about as complete as that of congressional committees. This isolation is as complete for programs housed in the same umbrella agency as for programs in different agencies. For instance, TANF, Medicaid, the State Children's Health Insurance Program, child welfare, mental health, substance abuse, and primary health care programs are all administered by the Department of Health and Human Services (DHHS), but for all their interaction with each other, they might as well be in the Department of Agriculture (which runs the Food Stamp Program), the Department of Housing and Urban Development (which administers public housing and rental assistance programs), or the Department of Labor (which administers employment and training programs including those that welfare recipients are expected to use).

State agencies form the next layer of safety net program silos, usually rivaling federal agencies in their complexity and isolation. To make matters worse, however, nothing guarantees that state agency and program structures conform exactly to their federal counterparts. More likely, the programs run by divisions of a single federal agency will be found in more than one state agency, and a single state agency will house programs coming down from two or more federal agencies. This structural complexity is almost guaranteed for the three core safety net programs, since TANF and Medicaid are nominally within the same federal agency (DHHS) while the Department of Agriculture sets rules and monitors performance of the Food Stamp Program. Federal public and assisted housing resources, in the meantime, are administered by public housing authorities, which are quasi-public entities and not part of either state or local government (and therefore not under the control of governors, mayors, or county officials).

At the bottom of the silos are the local public welfare, health, and employment agencies that face real clients every day. The public agencies often have little flexibility when dealing with clients, because of myriad rules and regulations, performance monitoring to ensure that they follow the rules, and financial penalties if they fail to comply.

Nonprofit agencies are sometimes at the bottom of the silos with the local public agencies, and sometimes find themselves outside. Many nonprofit agencies specialize in activities that meet the requirements of one or perhaps two particular silos, simplifying their lives by not trying to break out of or work across the silos. Many nonprofits, however—when they recognize that their clients need the resources of several different silos—find themselves working to break down the rigid silo walls to get their clients what they need. These nonprofits are the primary source of flexibility in the system. As a consequence, they are often the primary locus of cross-agency arrangements and facilitate the process of working through conflicting eligibility criteria, different perceptions of what clients need and what client goals should be, who can be served, what information will be shared across agencies to help a service team determine needs and assign responsibility for meeting them, what services and supports they can get, what the timing and patterning of service receipt should be, whether other members of a household will be included or excluded from similar benefits, and who will follow up with the client to ensure that desired outcomes are achieved.

Signs of Change

For a variety of reasons, some narrowly focused or "silo" systems of service delivery are beginning to change, although such change is always a time-consuming and sometimes painful process. Some methods of coordinating service delivery are "ordained" by government fiat. In the workforce development area, the "one-stops" designed to bring all relevant supports for getting and keeping a job into one location are an example of this process. Agencies develop other methods as they go along, in their sometimes painful pursuit of making abstract commitments work in practice. As safety net programs have increasingly accepted the complexity of their clients' needs and the value of addressing "the whole person," they have taken steps to improve their ability to work with clients on several issues simultaneously. For that reason, they have developed various mechanisms, including coordinated or merged application processes, case management with smaller or specialized caseloads, better communication among relevant agencies, shared databases for referral and service tracking, co-location to facilitate referral and potential teaming for case management, clear contractual obligations to serve each other's clients, and various degrees of services and systems integration. These issues have become important enough for the federal Administration for Children and Families to commission guidance papers describing options for TANF administrators in addressing mental health and substance abuse problems among their recipients (Derr et al. 2000; Kirby and Anderson 2000).

Regardless of the impetus for improving service coordination to benefit people with multiple issues or the available technical assistance, very few changes occur in the real world of service delivery without a lot of effort and a lot of leadership. The next section of this chapter provides examples of different service delivery mechanisms, ranging from the simple to the complex, and explains how they came to be what they are. The chapter concludes with a conceptual framework for describing service delivery mechanisms and for understanding and describing system changes that achieve more integrated service delivery.

Examples of Service Delivery Mechanisms at Work

So far, this chapter has been largely conceptual, describing challenges involved in helping people and households with complex needs. Here we present seven examples of service delivery, starting with one that looks at the performance of a single-focus program doing its single-focus work. Other examples offer a good deal more complexity.

Example 1: Work Incentive Offices in the 1970s

The Work Incentive program was established in 1967 to move families receiving AFDC into productive jobs, with the ultimate goals of increasing their self-sufficiency and reducing welfare rolls. Legislation over the life of WIN altered its emphasis several times with respect to long- versus short-term approaches to employment and who must participate.[2] The program's original emphasis was on longer-term investment in human capital through training and developmental services; its second emphasis was on short-term outcomes in the form of immediate, unsubsidized employment. The categories of adults receiving AFDC who had to participate or lose their benefits also expanded and contracted over the years. Toward the end, WIN adopted an approach that balanced short- and long-term strategies. In 1979, the year of the evaluation we use as an example (Mitchell et al. 1979), WIN offered direct job placement and training, employability planning, job search instruction, child care, transportation, various types of counseling, and other supportive services. It had about 1.6 million registrants nationwide, accounting for about a third of all AFDC households. WIN had offices in all states and some territories and was funded in fiscal year 1979 for $388 million.

   Responsibility for WIN was jointly held at all government levels, requiring at least a minimal level of "silo-breaking" and thus making it a good choice for one of this chapter's examples. At the federal level, administration was integrated; it was housed at the Department of Labor (DOL) but staffed by personnel from both DOL and the Department of

Health, Education, and Welfare (now the Department of Health and Human Services, HHS). This integrated structure was repeated in federal regional offices. Below the federal level, though, administration was not always integrated. Rather, most state employment security agencies and state welfare agencies each maintained separate WIN offices, and some WIN offices that were integrated were located separate from both of the parent agencies where welfare benefits and social services were processed. Thus, the pattern of dual organizational responsibility at the national level (but with the two systems maintaining separate local offices) continued, with considerable variation in the nature and functioning of links between the two.

Using a record-keeping system that DOL imposed nationwide, all state WIN programs were held to the same performance standards and indicators, on which they reported quarterly. Thus, DOL could tell which states and WIN offices within states were doing well and which were doing less well against the performance indicators. Federal WIN administrators wanted to know what factors made the difference, so they could potentially help the lower-performing states and offices boost their performance and help more AFDC families find and keep work. The evaluation was set up to answer this question.

Factors That Affected Success in WIN Offices

Success for WIN offices was defined by four measures: number of job entries per staff, average job entry wage, job retention rate, and average monthly welfare grant reduction. These measures were standardized to let the evaluators compare across offices and across states.

- *Identifying high and low performers:* High and low performers were defined after controlling for their socioeconomic and demographic environment. Factors included labor market conditions (unemployment rates, presence of low-wage industries, average employer size, and local employment growth) and demographic characteristics (local poverty rate, proportion of male registrants). These factors accounted for about one-third to one-half of the performance differences across offices and states. The study sample included 214 local offices in 10 states.
- *Things that made a difference:* After controlling for socioeconomic and demographic factors, three sets of program factors differentiated

high from low performers—state-level priorities, activities, and interaction patterns; the ways that managers in local WIN offices behaved; and staffing intensity (staff-participant ratio).

- *Factors that improved performance:* States did better when they had more frequent, often joint, training; more intensive and sophisticated monitoring; more technical assistance and a visible presence at local offices; more collaborative annual planning and budgeting with more involvement of field staff; more open upward communications of local to state offices; more lateral communication among local staff through statewide meetings, training sessions, and conferences; and more accurate, trouble-free reporting systems thanks to hiring technically trained staff and creating problem-solving procedures.

- *Practices that raised performance:* Local offices did better when they had a lower participant-to-staff ratio and when their manager emphasized frequent internal discussion and open sharing of information, maintained more accurate and timely reporting systems that allowed them to monitor their operations more frequently and intensely and discuss results with staff, allowed more flexibility regarding work rules and office procedures combined with greater accountability, cross-trained staff for different jobs and allowed them to trade functions, and dealt more directly and openly with conflict within the office. High-performing offices also worked differently with clients, offering many supportive services beyond child care, placing stronger emphasis on learning job search skills, focusing on developing jobs for individual clients rather than generating a large pool of job orders, employment and welfare staff interacting more closely regardless of their physical locations, and working more intensely with uncooperative clients.

- *Things that did not make a difference:* The state-level political-bureaucratic environment (e.g., more or less special treatment for some participants, interference in personnel or procurement decisions), organizational structure of state programs (size, location within host agency, number of local units supervised), or co-location, at either the state or local level.

What stands out in the results from this study of WIN offices is how much depended on *how people did things,* rather than on *how legislators and bureaucrats structured things.* Legislation and policy almost always focus on the structure, and it would be hard to imagine that one could legislate open communication, extensive training opportunities, or intensive interactions. But the "lessons learned" from this study, along with those emerging from the studies below, stress the importance of human interactions in achieving, or failing to achieve, desired program outcomes.

Managers of high-performing local offices devised ways to meet the challenge of clients with complex needs. They offered a wide array of supportive services, depending on need; and they evolved procedures for working with initially uncooperative clients, including brainstorming with colleagues to identify barriers and think through possible approaches, and showed flexibility in their direct interactions with clients until they found approaches that worked. The challenges posed by organizational and program structures certainly existed, but program staff at both state and local levels figured out how to meet and overcome them, with the result that structural factors such as colocation of staff did not predict which offices were high or low performers.

Example 2: Developing Institutional Arrangements during TANF's First Five Years

When the Personal Responsibility and Work Opportunity Reconciliation Act passed in 1996, eliminating the AFDC program and creating TANF, states got a lot more freedom to structure their programs as they saw fit and a lot more resources to work with. To balance these advantages (from the state perspective), new federal rules constrained states to place a major emphasis on work to meet strict performance standards or face substantial financial penalties and a time limit on the number of years that federal resources would support families on welfare, to name just a few factors that affected state decisions about how to structure their TANF programs.[3]

PRWORA did not mandate organizational changes, and for some years it was not apparent whether state welfare agencies and local offices would need to change much as they tried to meet the requirements of the new law. In past federal efforts to promote work among welfare recipients, which were numerous, welfare agencies did not substantially change their standard operating procedures (Meyers, Glaser, and MacDonald 1998). In the years that followed the passage of PRWORA, however, states and localities did indeed make significant changes in the welfare system, including how it is structured and how its policymakers and staff think about what they are doing—that is, institutional cultures changed, and a great variety of cross-agency working arrangements developed. Martinson and Holcomb (2002) attribute the widespread prevalence of these organizational changes to the flexibility bestowed on state and local agencies under TANF, the ample resources available through the TANF block grant that could be used to support innovative approaches and services, and the seriousness of the goal of promoting work and discouraging long stays on welfare. Example 2 describes key features of new approaches under TANF after the first five years of welfare reform.[4]

Changing Practices to Meet the Needs of TANF Recipients

Three focuses or strategies. (1) Strictly work first—insisting that every TANF recipient immediately try to get a job, sometimes even before being accepted for TANF cash assistance; offering very few assessment, education, training, case management, or barrier reduction services; (2) mixed services, still focusing on work first but also offering education and training, especially if the immediate job search does not result in employment; (3) enhanced mixed services, softening the work-first emphasis with a parallel focus on reducing barriers, recognizing that some people will need help with barrier reduction before they will be able to work.

Common barriers included learning disabilities, very poor reading and math skills, mental illnesses, substance abuse, not speaking English, threats of and aftereffects of domestic violence, and physical disabilities. Children's disabilities also sometimes posed barriers.

Changes over time. When TANF started, at least two-thirds of the states chose a strictly work-first approach, and most of the remainder opted for the mixed-services model. Very few began with enhanced mixed services. By five years into TANF implementation, the balance had shifted. Fewer than a third of states still pursued a strictly work-first approach, while close to three-fifths had shifted to enhanced mixed services. The most compelling reason for the change was that as welfare rolls shrank, the people remaining on them for long periods had multiple barriers to self-sufficiency or even to work at all. States recognized that they would not make substantially more progress in reducing the rolls unless they learned how to assist these harder-to-employ beneficiaries in finding and keeping work.

The process begins with assessment. TANF agencies using a strictly work-first approach do very little assessment. Everyone goes directly to job search, and no one looks very closely at clients until they fail to find a job. Once TANF programs moved away from that approach, assessment became important as a way to identify client needs and barriers to employment. Assessment was recognized as an essential step in identifying what services clients would need if they were to overcome their employment barriers. Identification of appropriate services was often accompanied by more intensive case management than in a strictly work-first approach, to ensure that the client got needed services and that the services were helping reduce the barriers.

Changes within welfare agencies. Roles within many welfare offices changed substantially. For years, welfare eligibility technicians had been trained to concentrate on the income and eligibility criteria for program entry and on little else. Under TANF, these agencies retained their responsibilities for determining eligibility, but once eligibility is established, agency staff have the additional responsibility of delivering a much stronger message about work and fitting into changed organizational structures that promote work. Instead of just determining eligibility, a new office might be one where (1) welfare office staff have integrated responsibility for eligibility and employment; (2) the welfare office covers both eligibility functions and employment functions, but different staff do each; or (3) the welfare office has responsibility for eligibility and contracts or has memoranda of understanding with other providers who cover the employment services.

Partnerships, links, and contracting for employment-related services. Types of agencies with formal roles in local TANF employment programs include the welfare agency itself and workforce development agencies, nonprofit and for-profit employment and training agencies, and sometimes public schools, community colleges, and other organizations. Partner agencies might provide employment services, case management services, services for hard-to-employ households (e.g., mental health or substance abuse treatment or domestic violence services), and other services, such as assessment or mentoring. In service-rich communities, it is not unusual to find welfare offices with contracts or understandings with 20 or more community-based providers. Many arrangements for service delivery exist in different counties, and sometimes even within counties. Examples include

- *Milwaukee, Wisconsin:* Five agencies (four nonprofit and one for-profit) run the TANF program, under contract with the state. They do everything from eligibility determination through assessment, assignment, referrals, and job placement.

- *Miami/Dade County, Florida:* After an initial period of several years during which local public-private boards had responsibility for administering the TANF program and its employment component, Florida shifted its strategy in 2000, giving all responsibility for welfare-to-work to the workforce development agency, which selected a new group of contractors and located their staff in its one-stop centers. The welfare department continues to do TANF eligibility.
- *Minneapolis/Hennepin County, Minnesota:* The TANF agency oversees eligibility and provides benefits. Two workforce development agencies (city and county) have responsibility for employment services, which they contract out to many local providers. An interagency work group consisting of top welfare and workforce development administrators makes policy, program, and fiscal decisions for the system.
- *San Diego, California:* The TANF agency oversees eligibility throughout the county and also contracts with nonprofit organizations for assessment, mental health, substance abuse, and domestic violence services when those are needed. In most of the county, which is divided into service areas, case management and employment services are provided by three contractors who in turn may contract out for certain services. In two areas of the county, welfare staff handle eligibility and welfare-to-work case management in house.

Arrangements for providing services to reduce barriers: Many TANF agencies took on employment-related tasks and at least as many developed contracts and memoranda of understanding with community agencies to provide some or all such services. Not all TANF agencies have put significant resources into services to reduce barriers, but if they do, they almost always contract them out; they usually include mental health and substance abuse treatment and domestic violence services.

Why so much change when it had long been resisted? Changes in federal governing legislation were occurring at the same time for both workforce development and welfare systems, both systems had increased resources that made it easier for them to come to the table, and some aspects of the changing legislation strongly encouraged or actually required interactions across agencies.

Example 3: Welfare-to-Work Grants

After Congress passed welfare reform in 1996, it provided additional resources in 1997 to help accomplish the new TANF program's work objectives by awarding special funding through the Welfare-to-Work (WtW) grants program. WtW was a time-limited strategy designed to cushion the effects of welfare reform on long-term welfare recipients, many of whom had significant barriers to employment.[5] WtW ran through the workforce development system under the Department of Labor rather than through TANF offices under DHHS, requiring by its very structure that at the local level two different agencies would have to figure out how to work together.

Funded at about $3 billion, WtW provided three rounds of funding that supported five-year grants to over 700 state and local workforce development agencies and nonprofit agencies. Grants were targeted especially to programs operating in high-poverty communities; those communities were to use WtW resources to assist the least employable, most disadvantaged parents who had been on welfare the longest as they tried to make the transition to work. In addition to welfare parents themselves, WtW was authorized to help noncustodial parents, usually fathers, increase their employment and their ability to support their children. Thus, WtW was one of the few federal programs in the welfare reform era to recognize that the fathers of children on welfare were often as disadvantaged in the workplace as the mothers and that helping fathers who were involved in their children's lives might ultimately help the children too.

Welfare-to-Work Grants to Serve the Hardest-to-Employ TANF Recipients

Program models. Three general program models for delivering services emerged across the grantees, each reflecting the primary approaches used in the WtW-funded programs:

- Enhanced direct employment models (with emphasis on individualized preemployment job search assistance, counseling, case management, and postemployment support)
- Developmental and transitional employment models (where the program emphasizes skills development, usually in a transitional, subsidized, or community service job)

- Intensive postemployment skills development models (where the dual objectives are job retention and skills development, working with individuals who have started a job)

Employment pathways. Regardless of the program model, most participants who became employed did so with just job search assistance or job readiness services, in keeping with the work-first focus of welfare reform. About one-fifth became employed after participating in a transitional or subsidized job, and less than 10 percent received job training or education. About 15 percent, though, received a mix of services from the program (job search assistance along with a transitional job and possibly training or education).

Innovative strategies. The grants allowed programs to develop a number of potentially promising approaches:

- Extensive involvement of nonprofit organizations as program operators and special service providers (e.g., services to special groups, including those with substance abuse, mental health issues, or limited English proficiency or those who are homeless).
- Collaborations with employers, in designing preemployment components, sponsoring workplace internships, guaranteeing jobs, or partnering for postemployment skills development.
- Transitional work components operated to some extent in nearly all the study grantees, with the intent to provide a bridge to regular employment, including a range of models such as paid community service jobs, part-time community service job plus wraparound education, supervised temporary employment, sheltered workshops, and on-the-job training.
- Special targeted programs for fathers were developed by some of the grantees, including mandatory employment services ordered by a court for those with child-support delinquencies, employment programs for fathers released from prison, and voluntary programs for low-skilled fathers to improve their employability with supportive services and counseling to complement job search assistance.

Policy and operational lessons. While program implementation challenges were prevalent, especially in the first two years of the grants program, important lessons emerged:

- When legislation includes detailed eligibility and fiscal provisions, implementation delays often follow. Legislation that is simple and "flexible within limits" is better.
- Temporary funding and authority impose added challenges—fewer agencies want to get involved when it is not clear that program funding will continue past a demonstration period.
- Programs benefit from public and private partnerships and collaborations at the local level.
- Carefully designed programs can reach populations with serious employment problems through systematic outreach and recruitment and a comprehensive package of services. Nonprofit community-based organizations can play a particularly effective role in this regard.

We come now to two examples of welfare-employment demonstration programs of the mid-1990s that took the fundamental goal of helping very poor families leave poverty, thought through what programmatic elements it would take to achieve this goal, put those elements in place, and observed the results. Although the demonstrations used different strategies and operated through different systems (one was public, the other private), both were quite successful. Example 4 describes the Family Independence Program (MFIP) that Minnesota developed under AFDC waivers in the mid-1990s. It also looks at what happened to the program after it went statewide under TANF and at recent efforts to develop a more integrated approach to services for welfare families with many barriers to work.[6] Example 5 describes the New Hope Project that was mounted in two Milwaukee neighborhoods at almost the same time as MFIP.

Example 4: Minnesota's Family Independence Program

MFIP's goal was to reduce poverty and improve children's outcomes among families on AFDC. About 14,000 families receiving welfare participated in the demonstration, which took place in county government welfare offices in seven Minnesota counties from April 1994 through June 1998.

Intervention. MFIP's designers knew the challenges that welfare families face in trying to leave poverty through work, including inadequate education, poor work skills, little work experience, low-paying labor market opportunities, child care responsibilities, transportation barriers, and sometimes physical, emotional, or addiction issues. They wanted to structure their waiver demonstration to provide parents in welfare families the opportunities to acquire the education and skills that would help them get good jobs—jobs that would pay enough to lift the family out of poverty. They were less interested in moving families quickly off of welfare and seeing rapid reductions in the welfare rolls than in structuring their program to make work pay.

Under MFIP, a family was always better off financially if the parent worked—a situation that was very different from the AFDC rules that prevailed at the time of the waiver, which started reducing the cash welfare payment substantially as the parent began to earn more and which cut people off welfare completely long before their income reached the poverty threshold or went beyond it. MFIP accomplished the goal of making work pay by establishing progressive income disregards that let families keep their earned income and still receive a slowly decreasing level of welfare; by increasing supports for employment and skills improvement; and by providing child care, health care, and direct assistance to reduce health and other barriers. Families continued to be eligible for some benefits until their income reached 140 percent of poverty.

Evaluation design and methods. MFIP randomly assigned each family applying for welfare during the demonstration period either to MFIP or to "AFDC as usual." Many methods were used to evaluate the program's results, including baseline interviews with families and follow-up interviews at three, five, and eight years; implementation and process analysis through site visits and document review; and analysis of welfare and unemployment administrative records.

Results. Compared to families in the "regular welfare" control group, those receiving MFIP stayed on welfare longer but were significantly less likely to be poor when they left, children's outcomes (school attendance, school performance, and health) improved, and for welfare families headed by a married couple, marital stability increased. These effects included economic improvement but also effects beyond economics, such as children's well-being. Even more important, the results were most pronounced for long-stay welfare families that faced significant barriers to employment, and the effects lasted for several years after leaving welfare and through the follow-up period.

What happened when MFIP went statewide under TANF?
- *Immediate:* The income cutoff for losing benefits went down, from 140 to 120 percent of poverty, one-parent families were required to be working after six months on the rolls rather than two years, edu-

cation and training activities were restricted, the amount available for local offices to invest in helping each family overcome barriers was reduced by about one-fourth, and a time limit for receipt of welfare of 60 months maximum was imposed to comply with federal regulation.

- *Longer-term:* The result of the changes just noted was that the statewide program never achieved the poverty-reducing ability of the MFIP waiver demonstration. Furthermore, many families with the most complex needs were not leaving welfare, despite the time limit and pressures to work. These families make up ever-larger proportions of those remaining on welfare in Minnesota, as has been true in many other states.

After several years of administering MFIP statewide, Minnesota's TANF administrators recognized that they were facing a number of challenges. As in other states, many of those remaining on the MFIP rolls had multiple barriers to employment, falling into the second and third groups of hard-to-serve households we described early in this chapter. To make matters worse, many of these barriers had not been identified or diagnosed until families had used up most of the 60 months on TANF that federal regulations allow, so there was not much time to help them before they would be cut off from assistance. Finally, and not surprisingly given what we have already discussed in this chapter, the service systems that could help with the problems identified—mental health, substance abuse, domestic violence, physical disability, children with special needs, child protection issues, and housing problems—were in their own silos with little communication or coordination among them or between them and MFIP agencies.

In 2005, Minnesota's Department of Human Services developed an Integrated Services Project (ISP) to address these issues and help its hardest-to-serve families make progress toward employment. On average, two-thirds of the families in eight ISP sites had two or more barriers (Martinson et al. 2007). As a testimony to the challenges of establishing full cross-agency coordination, it is interesting to see how these eight sites set up their programs, given that their target population obviously needed help from at least two and more likely three or four different service systems. Four of the eight relied on a service-brokering approach in which a case manager from the ISP agency worked with a family to help it access services as needed from other agencies, which remained in their silos. Three of the eight sites developed multiagency teams, bringing to bear the expertise of several different service sectors through coordinated case plans and consistent follow-through with all team members. Only one of the eight actually integrated service delivery, combining mental health rehabilitation expertise into the county MFIP employment services program and bringing in new non-MFIP funding. Thus, most sites focused on operational rather than systemwide service integration. Among other reasons for not integrating their services, the ISP programs were small (few participants compared to their county's overall MFIP population), and they were run by nonprofit agencies. More system change might have come about if county MFIP agencies had been involved, if the population to be served had been larger, and if more time had been available to get the structures up and running.

Example 5: New Hope, a Nongovernmental Approach to Poverty Reduction

The New Hope demonstration project was a unique experiment in poverty reduction in that it took place *outside* public safety net programs, although many of the supports and incentives it offered were similar to those available through public programs, and participants could still receive public services for which they were eligible. The project, funded largely by foundations and operated in a community context, had long-lasting effects on participants.[7]

The New Hope Project in Milwaukee, Wisconsin

The goal of the New Hope Project was to make a reality of the American ideal that anyone who works hard will not be poor. It did so by supplementing wages for all households in the intervention, whether they had children or not, and by providing wage supplements and guaranteed jobs to stabilize income and other supports that often drain the low incomes of many poor and near-poor families—child care and health insurance. New Hope, the brainchild of a Milwaukee community-based organization, ran in two neighborhoods from 1994 to 1998.

    Intervention. New Hope was neighborhood based, involving nonprofit agencies in two Milwaukee neighborhoods with relatively high poverty rates. The project recruited about 1,300 households with and without children who lived in the study neighborhoods, had incomes below 150 percent of poverty, were willing and able to work at least 30 hours a week, and were 18 or older. New Hope is unique in its inclusion of single adults and childless couples as well as families with children, making its outcomes of particular interest to those who are concerned about all types of low-income households.

Each household recruited was randomly assigned to the New Hope intervention or "usual services." Those in the intervention group received assistance in their search for jobs and were placed in paid community service jobs if they could not find employment in the regular labor market. Earnings were supplemented to raise household income above the poverty threshold. Participants received access to subsidized health insurance and child care during the three years of the demonstration, as long as they worked full-time. All work supports were available from a single agency, whose procedures for applying for and receiving these supports were relatively benign and unbureaucratic—a form of a "one-stop." The income level at which one could no longer receive cash supplements or subsidized child care or health insurance was significantly higher in New Hope than in most public welfare or safety net programs, giving participants a better chance to earn their way out of poverty and stabilize their incomes.

Evaluation design and methods. Evaluation methods included baseline and two, five, and eight-year follow-up interviews with participants and controls; implementation and process analysis through site visits and document review; analysis of program, welfare, and unemployment administrative records; and teacher reports for school-age children.

Results. New Hope's services to the intervention families fulfilled the goals of the program:

- Compared to control households, households that received New Hope services increased their work and income levels, even years after program benefits ceased. Intervention families had more stable employment, had higher wages, and were less likely to live in poverty than control families. Community service jobs were important stepping-stones for increasing employment and were used by 30 percent of participants. Effects on reduced poverty lasted for at least five years.
- New Hope also had effects that went beyond simple economic improvement, particularly for children. Children's school performance improved, and they were more involved in positive social behaviors and less involved in negative ones. Adolescents were more likely to be involved in structured out-of-school activities, such as

youth groups and clubs. Parents also improved in noneconomic ways, particularly with regard to their physical and mental health and their knowledge of and ability to use resources in the community.

What happened after the demonstration ended? New Hope ended without having its approach adopted in Milwaukee or elsewhere, despite demonstrated success. Its most central features, however, have become part of general practice. The earned income tax credit, which supplements the incomes of households that remain poor even with full-time work, is the single most important poverty-reducing program for families with children and working-age adults (Social Security has a greater effect, but only for the elderly). TANF offers child care and health insurance subsidies while beneficiaries are on the rolls and working, and both may be extended for a year after a family leaves welfare. So while nothing specifically called "New Hope" exists today, the lessons learned from the success of its approach have not been lost.

Both the MFIP and New Hope demonstrations made large, significant investments in well-thought-out interventions. They had time to develop to a steady state and sustained their interventions over several years, making them excellent candidates for evaluations that produced policy-relevant knowledge. Their evaluations used many research methods, giving the researchers the information needed to examine many aspects of the interventions to learn how they developed, how they conducted their daily activities, the impacts they had on participants, and the aspects of the interventions that were likely to be the most significant in producing those impacts. Both acquired the resources to do long-term follow-up with participants and controls to establish whether impacts continued after the services ended; the fact that the impacts did continue lends weight to the importance of both demonstrations.

The pressure on safety net and other programs to organize in new ways to serve clients and families with complex needs is not limited to cash assistance and employment programs. Every area of social services inevitably encounters some clients with needs that require coordinated services from several agencies offering quite different services. Whether we are talking about adults in need of protective services, women victims of domestic violence or sexual assault, children in the welfare system, pregnant and parenting teens, or formerly incarcerated people returning to the community—many in each group will have complex issues that would benefit greatly from support services coordinated across two or more agencies or systems. Examples 6 and 7 illustrate the reality of this universal situation for two very different populations with very different issues—young people and those experiencing homelessness.

Example 6: Service Integration for Youth in a Largely Rural County

YouthZone/Garfield Youth Services

YouthZone/Garfield Youth Services provides services and supportive activities for all youth in Garfield County, Colorado, a rural county on the western slope of the Rocky Mountains.[8] Its core focus is on prevention and services related to alcohol or drug abuse and youthful criminal behavior. Its approach is global—it serves *all* youth in the county, not just the "bad kids," on the premise that all young people need the opportunity for positive activities and the encouragement and support to pursue them, which in turn will help them stay out of trouble. As its web site states, "We at YouthZone are dedicated to providing opportunities for all youth to become responsible, contributing members of society. We work with youth, their families, and the community toward this end."

Many of YouthZone's offerings are designed to prevent problems before they start, and many of them are fun. The agency offers mentoring (matching a youth with an adult or an older youth for social and recreational activities), helps teens get on the boards of directors of various nonprofit agencies in the community, conducts in-home and school-based parenting classes, and organizes outings and similar activities. For young people with issues, YouthZone/Garfield Youth Services participates in services integration and also facilitates systems integration and community organizing.

Services integration. For young people with personal or family issues, YouthZone participates in the community evaluation team (CET), a multiagency team that also includes mental health and social services, the courts and schools, and other relevant agencies as needed. The team meets regularly for several hours and handles several clients or families at each meeting. Youths often attend, as do parents in 90 percent of cases. The meetings produce service plans involving two or more agencies, to which the youth, parents, and relevant agencies agree. This strategy cuts the time needed to arrange the elements of a services package from several days to half an hour. In addition, the agencies that have signed on to provide a service follow through more quickly than they did before the team began to function.

Systems integration. YouthZone has often worked with public agencies to devise new strategies to solve old problems. Over the years, these interactions have expanded to include more agencies and more levels of each agency, and agency practices have evolved to incorporate the new strategies until they become standard operating procedure. Good examples of this in Garfield County include the development of "host homes" and the CET. Host homes bridge the gap between prevention and treatment and provide a temporary emergency residence *in the county* for youths who cannot or will not stay in their own homes. They are a solution to the issue of too many youths being placed out of county and thus far away from the place where solutions might be worked out. The CET was developed to reduce the need for placing youths in secure detention, which almost always meant expensive out-of-county placement. It has become the basis for expanded coordination and policy development with CET agencies. Heads of CET agencies began meeting to do some long-range planning and to make policy decisions about service implementation. When it became apparent that these decisions were not necessarily filtering down to practice, casework managers from the different agencies were invited and began to attend the policy meetings. As a result, decisionmakers began to pay attention to practical issues of how strategies might work in practice and to incorporate viable approaches, and casework representatives were more committed to changes and in a better position to explain them and facilitate their adoption.

Links/community organization. YouthZone operates on a principle of increasing community involvement and asking regular citizens to participate in solutions to community problems involving youths.

- *The "glue" or "mortar" that holds the system together:* As a result of its "we're all in this together and we all have to help" attitude, public and nonprofit agencies and private citizens see YouthZone as *the* place for youth in the county and trust it to facilitate development of new services and programs in open and fair processes for the benefit of the whole community. When government agencies in the county identify a service need for a young person that they cannot fulfill, they turn to YouthZone. YouthZone considers whether it will develop the service, but over the years, it has become quite selective about what it will and will not undertake. In consultation with many stakeholders, it asks whether it is the right place for the service and what other agencies might be better suited to offering the service. Sometimes it decides to develop the needed service or activity, but sometimes the decision goes the other way and another agency meets the need. By respecting everyone's needs, opinions, and capabilities, YouthZone has become the "glue" or "mortar" that holds the system together.

- *Focusing on the priorities:* YouthZone/Garfield Youth Services began as a group of parents concerned about their children's exposure to alcohol and drugs. As much as it has grown over the more than 20 years of its existence, it has kept its direct services fairly tightly focused on substance abuse issues and, by extension, youth involvement in the justice system. Its prevention activities are much broader, but it has tried hard to let other agencies with more appropriate skills and training take on direct services for teen pregnancy, health, employment, and other issues.

- *Knowing the communities:* Garfield County does not have a huge population, but it is not homogeneous. Its several small communities have their own cultures and ways of doing things. YouthZone is run by long-time county residents who know those communities. When introducing a new program or activity, they work with local communities to adapt it so it will fit in with local ways. The basic premises and goals of the new activities remain the same, but by tailoring program operationalization to local circumstances, YouthZone has been very successful in seeing its innovative programs accepted throughout the county.

Effectiveness. YouthZone has long been interested in documenting its impact on youth and the community. Its programs have proven effective in significantly decreasing delinquent behavior and illegal drug use, while significantly increasing positive decisionmaking skills, prosocial development, and positive self-perception.

Example 7: Services and Systems Integration to End Homelessness

Many people who are homeless need only a little help to return to housing and stay there, while at the other extreme are people who have been homeless for many years and will never leave homelessness without a lot of help and support. Homeless assistance networks in most communities are fairly complicated, addressing needs for emergency shelter and also for longer-term assistance and support through transitional and permanent supportive housing. They may also offer everything from primary health care through mental health and substance abuse treatment to child care and youth recreational activities.

Successful Approaches to Homelessness

Over the 25 years that homelessness has been recognized as a national issue, many communities have evolved approaches that structure access to needed programs and services, including the services and supports available through regular public safety net programs. Below, we describe some of these approaches, drawing examples from communities that target different groups of homeless people and involve an array of safety net sectors to meet the various service needs.[9]

Engagement of street people. People who are homeless and living on the streets often have many complex conditions, any one of which may prevent the person from accepting help for one or more of the others. Many communities have outreach services designed to engage street people, but few outreach services are equipped to offer the range of help that will likely be needed. San Diego's Homeless Outreach Team (HOT) is an exception. Each HOT team consists of a City of San Diego police officer, a mental health or substance abuse specialist, and a benefits specialist (the latter two from county offices). The team, which focuses on street people with fairly obvious mental health issues, is able to do a mental health and substance abuse assessment, start the process of applying for cash and other benefits, and offer treatment as needed, all on the street. It can also offer housing, in either of San Diego's two safe havens. If the person is resistant to any help and also appears to be a danger to self or others or to be breaking the law, the person can be arrested or involuntarily transported to a hospital for mental health assessment.

Multiservice centers for newly homeless people. Many communities, recognizing the often wide-ranging needs of people who are newly homeless, have established multiservice centers where people can learn about available services and connect immediately with their representatives, work with a caseworker on a service plan, and get immediate assistance. The idea is to facilitate rapid access to services that can help end a homeless spell within a very short period of time. Some multiservice centers serve whole communities (Long Beach and Berkeley, California; Cambridge, Massachusetts; and Portland, Maine), while others serve special populations (veterans' multiservice centers in Philadelphia and Houston, a multiservice center for homeless youths in Seattle) and some in very large cities (New York, Chicago) serve only certain neighborhoods.

Centralized intake for families. Some communities (Columbus, Ohio; Hennepin County, Minnesota; Miami and Dade County, Florida; Montgomery County, Maryland; Washington, D.C.) have centralized their intake for homeless and about-to-be-homeless families so that they can combine their homelessness prevention activities with their assistance for leaving homelessness. Through assessment and triage, these centers determine which families that are about to lose housing can be kept in it and thus avoid homelessness altogether, which families will have to come into emergency shelter, and what those families need to be able to exit shelter and stabilize in new housing. They usually have a variety of funding sources they can bring to bear, depending on the issues at hand. Such resources may come from several different funding streams originating in different public agencies. They include money for arrearages in rent or utilities, security deposits and first month's rent, or money for moving; coordinating with any mental health, child welfare, or TANF caseworkers the family may have; arranging for child care or employment; dealing with domestic violence issues; and similar matters.

Integrating care within a single sector. Sometimes service delivery within a single service sector is itself so fragmented and ineffective that it takes a major effort just to pull that sector together. In the area of Los Angeles known as Skid Row, which is "home" to perhaps the largest concentrated population of homeless people in the country, health care was in such a fragmented state. A major foundation effort, later assisted by the county's Department of Health Services, brought together 19 partners, including the three primary health care providers in the area. Twenty-eight strategies were identified, along with a timeline for funding and implementation. At least half the strategies were funded within the first two years, increasing total care delivered, coordination of care among Skid Row providers and also with hospitals, access to care sites by providing transportation, and approval rates for SSI applications (while cutting time to approval from 12 to 4 months). These activities have evolved into a single service site incorporating dental, mental health, substance abuse, radiology, pharmacy, and optometry services along with primary care, with satellite teams visiting housing programs where formerly homeless people are tenants.

Integrated support teams for formerly homeless people with disabilities. People with several serious disabilities, including those with co-occurring mental illness and substance abuse, have been successfully housed and helped to maintain housing through integrated service teams. Sometimes the housing is in one place, such as a renovated hotel, and the services are available on site; more often, housing is scattered throughout the community, and the service team visits people in their homes.

The best-known model of this latter type is the Assertive Community Treatment (ACT) team, which has been used extensively with homeless people in New York City and is now in operation in Washington, D.C., Miami, and other communities. When adapted for use with formerly homeless people, an ACT team usually includes a social worker, psychiatrist, vocational trainer, substance abuse counselor, nurse or nurse-practitioner, and housing specialist. Through its own members (usually) or through links to other agencies (occasionally), an ACT team is able to work with clients to remove threats to housing stability from almost any type of problem a participant may experience.

Community mobilization to end chronic homelessness. Chronically homeless people—those who have been homeless for a year or more or have been homeless several times—usually have conditions requiring the services of health care, mental health care, substance abuse treatment, HIV/AIDS treatment, and sometimes employment services, in addition to their obvious need for housing and assistance to keep it. These needs cannot be met without the involvement of mainstream public safety net agencies. Communities around the country have been developing plans for ending chronic homelessness, and some of them have followed through to develop housing and supportive services and move people off the streets. Communities experiencing a drop in the number of street homeless people over the years of housing development include San Francisco, New York, Philadelphia, Portland (Oregon), Denver, Miami, and others. None of this success could have happened without significant public agency commitments and joint actions to create the housing and fund the supportive services that can keep people in it.

Thinking about System Change

As countless service agency staff lament, it is very hard to "serve the whole person." No matter how far back one goes in the world of safety net, social service, social assistance, or welfare programs, probably at no time did each not operate in its own world—in its own silo. Regardless of the population being served—from hard-to-employ welfare recipients to high-risk youths to people with serious mental illness to homeless people—differing eligibility criteria, enrollment processes, benefits coverage, or even simple things like hours or location of operation have been barriers to getting help to people with complex issues.

The process of breaking down the silos is one of changing systems. System change has interested people in many disciplines, in part because it seems to be so hard to do. Corporations care about system change because a poorly functioning corporate system means lower profits. Think of what happened in the United States when Japanese manufacturing firms began using total-quality-management practices, including just-in-time delivery of parts, to produce high-quality cars and electronics more efficiently, and therefore with higher profit, than firms in this country could do. One man, William Edwards Deming, helped Japanese manufacturers make these system changes.[10] Many U.S. firms tried to transform themselves into adept practitioners of the Deming approach. When their efforts failed, which they often did at least at first, it seemed to be because they tried to adopt specific tactics (e.g., just-in-time delivery) but did not appreciate the importance of changing whole organizational cultures toward more cooperative, less hierarchical and rule-bound approaches to production.

Leaving the business world for the world of education, some recent efforts to change whole systems have been quite successful. In the 1970s, for example, James Comer developed his approach to transforming individual schools to ensure that the most disadvantaged children got the support they needed to succeed in the classroom and beyond. Although he based his approach on his understanding of how children develop, a school must completely reorganize its governance, allocation of resources, approach to cooperation, attitudes toward and uses of assessment, and problem-solving orientation to make it work. Parents, teachers, and community members as well as administrators participate in making educational decisions.

Efforts of public programs to help vulnerable individuals and families progress toward greater self-sufficiency involve moving from "standard operating procedures" within several silos to new ways of doing things. The new ways almost always involve coordinated action across two or more programs or agencies, each of which has the resources and expertise to address one aspect of vulnerability but not other aspects. Communities that want to reap the benefits of more coordinated services have expended much effort in bringing systems together and forging new links and pathways among them, as we have seen in the numerous examples described in this chapter. Researchers have also gone to some trouble to track the process of change and understand what makes it go more or less smoothly.

Sometimes, as we saw in chapter 4, caseload or other program changes, such as dramatic declines in Food Stamp or Medicaid participation, alarm program administrators enough to lead to new procedures involving coordination across program boundaries. These procedures are designed to promote enrollment or retention of people who are eligible for benefits but who may not apply or may drop out for preventable reasons. Sometimes, too, new legislation establishes conditions akin to *requiring* different types of agencies to interact, such as what happened with TANF and the Welfare-to-Work grants program described earlier. And sometimes the failure of a particular group of people to make the progress expected of them pushes safety net agencies to analyze the reasons why and develop approaches that help to overcome these barriers. The solutions often lie in cross-agency work.

Classifying and Understanding Levels of Services and Systems Integration

Through past work with community efforts to change and after examining several analytic schemes for describing that change, we think it is useful to consider three levels of contact or working together that may occur between two or more agencies—communication, coordination, and collaboration. These levels are hierarchical—agencies cannot coordinate without communicating, and they cannot collaborate unless they coordinate. When enough agencies in a community are engaged in collaborative work, we may say that they have achieved a fourth level—coordinated community response. The hierarchy reflects the extent to which agencies pay attention to other agencies, perhaps change their own ways, and make a joint effort to establish and reach shared goals. As we describe these levels, their application to the many examples described above should be obvious.

Communication

Communication means talking to each other and sharing information. It is the first, most necessary, step. Communication may happen between front-line workers (e.g., a mental health worker and a TANF worker), middle-level workers, or agency directors. It may occur among these personnel in two systems, three systems, and so on up to all the systems in a community. Two agencies have reached the level of communication with each other if they have accurate knowledge of each other's existence, service offerings, and eligible clientele. They will also know how to access each other's services and may refer clients to each other. We deliberately speak here of "agencies" communicating. For two agencies to be regarded as "communicating," it is not enough that one or two caseworkers in one agency know and talk with one or two caseworkers in another agency. Knowledge of each other's offerings must be fairly widespread and should lead to significant cross-agency referrals.

"Communication" implies friendly, helpful communication, not hostile or negative communication. Agencies may never reach this first level of our hierarchy. Even when they know each other and sit on the same committees and task forces, when they really start working on integrating services, many will realize that they never really knew what their counterparts in other agencies did, the resources available to them, the types of services they offer, or the people they are authorized to serve. Even worse is the situation in which agencies do not interact in any way or, alternatively, interact negatively or hold inaccurate views of each other. In most communities at most times, most agencies operate toward each other at the level of communication or *below* this level. For many agencies, operating in a service delivery environment where communication, coordination, and collaboration are largely absent represents "business as usual"—and it takes work to get beyond it.

Coordination

Agencies have reached the level of coordination if in addition to communicating, they support each other's efforts to obtain resources for clients. At this level, agency staff work together on a case-by-case basis and may even do cross-training to appreciate each other's roles and responsibilities. Coordination or cooperation may happen between front-line workers or middle-level workers and may involve policy commitments for whole agencies by chiefs, directors, or agency heads. It may occur among these personnel in two systems, three systems, and so on up to all the systems in a jurisdiction.

Many different types of coordination mechanisms exist. Staff of one agency may sometimes work at another agency (outplacement); or, joint space may be made available where all agencies may work, such as a multiservice center or a one-stop (colocation). Multiagency teaming arrangements are a third mechanism. More involved coordination mechanisms include shared databases, shared application procedures, and other shared processes that nevertheless do not change the underlying goals or approaches of any participating agency.

Coordination does *not* involve major changes in the eligibility criteria or priorities of any cooperating agency. It merely means they agree not to get in each other's way and to offer the services they have available when it is appropriate to do so. It does not entail any significant rethinking of agency goals or approaches.

Collaboration

Collaboration adds the element of joint analysis, planning, and accommodation to the base of communication and coordination. Collaborative arrangements include joint work on developing shared goals, followed by protocols for each agency that let each do its work in a way that complements and supports work done by another agency. Agencies have reached the level of collaboration if they work with each other to articulate shared goals, analyze their operations to determine how they may achieve those goals, and make changes dictated by this analysis to improve their ability to serve their joint clients optimally. They may also share mission statements, do joint funding proposals, and work together in other ways.

Collaboration cannot happen without the commitment of the powers that be. In this respect, it differs from communication and coordination. If agency heads are not on board, supporting and enforcing adherence to new policies and protocols, then collaboration is not taking place, although coordination may still occur at lower levels. Collaboration may occur between two or more agencies or systems. Because collaboration entails *organizational commitments*, not just personal ones, when the people who have developed personal connections across agencies leave their position, others will be assigned to take their place. They will be charged with a similar expectation to pursue a coordinated response and will receive whatever training and orientation are needed to make that happen.

Collaboration may mean that agency staff members fill new roles or restructured roles; colocate, team, or otherwise work together with staff of other agencies; merge money; issue joint requests for proposals; apply together for new money to operate new programs in new ways; actively support each other's work; have mutual feedback mechanisms to ensure continued appropriate service and program delivery; and use other mechanisms and activities that reflect a purposeful, well-thought-out commitment to work together to reach common goals. When collaboration extends to include all or most agencies in a community focused on the same population with the same goals, we may call it a strong communitywide degree of organization or a coordinated community response.

Is More Always Better?

The communication-coordination-collaboration framework just described may seem prescriptive, suggesting that it is always better to collaborate than coordinate and coordinate than merely communicate. We do not want to leave that impression. Certainly, in some instances even communication across agencies may not be needed, and if it is not needed, it will not be either efficient or effective. If 60 or 70 percent of the people who need the services of a particular agency need *only* the services that the agency provides, then it will be most efficient for the agency to continue to work in its silo to help these clients. Furthermore, the agency may be good at what it does, so that operating in isolation is also effective as well as efficient. No community wants to lose the expertise of specialized agencies that successfully meet the needs of many people who have simple issues.

But what about the remaining people? This chapter has focused on what it takes to help people with multiple barriers succeed at getting a job and becoming self-sufficient, reaching a productive adulthood, getting and retaining housing, becoming a good parent and not needing child protective services any more, or whatever their goals are. These people need isolated agencies to come out of their isolation and work together. Because overcoming that isolation is so hard, people with complex needs often fall through the cracks and get no help at all. The approaches described in this chapter have been developed to address the needs of these hardest-to-serve individuals and families.

Conclusions—"Lessons Learned"

For decades, studies of service delivery mechanisms have discussed "lessons learned" as one of their most important report sections. Reviewing these sections leads a reader strongly to the conclusion that we have been "learning" the same lessons over and over. Studies of services and systems integration efforts from the 1970s articulate many of the same lessons as studies from the 1980s, 1990s, and now the 2000s. They are remarkably easy to summarize:

- It always takes longer than you think it will. However long you think it will take to get an approach up and running, double it. If new relationships among two or more agencies are involved, triple it, especially if they have never worked together before on anything.
- Clients have multiple and complexly interacting issues; funding and eligibility silos impede the ability of service agencies to help their clients. Break down the silos.
- People and agencies that have coordinated with each other in the past are likely to be the most successful at developing additional coordinative mechanisms or moving toward more intensive service integration.
- No single structure will work in every community. Each community has to evolve its structure for itself, paying attention to the location of talent, interest, leadership, and resources. Trying to impose a particular structure from without is more likely to slow things down than speed them up.
- Integrated services are good for clients with complex needs—they are more likely to get what they need, in a timely manner, and with due regard for all the issues they are trying to handle. But they may not be necessary for all clients. The motivation of any community to develop integrated service mechanisms or to integrate systems will depend on the scope of the problem being addressed and the resources available to address it.
- Having a way to track progress, get feedback, and use data to see how things are going can help the program development process along in many important ways.
- Having a coordinator, or some person whose job it is to keep things moving, helps. If carefully tended, a successful effort at service and systems integration has a tendency to widen in scope and have payoffs for the community beyond the original goals. Example 6 shows this happening in Garfield County, Colorado.

Why, then, do policymakers, managers, and practitioners seem not to have taken the lessons of the past decades to heart? Why do we appear to need to learn the same lessons repeatedly, without starting at least a step or two ahead of the game the next time we try to create structures to serve those with complex needs?

Some part of the answer to this problem lies with the array of challenges that the same evaluation reports also describe. As with the lessons learned, the challenges are similar across the decades, suggesting that even when they are met and surmounted in specific instances, communities have a tendency to relapse to the "status quo ante" of rigid silos unless very strong steps are taken to keep things open and moving forward. Challenges identified frequently across four decades of program and policy evaluation reports include the following:

- *"Turf" issues:* Agencies want to keep control of the services and clients they have traditionally served and are not always eager to share clients or yield control as would be necessary in an integrated service approach.
- *Agency "cultures":* Different agencies are staffed by people with different training, coming from different disciplines, and tending to see the world (and clients' problems) in specific ways. They are also subject to the rules and regulations that go with their specialty and typically ignorant of the rules and regulations governing other agencies. People who do cross-agency work have to learn each other's languages and come to appreciate each other's strengths and constraints.
- *Data privacy constraints:* All kinds of rules and laws govern who can share what information with whom and under what conditions. With good will all around, these constraints can usually be overcome to the benefit of clients, but it takes time. When an agency does not really want to work collaboratively, data-sharing issues can be used to resist full integration.
- *Inadequate resources:* Agencies do not have enough resources to do the work they already have and do not want to take the time to develop new ways of doing things or to focus on the hardest to serve among their clients or eligible population.
- *Characteristics of the population:* The population to be served is not big enough, popular enough, or considered "worthy" enough to warrant the effort that coordination or collaboration takes.
- *And of course, silos.*

What one *can* see across the decades is that lessons *are* learned locally and that challenges once overcome *locally* tend not to recur or are at least not as difficult to handle the next time they arise. Thus, Welfare-to-Work studies in the 2000s list the fact that "the agencies already had a good working relationship" as one of the factors facilitating collaboration. Locally, these agencies were able to capitalize on earlier investments in getting to know each other and working out feasible and useful cross-agency interactions—which perhaps happened during their state's experiments under AFDC waivers in the early 1990s or might go as far back as WIN in the 1970s. The problem for policymakers is how to get *most* places in the country to move beyond silos when that is necessary.

Evaluations of changes arising from TANF provide some of the answer: (1) set general program requirements and standards and then give states and localities the flexibility to decide how they will fulfill them; (2) give states and localities enough resources to make it worthwhile for different agencies to come to the table; and (3) focus on a population big enough, and of enough concern locally, to pull in the various agencies that constitute the safety net.

6

Program Administration and Institutions

The federalist structure of government in the United States creates both complexities and opportunities for planning, designing, implementing, and monitoring social safety net programs. The *federalist structure* means that both the national government and state or local governments have some responsibility for programs. The national government creates the largest safety net programs through legislation and funding commitments but then usually distributes program resources to states, counties, and independent entities, such as community action agencies and housing authorities, to administer them. These agencies in their turn often contract with nongovernmental service providers to deliver the services to clients, further complicating the structure.

This chapter describes those complexities, the interaction at various levels of government and the private sector, and some of the issues that arise because so many entities are involved. Before discussing these issues, we offer a simplified explanation to help the reader understand the relationships (see figure 6.1).

The figure shows the national government at the top, including Congress and executive branch departments, such as Health and Human Services, Labor, Housing and Urban Development, Justice, and Agriculture, and their component agencies. Executive branch agencies administer the programs that Congress establishes. Many programs—including Temporary Assistance for Needy Families, Medicaid, and the State Children's

Figure 6.1. The Federal Structure

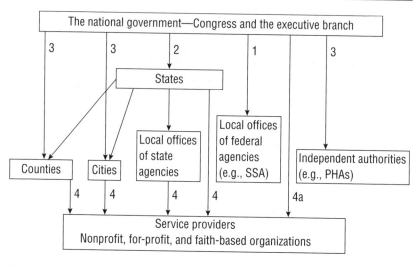

Key: 1 = completely federal programs; 2 = federal-state programs; 3 = federal to nonstate government agencies; 4 = partnering or outsourcing to nongovernmental service providers

Health Insurance Program—send resources to the states to administer the programs; states, in turn, allocate funds to counties, cities, or their own local offices or agencies. Federal agencies may also distribute funds to their own local offices (as they do for Social Security programs) or to independent quasi-governmental agencies such as housing authorities, or they may contract directly with service providers (the box at the bottom of figure 6.1). States, counties, and cities may also contract with nongovernmental service providers to interact directly with clients and deliver the program services.

Every one of the pathways represented by arrows in figure 6.1 is used by one government program or another; sometimes the same program will use several pathways. Sometimes because a set of pathways is favored in one era, the programs created at that time will follow those pathways. When there are reforms, programs may change directions and bypass the old pathways in favor of a different arrangement. The complexity that characterizes the American social safety net today comes from the fact that programs were created in different eras, each embodying the premises, priorities, and values of its own time.

Why We Have Such Complexity

The framework just described, within which safety net policies are administered, reflects the federalist foundation of the United States and the constitutional and fiscal relationships between the national government and the states. Most individuals in need of assistance come into contact with local governmental and nongovernmental agencies where the actual delivery of most services occurs. Between Congress and grass-roots services lies an intricate institutional and administrative web. It is not hard to see this web as fragmented and difficult to understand, but it is equally difficult to simplify it.

As a result of the political realities of the federalist system, many of the efforts to reform the safety net—whether the goal is to strengthen it or reduce it—focus on trying to improve the performance of institutions at all levels, simplifying administrative complexity, and ensuring both fiscal accountability and the desired impacts. Some of these efforts at programmatic and organizational reform have had a degree of success, but over time the safety net has become increasingly complex and somewhat overwhelming. Most programs that provide safety net services and crisis intervention for vulnerable and poor people operate at the local level but are often required to change as new regulatory and legal provisions made at every other level of government take effect.

The structure of American federalism figures importantly in the historical evolution of the social safety net since the 1700s, as described in chapter 1. Federalism defines how programs are structured institutionally, how they are financed, and how they are managed. The U.S. Constitution specifies and limits the role of the national government, generally reserving for the states all rights not specifically designated for the national government. The Constitution, however, also places responsibility for protecting the general public welfare with the national government, in addition to its other major role of preserving national security. Balancing these two federalist principles—states' rights and the national government's responsibility for public welfare—has been an ongoing theme in social and economic policy development. Understanding how this theme plays out helps one understand the structure of the social safety net.

The role of the national government has shifted periodically as the nation has grown, as different political priorities have emerged and dissipated, and as various social and economic challenges have arisen (chapter 1). A more active national role developed to address the severe and immediate crisis during the Great Depression of the 1930s and again in the 1960s and 1970s as a national consensus arose to confront poverty. Especially in the 1960s and 1970s, the public welfare role was defined quite broadly to include ensuring equal opportunity and, to some extent, equalizing across states poor people's access to services and benefits.

One of the more important political shifts that affected safety net programs occurred in the 1980s. From the beginning of his presidency, Ronald Reagan placed devolution on the national agenda in all aspects of government, in keeping with his basic political philosophy that favored a limited government, particularly at the national level. The gradual expansion of the federal role that had been going on since 1935, thus, reversed somewhat in 1981, and since then, there has been more devolution of authority to the states for carrying out programs that are fully, or mainly, funded by the national government. Support for restructuring the roles of different levels of government also likely resulted from growing concerns about the effectiveness and cost of safety net programs at a time when all levels of government were facing growing fiscal constraints. These concerns also led to increasing attention to program accountability and performance.

The intergovernmental framework of U.S. social safety net policies thus reflects an ongoing challenge to balance the national government's obligations to preserve and support the public's welfare with respect for states' rights and concerns for fairness in the face of clearly unequal treatment of people in identical circumstances who live in different states. There is also a need to balance the respect for states' rights with the federal government's responsibility to maintain a reasonable level of oversight and accountability for federally funded programs. The specific details of these intergovernmental responsibilities change as priorities, concerns, and fiscal and political situations change.

Federal, State, and Local Program Delivery Arrangements

Four general administrative models for funding, administering, and overseeing federally authorized social programs account for almost all the major safety net programs: totally federal programs, intergovernmental federal-state partnerships, intergovernmental partnerships with other government entities, and federal-direct-to-nongovernmental entities approaches. Totally federal programs are depicted above in figure 6.1 by the arrow labeled "1." Federal-state partnerships are depicted by the arrow labeled "2." Federal partnerships with counties, cities, and quasi-public entities, such as public housing authorities, are shown by the arrows labeled "3." Partnerships or contracts with nongovernmental service providers are labeled "4," with the special case of federal-direct-to-nongovernmental entities labeled "4a."

Federal-Only Model

Some safety net programs are administered and implemented entirely by the federal government. This pathway is depicted by the arrow labeled "1" in figure 6.1, running from the national government to local offices maintained by federal agencies. Federal law and regulations specify the rules and details of these programs, and federal employees administer the programs, including direct involvement with clients. Programs of this type include major pension and health programs for the elderly (e.g., Social Security and Medicare), programs for the disabled (Social Security Disability Income and Supplemental Security Income), and programs that operate through the income tax system (e.g., EITC).

One major example of a federally administered safety net program with a complicated application process is Supplemental Security Income (SSI), which provides cash income to very poor aged, blind, or disabled adults and children. One does not need to qualify for regular retirement benefits under Social Security to be eligible for SSI. While individuals may apply for SSI electronically, by mail, or in person through the nationwide network of Social Security offices staffed by federal employees, to succeed in qualifying for benefits almost always requires assistance from a caseworker in a local office or an advisor or other advocate with special training.

The EITC is another federal program with a somewhat more straightforward process. Low-income workers, especially those with children, receive benefits by filing regular federal income tax returns; the federal Internal Revenue Service processes the tax returns and provides the individual a payment from the tax system based on the credit.

Federal-State Model

TANF, Medicaid, SCHIP, Food Stamps, and many other safety net programs are partnerships between the national government and the state governments, as shown in the arrow labeled "2" in figure 6.1. Federal legislation defines the program, states (and any entity they choose to include for various activities) administer the program, federal and state governments usually share responsibility for funding, and federal agencies monitor and conduct quality assurance activities. Federal programs with this model include many within the Department of Health and Human Services and the Department of Agriculture.

Structure (federal plus state) and funding mechanism are not synonymous. The federal-state model is used for some open-ended entitlements (Medicaid, SCHIP, out-of-home placement for abused and neglected children) and for some block grants with capped funding (TANF and the social services, mental health, substance abuse, child care, preventive health, and other block grants), and other funding structures. Funding for the Workforce Investment Act is also distributed under this model but is neither a block grant nor an entitlement. Neither block grants nor WIA funding require state matching funds, but Medicaid and SCHIP do have such requirements.

The Food Stamp Program is an interesting variation on the federal-state partnership model. It is an entitlement, administered through the same state welfare agencies that administer TANF. But all funding for the actual benefits is federal—there is no state match requirement as there is for most other entitlements; the funding for administrative costs, though, does require a state match.

Federal-Local Government Model

In this model, depicted by arrows labeled "3" in figure 6.1, federal agencies transfer their program resources directly to local government entities, which include counties, cities, other agencies such as public housing authorities, and Indian tribes. This model is common in HUD programs. Public and assisted housing resources from various programs go directly to public housing authorities, which are not directly under the control of cities, counties, or states. Community Development Block Grant (CDBG) and HOME dollars go directly to "entitlement jurisdictions," which are cities and urban counties (minus the cities) of a certain population size. Funds for some programs have extensive federal conditions that must be met; other programs have few requirements attached to the federal funding. CDBG and HOME funds, for example, allow broad local discretion.

Direct-to-Nongovernmental Entities Model

The pathway marked "4a" in figure 6.1 is relatively rare these days but was common for programs created in the 1960s. One of the first programs to use this model was created by the Community Mental Health Centers Act of 1963. This act established a whole new source of federal money for mental health services; but, because it was created in response to very negative assessments of state mental health agencies at the time, the act bypassed them in favor of new nonprofit entities. Community mental health centers proliferated throughout the country, becoming the direct recipients of federal funds for establishing a new array of community-based services for people with serious mental illness. When these resources were consolidated into the Mental Health Block Grant and sent directly to states in the early 1980s, it caused a good deal of consternation and required some major realignments of working relationships among state and county mental health agencies and the community mental health centers.

Programs under the Office of Economic Opportunity established by the War on Poverty also tended to take this form, and for the same reasons—that is, the public lacked the confidence that some of the older, more established pathways for federal funding would take up the cause of the War on Poverty. Community action agencies were the primary example of a local nonprofit agency in this case. Many still exist, especially in smaller communities and rural areas, but their core funding no longer comes directly from Washington.

Some important examples of this model are still active today. The U.S. Department of Health and Human Services awards grants to over 1,400 public or nonprofit organizations or local school divisions to operate Head Start Centers, which provide early childhood education to low-income preschool children. The Job Corps is also a permanent, national, intensive, mainly residential program for very disadvantaged youth, operated by dozens of Job Corps Centers around the country. The national Job Corps office in the U.S. Department of Labor contracts directly with private businesses and nonprofit organizations to operate the centers. National grant programs authorized for a specific period of time, rather than permanently, also fit into this category as—when a federal agency makes grants to public or nonprofit organizations or private businesses to provide specific services or operate a type of program. Under the Prisoner Reentry Grants (Department of Labor and Department of Justice), Welfare-to-Work Grants (Department of Labor), and Job Opportunities for Low-Income Individuals Grants (DHHS), for instance, national offices issue grants periodically under special announcements that indicate the types of organization eligible to apply for funding.

Roles for Nongovernmental Entities

Nonprofit agencies have long been critical to the social safety net. Their relationship to government agencies at every level is depicted by the arrows labeled "4" in figure 6.1. Different safety net programs are more or less likely to contract with nonprofit agencies to deliver actual services to actual clients. Furthermore, the inclination fluctuates from time to time depending on resources, on what services are required, on which entities have the expertise to deliver them, and sometimes on local preference and experience as well.

Businesses are also sometimes directly involved, as in workforce development programs, where they may offer jobs to participants, serve as training sites, and sponsor subsidized workers. In some localities, private businesses are contracted to operate the local One Stop Career Centers. In general, though, as social service delivery has for most of its history been quite "unprofitable" (i.e., resources were not adequate to allow service delivery plus a profit margin), for-profit firms were largely absent from the field (with the important exception of Job Corps). The situation has changed somewhat in recent years as states automate their eligibility and benefits transfer functions and sometimes other aspects of their work, and private companies often receive government contracts for computer technology systems.

Finally, recent years have seen increased involvement in social services by small faith-based organizations. Major, large faith-affiliated service agencies such as Catholic Charities, Lutheran Social Services, and Jewish Vocational Services with long histories of service delivery and federal funding continue, but the new development is that smaller faith-based agencies and even individual congregations now have a role as well.

Nonprofit Community and Faith-Based Organizations

Much of the federal and state funding for social safety net programs is funneled through governmental agencies, and most cash benefit programs are implemented by government agencies. The delivery of services at the local level, however, often occurs through a combination of public agencies and nonprofit organizations. Operating as contracted providers of services for various government programs and providing direct services of their own with mainly private funds from donations or philanthropic grants, community-based nonprofit service organizations have a long history in the United States.

Nationwide, countless nonprofit organizations are in operation. According to some research in this area, the over 12 million such organizations can be categorized into five groups based on their primary purpose (Salamon 2002): service, advocacy, artistic and expressive, community building, and value guardian (that is, serving as a vehicle through which individuals and groups can pursue charitable and voluntary activities of their own choosing). Some of the nonprofit service agencies are faith based—that is, they are churches or religious organizations or are affiliated with a religious entity. Others are secular. Still others are in between; they have a religious affiliation but hire staff of all religious persuasions and do not require any religious observance of their clients.

The service purpose of both secular and faith-based community organizations and their receipt of public funds are particularly relevant to the social safety net. To some extent, nearly all government agencies that run safety net programs contract out for the provision of various services, and many of these contracted providers are community-based nonprofit organizations. The organizations may also receive funds from philanthropic foundations, private donations, or directly from the federal government by submitting applications and receiving special program grants. Community-based nonprofit agencies operate many social services programs, crisis and emergency facilities, child care and senior centers, homeless shelters, foster care group homes, feeding programs, employment centers, and health facilities.

The extensive involvement of nonprofit agencies in the delivery of public services has not always been the case, however. In the 1950s, public agencies provided most public social services, while nonprofit agencies provided services supported mainly by charitable contributions (Kennedy and Bielefeld 2002). In the 1960s and 1970s, when federal programs designed to reduce poverty expanded, nonprofit organizations assumed major responsibility for delivering public services. They often received funding through federal grants in addition to contracts from state and local agencies. In the 1980s, dramatic federal budget reductions in all domestic programs strongly affected nonprofit agencies. Their role diminished considerably, although many continued to operate in their specialized areas (e.g., child care, employment and training, homeless services, emergency services, mental health treatment).

The role of nonprofits expanded again in the 1990s for two related and somewhat controversial reasons. First, beginning in 1996, Congress included provisions in several laws requiring states to allow faith-based organizations to compete for program contracts in the same way as secular organizations and to allow individuals to choose whether to receive services through faith-based or secular providers when both were available, a provision known as "charitable choice." Three major block grants that fund social safety net programs have the charitable choice provisions: TANF, the Substance Abuse Prevention and Treatment Block Grant, and the Community Services Block Grant.

The second reason for the expanded role of faith-based services also applies to all social services providers. As a result of the welfare reform law of 1996, states received a surplus of funds, at least in the initial years of TANF. Many state TANF agencies decided to use more of their block grant "surplus" funds for employment and training, child care, and other supportive social services—all of which had traditionally been provided by nonprofit service organizations, including those that are faith based.

Reinforcing the importance of faith-based services, President George W. Bush raised public and political visibility with his Faith-Based Initiative coordinated by the new White House Office of Community and Faith-Based Initiatives. Eight cabinet departments and two other federal agencies were also directed to establish community and faith-based offices.

The controversial aspect of the expanded role for faith-based organizations stems from to the constitutional protection of freedom of religion and the required separation of church and state. Like other nonprofits, faith-based organizations have historically collaborated with public programs to provide various services. In the past, they had to comply with requirements to abstain from religious activity and proselytizing and could not discriminate on the basis of religious belief in hiring employees. The charitable choice provisions in the 1990s were premised on a belief that faith-based organizations and houses of worship provide important and effective services because they are close to the people and can harness the power of volunteers in a compassionate community. At the same time, though, some feared that the charitable choice provisions blurred the line between church and state because the new law exempted them from the nondiscrimination employment provisions, allowing even those receiving public funds to use religion as a factor in hiring (Gill 2004; Kramer et al. 2005).

As of 2008, evidence of whether faith-based organizations are more successful than secular nonprofits at addressing problems facing vulnerable populations is inconclusive. Neither does evidence show if faith-based providers have maintained an adequate separation of church and public activities. There is no doubt, however, that the historically substantial role of faith-based organizations in the provision of safety net services has expanded since the mid-1990s. Research does indicate that, like small nonprofits generally, some small faith-based organizations have more administrative challenges than do larger programs in dealing with federal program and fiscal reporting requirements and in implementing regulatory procedures (Kramer et al. 2005). Such issues have raised new questions about government accountability for the expenditure of public funds on their specified purposes and how to monitor such programs, including those that involve faith-based organizations.

Private For-Profit Firms and Public Social Services

The expanding role of community and faith-based organizations is one dimension of privatization that has become increasingly common in social services since the mid-1990s. As it relates to faith-based organizations, the shift reflects political ideology—the belief that faith-based organizations and religious communities are well suited to help people change their ways and eschew socially unacceptable lifestyles (we term this a *belief* because there is still no evidence on these issues). The inclusion of faith-based organizations in delivery of public services also falls within the growing trend to outsource various functions as a way to address financial constraints and to improve efficiency and performance. Another sign of the growing emphasis on better management, greater efficiency, and outsourcing is the involvement of for-profit firms in safety net programs.

Since the early 1990s, the federal government has increased its stress on managing for results, becoming more efficient, and getting more for each government dollar. The Government Performance and Results Act of 1992 (GPRA) requires all agencies to develop annual performance plans with clear goals and then track progress toward them (Kramer et al. 2005). A major thrust of this development is outsourcing—having private organizations and firms do the actual work and leaving a smaller government workforce to oversee and administer the programs. The Government Management Reform Act of 1994 (P.L. 103-356) states:

> To be successful in the future, government must, like the private sector, adopt modern management methods, utilize meaningful program performance measures, increase workforce incentives and flexibility without sacrificing accountability, provide for humane downsizing opportunities, and harness computers and other technology to strengthen service delivery.

Since 2001, the President's Management Agenda (PMA) has also specified that each agency focus on continuously improving five areas of management: strategic management of human capital, competitive sourcing, improved financial performance, expanded electronic government, and budget and performance integration (Office of Management and Budget 2002). The core feature of the PMA is to improve performance by using sound management planning practices, setting clear goals, and using technology efficiently.

The Issue of Privatization

Privatization refers to the provision of publicly funded services and activities by nongovernmental entities. Support for privatization is part of the PMA principle of competitive sourcing, which includes contracting out functions to nongovernmental entities and companies. It is not a recent phenomenon—privatization has increased at many historical points, including during the late 19th century, the New Deal and Great Society periods, and the Reagan administration.

But the nature of the approach to privatization operating during George W. Bush's presidency was somewhat different, raising new concerns about safety net programs and providers, their ability to meet performance expectations, and how setting and enforcing performance goals may affect the way that state and local public agencies set priorities and award contracts. More specifically, evidence suggests that some programs (whether operated by public agencies or contractors) may make narrow program decisions about whom to serve and what types of services to provide based on whether they expect to meet performance goals and targets. Program administrators might, in effect, decide to serve the easiest people, which will make the agency look more successful, rather than responding to the broader mission of serving those with the most serious problems. When contract agencies behave in this way, it may leave government agencies to work with the hardest-to-serve people, those who require the most resources to succeed and those with the least likelihood of success. Under these circumstances, the private contractors will look "good," and the government programs will look "bad" on standard performance measures, unless someone analyzes success rates based on the barriers faced by the clients served. Accountability policies and clear guidance along with performance measures could minimize this tendency to serve some clients and not others. In general, though, government performance policies thus far have not been sophisticated enough to include accurate measurement or flexible enough to allow program managers to adapt quickly to changing circumstances and needs (Radin 2000).

Publicly funded services and activities may be privatized through various methods, including contracts, formal agreements, vouchers, grants, subsidies, public-private partnerships, and collaborative service delivery. In general, though, the term *privatization* usually refers to formal contracts for services from a government agency to a nongovernmental one, whether nonprofit or for-profit.

The traditional approach to contracting in social services had involved noncompetitive, quasi-grant arrangements, primarily with nonprofit organizations. The increased emphasis on competition and performance contracting for the delivery of social services, however, is more consistent with private sector initiatives focusing on efficiency and customer service.

With the new flexibility allowed under welfare reform, large for-profit private companies (e.g., EDS, Lockheed Martin, IBM) moved more directly into the welfare market. Before welfare reform, private companies were involved only in special programs for poor people, such as operating Job Corps residential centers for disadvantaged youth, collecting and enforcing child support payments, or developing computerized reporting systems for human services agencies. Since welfare reform, states have been considering additional privatization options because of cost constraints and the pressing need to meet higher performance standards specified in new federal goals. For example, Texas uses an automated system for processing cases called the Texas Integrated Enrollment System (TIES), which has recently been privatized. The TIES system integrates eligibility determination for 15 safety net programs, including food stamps, TANF and its predecessor AFDC, and Medicaid. Thus, with new private sector options opened by welfare reform, companies are now testing the government services waters in ways different from the past, including contracting to process some program intake functions.

Arguments for and against privatization abound. One strong argument in favor of privatization, from government's perspective, is that it increases flexibility, which results from reduced bureaucratic complexity and procedures. Governments do not have to take on additional permanent staff when they launch a new program. Instead, they can issue a request for proposals and see whether any private organization can make a case for why it should get the chance to deliver the services. Then, if government funding is reduced at some point, the government can simply terminate the contract when it comes up for renewal, rather than having to lay off permanent public employees. Another strong argument in favor of privatization is that costs should be lower and efficiency in service delivery will be greater if different private agencies must compete for contracts and can be held to clear performance criteria. Administrators of safety net programs want their agencies to have the greatest possible impact; many people believe that privatization is the best way to reach this end.

In contrast to the arguments *for* privatizing safety net programs are several strong arguments *against* it. The most prominent of these are that privatization may dilute the quality of benefits and services provided, will negatively affect public sector employees, or will "skim off" the easiest clients to serve while overlooking the more difficult ones.

The jury is still out on which set of beliefs about privatization is correct. Once adequate research evidence is available, it will likely reveal mixed results. Privatization will prove to be very useful for some functions of some safety net programs some of the time and under some circumstances, and government provision of services will prove to be most useful for other functions under other circumstances. We say this not to be cynical but to be realistic. No magic bullet will make all social safety net programs achieve great results all the time and in every community. Neither communities nor safety net programs nor nongovernmental organizations are standardized. As we discussed in the conclusion to chapter 5, to work best, safety net programs must be fitted to the specific circumstances of each community and clientele. As usual, one size does not fit all.

Intergovernmental Funding Mechanisms

As described above, federal agencies pass funding on to states, local governments, and nongovernmental agencies through various arrangements. While states also use their revenues to fund certain social programs, such as general assistance or state earned income tax credits, most of the safety net activities discussed thus far have considerable federal involvement. Here we summarize the most common intergovernmental funding arrangements:

- *Federal-state partnership.* A program is federally mandated as a federal-state partnership, with federally developed rules and regulations, administered through the states, which decide how to deliver services, and both levels of government contribute funding. States may be required to provide matching funds to receive the federal grant.
- *Federal grant-in-aid.* A program is federally mandated and funded, with federally developed rules and regulations, administered through states or local governments or by other grantees (e.g., nongovernmental entities).
- *Federal block grant.* A program uses federal block grants to states or localities, which decide how to deliver services.
- *Federal program grant.* A program is federally authorized, with federal guidelines, administered by grantees that receive the funds and may be state or local governments or private entities. Depending on the program, the federal government may fund the entire cost, or grantees may be required to contribute a share.

Some federal sources require a local match, the amount of which is usually specified in the authorizing legislation. Others, including block grants, generally require no state or local match. Match or no match requirement, funding may be either open-ended (entitlements) or capped funding (table 1.1 in chapter 1 identifies which safety net programs are open-ended entitlements and which are capped). Other dimensions on which safety net programs vary are their geography and how funding levels are determined. Most safety net programs go to every jurisdiction in the country—urban and rural, large and small. But some go only to communities of a certain type. HUD block grants, such as the CDBG and HOME programs, for example, go only to urban areas. Some housing programs go only to rural areas or Indian tribes. Resources from the School Breakfast and School Lunch programs run by the Department of Agriculture go only to schools that meet certain criteria for the proportion of low-income students, as do compensatory education funds administered by the Department of Education. Many federal resources are allocated by formula, and not all formulas are the same. Common elements in block grant formulas are a jurisdiction's population, the unemployment rate, and the poverty rate, but most block grants also have elements in their formula that reflect their special purpose, be it education, nutrition, housing hardship, or other factors.

Each type of funding stresses a form of interjurisdictional governance. An open-ended entitlement may be fully funded by the federal government (e.g., food stamps, SSI, foster care payments for child welfare) or require matching funding from the state. When matching funding is required, the state match can vary from program to program and will certainly vary from state to state. For instance, Medicaid and SCHIP both require states to match, although the match amount varies from state to state according to poverty levels and other factors. In general, federal sources supply 50–76 percent of funds for these health insurance programs, and states must meet the remainder.

In contrast, capped funding supports a different form of interjurisdictional governance. Capped funding may be provided in the form of block grants, which may include a state match requirement. In the case of TANF, the block grant is distributed to states by formula with a requirement that states maintain their pre-TANF spending (referred to as a "maintenance of effort" requirement). In the case of child welfare services, the block grant requires a state match.

Other safety net programs use different capped-funding mechanisms. Public housing funds, for instance, are distributed as direct grants to public housing agencies as capped-dollar amounts, although they are often spoken of as covering a particular number of housing units. Creative housing authorities are often able to squeeze more units out of a fixed-dollar amount. It also happens, however, that annual adjustments of funding allocations do not keep pace with the rise in local housing costs, forcing housing authorities to juggle resources or, as a worst case, cut the number of households they assist. Nor do public and assisted-housing dollars go equally to jurisdictions with equivalent circumstances. In times past, housing authorities had to apply for funding, and some were more assertive than others. In general, the number of poor households in a jurisdiction and the number of assisted-housing slots are highly correlated, but even so, some jurisdictions have more than "their fair share" of assisted-housing units, thanks to their success in gaining units in past years.

Some of the basic features of open-ended entitlements versus block grants can be seen in the shift from AFDC to TANF. Before 1996, federal and state governments jointly funded AFDC, and states operated it under federal guidelines that governed eligibility and spending. Cash benefits were entitlements for anyone meeting income and some other criteria. The program also had open-ended entitlement funding from the federal government that required a state match, the exact percentage of which varied by state according to a prescribed formula but which averaged about 60 percent.

The 1996 welfare reform law changed the financing to a block grant. The amount of each state's initial TANF block grant (set for a six-year period) was considerably higher than any state actually needed to pay its welfare benefits. The generous funding was in large part intended to provide financial motivation for states to support the new reform. The block grant funding formula guaranteed that states would receive the same amount of federal funding under the new program that they had received under AFDC in the mid-1980s. Nearly all states experienced caseload declines between 1984 and 1996, resulting in a windfall of sorts, because the block grant would provide more funding than they needed to pay out in cash benefits and more than they would have received in 1997 under the old entitlement program. Compared to earlier AFDC financing rules, every state experienced a TANF "surplus" of funding, at least during the first five years after TANF replaced AFDC.

A change to a safety net program's funding mechanism can have major impacts on how services are delivered. When welfare policy shifted in 1996 from an open-ended entitlement (AFDC) to a block grant (TANF), several changes occurred. State fiscal discretion increased, since block grants have less direct federal oversight or accountability mechanisms. The change also increased state policymaking discretion, leading to more state-initiated changes in policy and funding and more variation in program design. These areas of increased flexibility and "surplus" funding, however, were balanced against another aspect of block grant funding—periodic congressional reauthorization, in contrast to open-ended entitlements that almost always are permanent programs. When TANF was reauthorized in 2006 (the program survived on continuing resolutions for several years), states found themselves facing increased performance expectations but no more resources, and caseloads were increasingly filled by families with many barriers to leaving the welfare rolls through employment.

Despite all the flexibility, experimentation, and caseload changes in TANF, the underlying structure and administration remain relatively unchanged from the AFDC days. States are still ultimately responsible for the program and able to set rules. State agencies either administer TANF or delegate much of the responsibility to counties. And at the ground level,

TANF is still delivered jointly with other benefit programs, such as Food Stamps, Medicaid, and SCHIP, meaning that administrative costs and some staff service costs are shared across programs.

The Devolution Debate

The interplay of federal and state agencies and funding in most safety net programs naturally prompts discussion of which level of government is best able to carry out which functions and about which type of federal program is best. Some discussions reflect different perspectives on the role of government in general and the role of the national government specifically, while others center on the accountability that underlies government policies on performance that have been especially prominent since the early 1990s. Because there are no easy answers and certainly no definitive answers, the nation has gone through decades-long pendulum swings from centralization to decentralization and back again, as fairness and equal treatment across state and local jurisdictions wars with the conviction that the government closest to the people knows best what the people need and how to help them.

Since the days of Thomas Jefferson, James Madison, and Alexander Hamilton in the late 1700s, Americans have struggled over the benefits and drawbacks of centralized versus decentralized government. Historian Mary Furner (1996, 1) sees this struggle as actually part of the nation's political character: "Periodic reversals in the size and scope of government and changes in the balance of power between the state and national governments," she writes, "define us as a people." She also points out that public and political support for devolution (decentralization) has appeared five times, each after periods of government growth, which contributed to "revulsion against government." After the Civil War, for example, national government actions expanded until states' rights reaction in the late 1870s undid many of its programs. Following World War II, rapid economic growth and the civil rights movement led to increased centralization of government at a national level. With the economic downturn of the 1970s, centralized government became less desirable, and again the calls for devolution and smaller government mounted.

The federal system presents unavoidable tensions because centralization and decentralization each have advantages and disadvantages. Two particularly salient tensions for safety net programs inherent in Ellwood's dilemmas are equality versus individualism and uniformity versus diversity.

With a foundation in the Declaration of Independence, the principle of equality pervades U.S. law and demands that equals be treated equally. In the modern state, those on both ends of the political spectrum agree that, in theory, if two people, families, or corporations are in equal circumstances, then they should pay the same tax and receive the same benefits from the government. The concept of equality, however, is directly challenged by Americans' desire for individual freedom, which is also constitutionally protected. Freedom of choice among individuals allows them to decide where to live, work, buy property, and start businesses. From a political perspective, individual freedom also means that people are able to "vote with their feet" and move to a jurisdiction consistent with their perspectives and best suited for them. The dynamic economic and social progress of some communities undoubtedly results from the combined individual initiative that promotes prosperity. The concept of states' rights evolves out of this strong embrace of individualism. Government closest to the people can, in theory, best make decisions for the good of the people in a local jurisdiction.

Another result of the state diversity, though, is that it often produces inequality across jurisdictions in prevailing wages, public benefits and services, economic opportunities, and—because of the mix of federal and state responsibilities—the social safety net. One reason that food stamps was established with more federal standards and benefit levels was specifically to smooth out some of the cross-state differences in AFDC policies by providing benefits designed to equalize across states the combined benefits from welfare plus food stamps. The 1996 change from AFDC to TANF, perhaps representing a devolution cycle in Furner's terms, expands state discretion in TANF well beyond what had existed under AFDC and raises some new concerns about cross-state inequities.

In contrast to local diversity, standardized national policies can, again at least in theory, improve the efficiency of programs and ensure that all similar beneficiaries of various public services are treated equally. Delivering a good or service through one provider on a mass scale can decrease inefficiencies and overhead costs. It can also help ensure that beneficiaries receive equal treatment. A uniform program, however, does not always lead to equal provision of goods or services in the real world. Agencies and programs may not be well managed. Entrenched bureaucracies may stifle innovation and progress. The top decisionmakers may be far removed from the people in need of assistance and not be able to respond appropriately when new situations arise.

State and Local Government Roles

In comparison to the federal government, which is somewhat distant from individuals and communities, states and localities control many of the goods and services that affect people in their day-to-day lives, such as fire and police protection, education, land use, and transportation. In states and localities, public sector employment is devoted largely to carrying out those functions, including large parts of the social safety net. In addition to enacting their own programs (which many states do), states are responsible for administering federally funded programs, and state legislatures have the power to assign primary administrative and operational responsibility for federal programs to state, county, or city government agencies. State legislatures also determine how to meet the state's share of funding when a state match is required to secure federal funds. Some states go one step further and require a local funding share from their counties and cities. In addition, state legislatures and governors are responsible for coordinating state laws, programs, and rules with federal programs and rules.

Welfare policies illustrate how integral state and local governments are to the functioning of the federally developed safety net. Two structural models govern state welfare programs and the related social and crisis intervention services, neither of which changed with the welfare reform of 1996. The first model is a *state-supervised and state-administered* structure, whereby the state government maintains responsibility for supervision and delivery of human services, with state staff working in the local offices. Most states have this structure.

The second model is a *state-supervised and locally administered* program, whereby the state maintains overall supervision and oversight of services but local governments administer the program and deliver services. In this case, the local level is usually the county but may also be the city or town. About seven large states, including New York and California, have this structure. No evidence indicates that one structure is better than the other; the choice is mainly a reflection of state history and the intergovernmental sharing of responsibilities for financing and service provision.

In the case of AFDC/TANF, the 1996 reforms actually strengthened federal financing of cash welfare for poor families with children. Whereas under AFDC, the federal government would contribute additional money for every additional dollar spent by the states or localities, today, under TANF, states and localities operate with fixed-funding amounts from federal block grants. Any additional spending that might be needed must come entirely from state sources; there is no longer a federal financial safety net if caseloads rise. As a result, state incentives to spend less of their own money have in many ways increased the importance of the federal financing. Instead, states have their own pressures to contain costs and thus focus much attention on management and cost-control functions.

Who Should Do What?

In their classic book on reinventing government, Osborne and Gaebler (1992) note:

> Business does some things better than government, but government does some things better than business. The public sector tends to be better, for instance, at policy management, regulation, ensuring equity, preventing discrimination or exploitation, ensuring continuity and stability of services, and ensuring social cohesion. . . . Business tends to be better at performing economic tasks, innovating, replicating successful experiments, adapting to rapid change, abandoning unsuccessful or obsolete activities, and performing complex or technical tasks. The [nonprofit] sector tends to be best at performing tasks that generate little or no profit, demand compassion and commitment to individuals, require extensive trust on the part of customers or clients, need hands-on, personal attention . . . and involve the enforcement of moral codes and individual responsibility for behavior (45–46).

That being said, little empirical research has been conducted—and therefore little evidence is available—to calculate the relative effectiveness of the private, public, and nonprofit sectors *when it comes to delivering safety net services* (Nightingale and Pindus 1997). It is yet to be determined whether private companies will find it profitable to continue to pursue contracts for deciding safety net program eligibility or managing benefits. Nor is it clear whether private businesses are indeed more efficient than nonprofit or government agencies in providing social services to individuals through contracts from government, or whether the federal, state, or local government is best to administer certain programs.

Many believe, for example, that if a more equitable income distribution is a goal, the national government should be responsible for the programs involved, because state and local governments face clear disadvantages in trying to redistribute income, and it is hardly the role of the private sector. Paul Peterson (2005) explains the difference between redistribution (sharing the pie) and infrastructure development (making the shared pie bigger). With redistribution, something is taken from the "haves" and given to the "have nots"—an activity best done at a level of government that has both a wide territorial reach and is free of immediate economic competition from similar jurisdictions. States may not want to compete with nearby jurisdictions by charging their citizens higher taxes to support higher welfare services. So when the federal government is the one that sets a minimum benefit level in particular programs, it can prevent a "race to the bottom" and keep the social safety net reasonably intact.

Similarly, no state or local government wants responsibility for certain politically difficult purposes and programs, either because the challenge or cost is too high or the possibility of failure too risky politically. Such programs, too, are best left to the national government. Making changes to Social Security retirement benefits and Medicare, for example, are clearly high-stakes undertakings, because these programs serve not only the poor but also the middle- and upper-income elderly and the latter constituents have the political clout to resist changes that will leave them worse off. Decisions about these types of programs are best kept in the national policy domain.

In general, when the public sector appears to have problems administering safety net programs (e.g., high cost, low performance), public officials may consider privatization. But privatization is not always a satisfactory answer; all three markets—the public sector, nonprofits, and private businesses—have their successes and failures. According to Osborne and Gaebler (1992, 47), "The determining factors have to do with the incentives that drive those within the system. Are they accountable for their results? Are they free from overly restrictive rules and regulations? Is authority decentralized enough to permit adequate flexibility? Do rewards reflect the quality of their performance?"

Conclusions

The discussions above highlight the complex interplay among government entities and among the public sector, the nonprofit sector, and private businesses in financing and administering social safety net programs. There are, however, no clear answers about which structure or which funding mechanism is best, and in all likelihood no one approach will ever be best for everything.

Regarding the various funding strategies, we can draw a few general conclusions. First, programs with open-ended entitlement funding have more stable funding from year to year because federal support is guaranteed. Second, programs with capped funding potentially face less fiscal stability because Congress must appropriate funds, usually annually. They are thus subject to more political review, with the consequence that their budgets could be reduced or their programs eliminated due to fiscal constraints or new political directions. Finally, while block grants provide more flexibility for states to design policies, national government regulations for those grants sometimes become stricter to ensure fiscal accountability for the federal funds and to guard against the substitution of federal funds for what the states or local governments would have spent (the rationale for maintenance-of-effort requirements).

No clear evidence points to which level of government is best positioned to administer social safety net programs or suggests any simple answer about whether the private sector is better able than the government to provide services to poor and vulnerable people. In general, the trend since the 1990s has been for the federal government to limit itself primarily to financing roles and for state and local governments to take on more administrative and operational roles. But that trend may reflect fiscal pressure more than a sound public policy rationale about how to best protect and serve the poor and vulnerable. Raising taxes to expand social programs (or any programs) is unpopular; few federal politicians are willing to raise taxes for state and local politicians to spend. The same dynamic holds true for state and local politicians. As a result, governments currently focus on regulating the programs they subsidize and attaching requirements to the financing they provide to control or limit the actions of administering entities and individuals in need of assistance. Examples include work requirements for TANF recipients and financial matching or maintenance-of-effort requirements as well as work participation rates for states.

The vast majority of administrative and structural choices are, in fact, made pragmatically. Each social safety net program lends itself to a level of governance that best suits its design and purpose; each level of government is able to address the efficiency and responsiveness concerns of programs in different ways. Each community may have some unique needs and social problems that suggest one type of administrative arrangement rather than another. One might make a reasonable case for having a national income guarantee or national health insurance or even nationally administered public education, on the grounds that the Constitution places responsibility for the general public welfare with the national government. In other instances, local control of programs may make more sense when services must be provided quickly in crisis situations and compassionately to those who are particularly vulnerable.

An ongoing trade-off, though, continues between allowing maximum local control and ensuring accountability for federal funds. And this trade-off exists with the historical backdrop of individual and community freedom and independence. The rights of states to control public education are not likely to give way to national objectives to guarantee equal educational opportunity to all children regardless of wealth or the tax base in the communities in which they live.

The policy decision to devolve TANF to the states but not the EITC or SSI suggests a willingness on the part of the federal government to downplay its role in ensuring a social safety net for poor families with children and a working-age adult—a constituency with little political influence. In regard to Medicaid, though, the situation is more ambiguous. Whether the nation wishes to have a health insurance system for all or a health safety net for the poor is an unanswered question, in addition to the question whether the national government should play the lead role in either case. These issues arise especially in a politically risky environment with spiraling health care costs and a powerful health care industry on one side, a general public desire to expand health care coverage to all children, and clear consequences in terms of bad health, delayed care, and more costly ultimate care among uninsured people. There are periodic proposals to turn Medicaid responsibility entirely over to the states (e.g., in the form of block grants), which would then give states the unpopular task of dealing with service utilization and payments to hospitals, doctors, and other medical providers. At the same time, Congress continues to try to expand eligibility to children of families with higher income levels and increase the funds available. As of now, the direction Medicaid will take is still unclear.

The trade-offs and ambiguous political consensus around providing a social safety net have resulted in a patchwork of programs, some of which reflect centralized authority and some decentralized authority— as well as some that shift back and forth between centralization and devolution. It might be intellectually desirable to have a simple, straightforward social safety net, but the reality in the United States is that such a singular system for the entire social safety net might not be feasible, at least not in the immediate future. Meanwhile, policymakers and the general public need to understand which programs seem to be accomplishing their intended purposes. Evaluation and accountability for results are a critical issue and are the subject of the next chapter.

7

Policy Analysis, Evaluation, and Performance Monitoring

In discussing the various issues and programs involved in social safety nets, every preceding chapter has highlighted the types of questions that arise with respect to safety net policy and has included findings from policy research, evaluations, and program monitoring activities that provide answers to those questions. Our focus up to now has been substantive, not dwelling on how the data were collected but considering what they have to tell us.

We now reverse directions and look at the approaches one might use to collect or analyze information relevant to particular types of concerns, be they those of legislators, administrators, advocates, office or program managers, or the general public. We focus on the nature of the questions asked, which are remarkably similar, whether the policy goal is reducing poverty, ending hunger, increasing employment, or improving health. We are interested in how to answer such questions as

- Should I vote for this policy change?
- What happened as a result of that legislation?
- Who needs what types of help?
- What works?
- What will it cost?
- Does the assistance get where it needs to go and does it get there efficiently and effectively?

- Why are eligible people not applying for benefits?
- How can I improve the performance of Office A so it matches or exceeds that of Office B?

We refer to examples in previous chapters but do not duplicate material found there. To balance the emphasis on TANF and the work issues covered in chapters 4 and 5, this chapter selects its examples from Medicaid and SCHIP, child care and child support enforcement, and more general policy questions such as "What program changes could cut poverty in half?" or "What will retirees look like and what will they need in the 21st century?" It also describes the role of research evidence in effecting a significant change in direction for policies to end homelessness.

This chapter discusses many approaches used to answer policy and performance questions, but it is no substitute for a textbook on evaluation methods. Rather, it tries to organize the types of questions that policymakers frequently have about safety net programs and summarize the different ways that policy analysts, evaluation researchers, and program managers have tried to answer them.[1] Thus, in this chapter, the reader will find examples of policy research using many different methodologies but will not find details of methodological procedures or comparisons of methodological strengths and weaknesses.

Questions That Legislators Might Ask

Elected officials in Congress, state legislatures, governors' and mayors' offices, people on city and county councils, and members of boards and commissions at every level of government routinely face choices about what to do to achieve certain goals. Making choices never stops. Circumstances change and affect success at reaching a goal, goals change, expectations for what government should be doing change, and people in policymaking positions change and with them the alliances and power balances that were responsible for past decisions. Such changes often stimulate reexamination of important policies.

When faced with the need to make a new policy or change an old one, people in legislative positions do many things—they look to their constituencies and register what they want, they consult their colleagues and examine what might stand a chance of passage, and sometimes they gather information about what might happen if they opt for various alternative policies. When they are in an information-gathering mode, they may ask such questions as, Should I vote for or adopt this policy? How many people need this change? Who would be affected? Who would become eligible, and who would lose eligibility? What would happen if the policy were in place?

Policy analysts have responded to such questions in a variety of ways, including analyzing national databases and using computer simulations. If the questions are of sufficient importance and the potential impact of sufficient magnitude, policymakers may waive program rules, allowing communities to "try out" policy options and see what happens. Welfare reform was preceded by at least five years of waivers of AFDC requirements to allow states to try different things; waivers have been used within the Medicaid program to try a variety of practices from home- and community-based care to managed care to innovative practices that states may propose. Alternatively, policymakers may authorize experiments to see "what would happen if." Some approaches explored under waivers may also be experiments, such as the Minnesota Family Investment Program described in chapter 5.

Analyses Using Large National Databases

Many federal government agencies support routine data collection through national surveys that provide a great deal of information relevant to safety net policies. Some of these surveys are cross-sectional, meaning that they are conducted over and over again but with a new sample of respondents each time. Some have "revolving" samples, meaning that respondents are interviewed several times to provide longitudinal data for each household, but a certain proportion of the sample is replaced with new households for each survey wave so eventually none of the "original" households remain. Finally, some national surveys follow the same households and their children's households over many years to see how they develop and change and how they respond to changing conditions.

National survey databases most commonly used to address the issues we have been examining in this book tend to be of the second or third type, yielding some ability to track the same people over time. These include the following six:

- *The Current Population Survey* (CPS): The Census Bureau has conducted the CPS monthly for more than 50 years for the Department of Labor's Bureau of Labor Statistics. Each household is interviewed monthly for four months, then not interviewed for eight months, and then interviewed monthly again for another four months before being replaced by another household. BLS's primary purpose in funding the CPS is to collect data for monthly employment and unemployment statistics, but the CPS provides a good deal more information. In addition to the basic monthly survey, certain months have special supplements. The March CPS gathers income and poverty-related information for the preceding calendar year, making it a very valuable annual tool for assessing changes due to economic conditions or shifting policies.

  Sometimes purposes served by a separate national survey may be subsumed into the CPS. This occurred, for example, with the National Food Consumption Survey (NFCS) that the Department of Agriculture's Food and Nutrition Service, which runs the Food Stamp Program, sponsored only twice, in 1977–78 and 1987–88. At about the time another wave of the NFCS would have been expected, public concern was growing about households that routinely did not have enough food to eat because of inadequate income (known as "food insecurity"). It was recognized that the NFCS did not do a good job of measuring food insecurity and that researchers had recently developed a variety of ways to measure it. After due deliberation and consultations with experts, the Food and Nutrition Service opted to "buy into" the CPS, funding a special annual supplement on food insecurity and dropping the NFCS.

- *The Survey of Income and Program Participation (SIPP):* SIPP data collection began in 1984. For SIPP, the Census Bureau interviews between 14,000 and 36,000 households a month in four-month waves, for periods covering a total of 2.5 to 4 years, depending on the panel. SIPP's main objective is to provide accurate and comprehensive information about the income and program participation of individuals and households in the United States and about their principal determinants. SIPP offers detailed month-by-month information on cash and noncash income. The survey also collects data on taxes, assets, liabilities, and participation in government transfer programs. It includes topical modules that are usually assigned to a particular month and done once a year. These modules cover personal history, child care, wealth, program eligibility, child support, utilization and cost of health care, disability, school enrollment, taxes, and annual income. The core SIPP data provide a broad context for understanding the specific issues covered by each module. By collecting information relevant to many government programs in one comprehensive survey, SIPP allows government and other policy analysts to evaluate the effectiveness of federal, state, and local programs.

- *The American Community Survey (ACS):* The ACS is the Census Bureau's answer to problems with decennial census data. Census data for many uses often do not become available for two years after a decade begins and toward the end of every decade are significantly out of date. The ACS is done more frequently, being sent to a small percentage of the U.S. population on a rotating basis. The ACS began in a small sample of communities in 1995, from which it has expanded every year. In 2008, data became available for all areas of 20,000 or more. Over time, data will be accurate for even smaller areas; beginning in 2010 and for every year thereafter, the nation will have a five-year period estimate available that shows change over time even for neighborhoods and rural areas. The ACS lets communities see how they are changing in the years between each decennial census. The ACS covers all the questions on the census long form, including demographic, educational, and employment characteristics of each household member and information about the housing they currently occupy. Data from the ACS help determine how more than $300 billion in federal funds are distributed annually and inform decisions on policies, programs, and services for communities.

- *The National Health and Nutrition Examination Survey (NHANES):* NHANES, which began in the late 1950s, is the largest and longest-running national source of objectively measured health and nutrition data. Through physical examinations, clinical and laboratory tests, and personal interviews, NHANES provides snapshots of the health and nutritional status of the U.S. population that can be compared from year to year. This survey is the responsibility of the National Center for Health Statistics, part of the Department of Health and Human Services. Findings from NHANES provide health professionals and policymakers with the statistical data needed to determine rates of major diseases and health conditions (e.g., cardiovascular disease, diabetes, obesity, infectious diseases). They also identify and monitor trends in medical conditions, risk factors, and emerging public health issues so that appropriate public health policies and prevention interventions can be developed. Four rounds of NHANES were carried out over four-year periods with about a year in between. In 1999, NHANES became a continuous survey, collecting data every year.

- *The National Survey of Family Growth (NSFG):* The NSFG, conducted by the National Center for Health Statistics, gathers information on family life, marriage and divorce, pregnancy, infertility, use of contraception, and men's and women's health. The survey results are used by DHHS and others to plan health services and health education programs and to do statistical studies of families, fertility, and health. The first five cycles of the NSFG were conducted between 1973 and 1995 with only women as respondents. Cycle 6, which began in 2002, included men for the first time, acknowledging that men as well as women were involved in family growth and dynamics and that their perspectives should also be assessed. To make this happen, major portions of the National Survey of Adolescent Males were incorporated into the NSFG, and the former survey was no longer conducted, in the same way that some aspects of the National Food Consumption Survey were turned into a topic module for the Current Population Survey and the NFCS ended. Cycle 7 of the NSFG, which began in 2006, changes it to a continuous survey that, by 2011, will provide annual national samples of data on these important family growth topics.

- The *Panel Study of Income Dynamics (PSID) and National Longitudinal Survey of Youth (NLSY):* These are multiyear panel studies whose first cohorts were interviewed decades ago. Tens of thousands of studies have used data from these two surveys over the years to answer myriad policy questions related to safety net issues.

  ○ The PSID began in 1968 with about 4,800 families to gather information about economic, educational, health, and social behavior over whole lifetimes. In 1997, a Child Development Supplement was added to learn about the children and caregivers in PSID families. This ongoing supplement adds information about children's education, health, cognitive and behavioral development, and time use to the core PSID data. The PSID now includes close to 8,000 families and more than 65,000 individuals, expanding through a process of following not only the original families but also their children as they grow up and form families of their own. For original sample members, up to 40 years of their lives had been documented as of 2008. The Survey Research Center of the University of Michigan's Institute for Social Research conducts the PSID, which has numerous public and private funding sources.

○ As useful as the PSID is, it nevertheless depicts only one cohort of people—those in low-income households whose household heads were under 60 in 1968. Their experiences reflect the conditions of their particular time and place. One could think of the PSID as covering two cohorts if one thought about the children of these families as a second cohort, but the second generation came of age over a period of years and is not usually considered a cohort in a research sense. The NLSY began in 1979 as a single cohort of 14- to 22-year-olds that is still being followed. But, cognizant of the need to have similar data reflecting the contextual reality of young people in the 1990s and beyond, the Bureau of Labor Statistics funded a second NLSY cohort in 1997. A connected Child Sample is sponsored by the National Institute of Child Health and Human Development. Each cohort of the NLSY addresses key questions about the economic, social, and academic experiences of respondents and examines the complex issues surrounding youth entry into the workforce and subsequent transitions in and out of it. The 1979 cohort completed its 22nd round of data collection in 2007; the 23rd round began in 2008. The 1997 cohort is currently in its 11th year. The cohorts both involve large samples with oversamples of African American and Hispanic youth to ensure sufficient sample sizes to examine the experiences of these populations.

Other ongoing national surveys frequently used to answer the types of policy questions raised in this book include the National Health Interview Study, the Medical Expenditure Panel Survey, the Early Childhood Longitudinal Study, the National Educational Longitudinal Survey, and the American Housing Survey, to name a few. And of course, the decennial census itself has long been the ultimate source of population and housing data that provides information accurate down to the block level.

Example 1: What Supports Help Families Leaving TANF to Remain off Welfare?

Many researchers have used the large national databases just described, as well as others, to examine the consequences of myriad provisions of the Personal Responsibility and Work Opportunity Reconciliation Act of 1996 and other legislation involved in welfare reform. For example, researchers have synthesized research conducted since the beginning of welfare reform in 1996 to assess the well-being of families who leave and remain off welfare and have supplemented their conclusions with tabulations from the CPS, SIPP, and the National Survey of America's Families (Acs and Loprest 2007a).[2] They have also used two waves of SIPP to study whether Medicaid, food stamps, and other publicly funded benefits serve as supports for work, leading to increasingly stable employment and reducing the odds that families will have to go back on welfare (Acs and Loprest 2007b). They find that leavers who use food stamps as a transitional benefit (i.e., they receive food stamps in the month they exit TANF but subsequently leave the rolls) are less likely to reenter TANF than leavers who did not receive food stamps at the time they exited TANF. From a policy perspective, these results suggest that the use of some public benefits, in particular food stamps, can serve as supports for work, helping families to make more durable transitions off TANF and maintain steady employment. It was also true that many who stopped receiving food stamps went back to them much more frequently than they went back to TANF, indicating that TANF leavers are using food stamps as a "cushion" when times are tough, to tide them over and help them avoid returning to welfare.

Example 2: How Many People Are Eligible for Medicaid and SCHIP and How Many Will Actually Enroll?

Researchers analyzed CPS data to estimate the number of adults and children eligible for Medicaid and SCHIP, the proportion who could be expected to actually enroll, and the characteristics differentiating those who did and did not enroll (Giannarelli et al. 2005). They also estimated the number of people who remained without any type of health insurance for an entire year. They found that about two-thirds of eligible people actually enrolled and that enrollment rates differed by age and disability status. Participation was highest for children (73 percent) and disabled individuals (74 percent), lower for eligible adults (60 percent), and lowest for eligible elderly people (40 percent). These results give policymakers a sense of the gap to be overcome if all low-income Americans were to enroll and receive the supports for which they are eligible—and which much research has shown will lead to improved health outcomes.

Analyses Using Microsimulations

Simulations use computer technology and existing population databases, such as those described above, to make estimates of what would happen under different scenarios. Simulations are common in many fields, including engineering, architecture, and various branches of science. Social science and policy analysis are no exception. One such simulation program is the Urban Institute's Transfer Income Model, usually referred to as TRIM. TRIM is a comprehensive microsimulation model widely used by government and academic analysts for simulating the effects of different policy, economic, and demographic scenarios on households and individuals. Models such as TRIM are called "micro" simulations because they look at individuals and households rather than larger entities such as counties, states, or nations. Over the years, TRIM has gone through constant development; the version now in use is TRIM3. Most TRIM simulations use data from the Current Population Survey, but any database can be used, and many have been, as long as their variables can be made to conform to TRIM specifications. We saw the results of one analysis using TRIM in chapter 4, in a study that estimated the effects of PRWORA restrictions on participation by legal immigrants in the Food Stamp Program. Two other brief examples are given below.

Example 3: How Much Could Different Policies Reduce Poverty?

The Center for American Progress (2007) recently used TRIM estimates to report the effects of different policy options on reducing poverty. Options examined using TRIM, separately and together, included increasing the minimum wage, expanding the earned income tax credit and the child tax credit so they affect more poor working households, and increasing child care assistance so more parents could work. Each option had a significant effect in reducing poverty; taken together, these four options would move one in four poor people out of poverty. For a policymaker interested in reducing poverty in the United States to the level of many other industrialized nations, these simulations offer guidance on the most effective measures to reach that goal.

Example 4: How Much Could Different Policies Increase Child Support Payments?

A different example shows how TRIM has also been used in a different area of policy concern—to estimate the potential effects of certain changes in laws governing child support. Wheaton and Sorenson (2007) test what would happen under certain conditions: (1) if custodial parents received a higher proportion of child support collected by enforcement agencies (i.e., if the "pass-through" were greater); (2) if states did not reduce the value of other benefits in relation to the additional funds received (i.e., if the additional funds were "disregarded"); and (3) if collections from noncustodial parents increased because they knew the custodial parent would get more of the money. Analyses showed that if all states adopted the proposed pass-through and disregard policies, the average amount of child support distributed to TANF families would more than double, from approximately $337 to $806 per family per year. Sixty-five percent of child support collected on behalf of TANF families would be distributed to the families, up from 27 percent before the expansion. In addition, the behavioral response to the more generous pass-through and disregard could increase the number of TANF families with a child support collection by 9 percent, which would add to the benefits of the policy change to families and decrease costs to government.

Example 5: What Will Retirees Look Like in the Future, and What Are the Implications for Social Security?

TRIM is a static microsimulation model, meaning that it looks at a population at one point in time and changes program rules to see what will happen. Another widely used type of simulation—dynamic microsimulation—actually ages a population over a number of years. In dynamic microsimulation, people get born, go to school, graduate or not, get married (if the computer can find them a suitable mate), get and lose jobs, change addresses, retire, die, and so on, all in accord with known probabilities or the probabilities that correspond to the population changes or policy options being tested. These simulations look at what is likely to happen with a population over time so that policy-makers can judge the implications for needed benefits and services. DYNASIM (Dynamic Simulation of Income Model), also developed at the Urban Institute, is one such model. In one recent use (Smith and Toder 2005), DYNASIM projected the population and analyzed the long-run consequences of changes in retirement and aging patterns. Results indicated that the retired portion of the population would increase in the next two decades and that its demographic composition would change. Newly eligible retirees would be increasingly better educated, but that trend would level off after 2012. Larger shares would be divorced or never-married and smaller shares married or widowed. The share of whites would decline, while shares of other groups, especially Hispanics, would increase. These changing demographics of the retiring population will affect Social Security financing and retirement policies. In particular, while economic growth will reduce poverty, there will be more retirees in groups that historically have been at higher risk of poverty and who may need more, or perhaps different, supports from Social Security.

Results of Activities Implemented under Waivers

All the major safety net programs in the United States operate under complex rules and regulations that limit what states and localities can do, for whom, when, where, and for how long. A few rules and regulations in each safety net program are very important in defining the program's basic characteristics. Waivers are one way Congress allows federal agencies to provide options for states to modify one or more major rules to see what will happen. They are the equivalent to doing a pilot study of changed program rules before deciding whether the change should be made universal and permanent.

From 1992 through 1996, DHHS used waivers of major AFDC provisions to learn what would happen under various options being considered for comprehensive welfare reform (described in chapters 1 and 3). During this time, 37 states implemented at least one major waiver of AFDC rules in the areas of terminations and time limits, work exemptions, sanctions for noncompliance with work requirements, earnings disregards (how much a family could earn and still remain on welfare), and family caps (no additional cash assistance for children added to the household after eligibility determination). The Minnesota Family Independence Project, described in chapter 5, was one of these, and others have been mentioned throughout previous chapters. Because we have already looked in considerable detail at AFDC waivers, we do not present additional examples here. Instead, we use this chapter to describe some waivers involving Medicaid.

The Centers for Medicare and Medicaid Services (CMS) within DHHS presides over several types of waivers. One type (Section 1115) covers research and demonstration projects and can be used to test substantially new ideas and evaluate policies and approaches that have not been demonstrated on a widespread basis. The most common basic provisions waived are those requiring statewide coverage (to allow states to test a policy in just a few cities or counties) and those that commit federal matching funds for services that Medicaid otherwise would not cover. Evaluations of their impact on outcomes of interest to CMS are expected to be part of the demonstration's activities.

A second type of Medicaid waiver is Section 1915(b), Managed Care/ Freedom of Choice, which allows states to try different approaches to mandatory managed care rather than fee-for-service health care. A third type is Section 1915(c), Home and Community Based Services, which allows flexibility in types and duration of services and the point of service delivery (in the community rather than in institutionalized settings). The bottom-line requirement for these waivers from a federal perspective is that they be cost neutral to the federal government.

States have used these waivers to expand medical coverage for specific people who might not otherwise be covered on the basis of income or where they live (at home rather than in a nursing home) and to expand care to include nonmedical services, such as respite, case management, and physical accommodations (e.g., ramps, handrails) that make it possible for people to remain at home. Many have also used waivers to improve care and treatment for people with behavioral health problems (mental illnesses and substance abuse disorders), sometimes trying to integrate behavioral health and primary health care but more commonly "carving out" behavioral health care for separate service delivery options.

State activities under Section 1915 waivers have not been as systematically or carefully evaluated as waivers under Section 1115, as mostly they need to prove only that the changes are cost neutral to federal Medicaid. These waivers have become mechanisms that allow states to offer more services to more people under Medicaid than official rules would allow— states are using them, in effect, to move toward health care reform "under the radar screen."

Example 6: Evaluations of Medicaid 1915 Waivers

Evaluations of 1915 waivers have taken two forms. While some assess cost neutrality, many more examine implementation issues and address the question of what the new state approaches may contribute toward overall health care reform. An example of the first type of study occurred in Florida, where researchers analyzed the effects of five Medicaid waivers for home and community-based care for frail elderly people on inpatient hospital days, outpatient days, nursing home days, deaths, and total Medicaid claims. They found that different levels of client impairment and different service mixes affected use of care and therefore expenditures, with one of the five programs costing significantly more than the others. The probability of death was not affected (Mitchell et al. 2003). Examples of implementation evaluations are given later in this chapter.

Experiments and Quasi-Experiments

A true textbook experiment involves randomly assigned treatment groups and control groups. As discussed in chapter 5, the Minnesota Family Independence Program was a true experiment implemented under an AFDC waiver. The experiment randomly assigned people to different "treatment" or "control" groups. Results were sufficiently promising that Minnesota used the MFIP model that combined financial incentives with mandatory work requirements, albeit with significant modifications, as the basis for its statewide TANF program. The Milwaukee New Hope Project, also described in chapter 5, was another true experiment that assessed the effects of providing wage supplements, community service jobs, counseling, and support services to improve low-income workers' ability to move out of poverty.

Quasi-experiments are more common than true experiments because true experiments are hard to do. No social experiment carried out over several years in communities of different structures and interaction patterns is ever "under control" in the same way as experiments conducted with laboratory rats or clinical drug trials. Quasi-experiments use naturally occurring variations or compare jurisdictions with and without innovations to assess the effects of different practices. For instance, Wisconsin and Washington tested different approaches to helping welfare families move into employment by comparing the experiences in "treatment" counties— those that used the new approaches—to experiences in "comparison" counties—those still using the old approaches or those without any relevant programs (Long, Nightingale, and Wissoker 1994; Pawasarat and Quinn 1993). Very sophisticated statistical and econometric analysis is typically used in quasi-experimental evaluations to adjust for the lack of random assignment (e.g., control for what is referred to as statistical selection bias).

Statistical Approaches to Compensate for Not Using Random Assignment

Random assignment is the "gold standard" of research designs because it offers the best hope that results are not influenced by preexisting differences in who gets an intervention (the treatment) and who does not. In most settings of interest to social policy, however, random assignment designs are not likely to be possible, usually for logistical reasons, such as not being able to assign individuals randomly to different groups or not having ideal data. Therefore, researchers have developed various nonexperimental ways of selecting a set of people or communities as comparison groups not receiving the intervention and have sought to "equalize" the intervention and nonintervention groups through statistical means.

Several approaches have been developed to do this, among which difference-in-difference, instrumental variable, regression discontinuity, propensity score matching, and variations and combinations of these and other techniques are quite common. Each has generated an extensive literature assessing its advantages and disadvantages and the conditions under which it is most and least likely to produce unbiased results (compared with the results that would have been achieved by random assignment). The details are too complex for this chapter, but readers interested in them might want to start with the four issues of the *Journal of Policy Analysis and Management* from volume 27(2) (Spring 2008) through volume 28(1) (Winter 2009), which contain numerous short articles debating the case for and against alternatives to random assignment. Here we note the general conclusions, which are that most of these alternative techniques work best when the treatment and comparison groups start out very similar in demographics and geography (coming from the same place) even before matching or other statistical equalization techniques are applied; that variables are measured with the same instrumentation (which should be precise and stable); and that baseline measures of outcome variables are obtained (Pirog et al. 2008).

Analyses Using Variations in Program Rules and Other Policies

Given the great variations in how safety net programs are run in different jurisdictions, keeping track of who is doing what, where, is not easy. Without this knowledge, though, it is practically impossible to assess the effects of different program rules and practices on outcomes for clients and beneficiaries. And without knowing these effects, it is impossible to make policy decisions that select the right set of rules to achieve the outcomes intended by the programs' creators. For example, one might want to know whether TANF programs with a higher income disregard have a greater long-term effect on reducing poverty than TANF programs with little or no income disregard, or whether the length or severity of TANF sanctions affects a family's long-term prospects for leaving poverty. If these policies have significant effects, policymakers might want to set their state's rules to align with policies that have the greatest likelihood of moving families out of poverty.

It is extremely valuable, therefore, for policy analysts to have a source that keeps track of safety net program rules. For TANF, DHHS supports the ongoing maintenance of such a tool in the Welfare Rules Database, which policy analysts may access through an annual *Welfare Rules Databook* (http://www.urban.org/url.cfm?ID=411685) or directly if they wish to manipulate the information themselves (http://anfdata.urban.org/wrd).[3] The Welfare Rules Database provides information about TANF rules and rule changes since 1996, including eligibility requirements, financial incentives to work, sanctions, time limits, treatment of various types of non-TANF income, and so on. Example 7 demonstrates how this information may contribute to sophisticated analyses of the effects of individual policies and policies considered as a group on family poverty in the short and long term.

Example 7: How TANF Rules and Other Policies Affect Family Poverty

McKernan and Ratcliffe (2006) wanted to improve on analyses that tried to discern effects of welfare reform on poverty, which usually have shown either mixed or no effects. Noting that most research was not able to isolate the effects of specific welfare policies and that some might be expected to increase poverty (e.g., the family cap) while others might be expected to decrease it (e.g., higher income disregards), they undertook analyses to distinguish the effects of specific policies and practices as they varied from state to state and over time. They used monthly SIPP data from 1988 through 2002 and monthly state-level policy data for the same period to span the pre-TANF years of AFDC waivers and the first six post-TANF years. They tested the effects of 19 specific policies on poverty at the time a family was first measured and at 12 and 24 months thereafter. Fourteen policies pertained to TANF—eligibility requirements (family cap, vehicle asset exemption, earned income disregard), benefit levels and earned income disregard during month 12, sanctions (amount and duration), treatment of child support income, and time limits. Five other policies included in the analysis pertained to the applicable minimum wage and federal and state EITC income and refundability.

Overall, these researchers found evidence that more lenient eligibility requirements for welfare receipt (e.g., no family cap, higher earned income disregard, no explicit net income test) and more generous financial incentives to work (higher state minimum wage, more generous treatment of child support income, higher state EITC) generally reduced deep poverty. The six time-limit policies examined did not have consistent effects; the researchers suggest that some stricter time-limit policies may result in less poverty.

Questions that Program Administrators Might Ask

Many times, policies are set in place and people in charge of making them work need information about how things are going, what might make programs and services better, and what differentiates places where the changes are going well from places where change efforts have bogged down. Of course, administrators and staff want to know about the impacts of policy changes on clients; for such questions, they seek answers using research techniques very similar to those described above, including analysis of large national databases and special surveys.

Many times, however, program administrators need to know what is happening with policy implementation long before they will start learning anything about program impacts. Spending money on impact evaluations is pointless unless we know that a program exists and is working mostly as expected and intended. Even when a program is fully operational, program administrators will be interested in differences in program performance across counties, offices, and even staff, as a way to pinpoint how to make the program better—that is, more responsive to client needs, more able to help clients achieve good outcomes. Program administrators, then, need answers to a range of questions: Does the program *as practiced* look like we thought it would? Are we getting the clients we expected? Are we able to get clients the services they need? Is it working better in some places than in others? Is it working better for some clients than others? How could we fine-tune it?

Some of the most common research techniques used to answer these questions are implementation and process analysis, special surveys, and analysis of caseloads and client characteristics.

Implementation and Process Analysis

The many examples presented in chapter 5 that describe service delivery and service integration mechanisms drew heavily on research using implementation and process analyses to learn how different aspects of welfare reform were progressing. Implementation and process analysis use many of the same data-gathering techniques (key informant interviews, case record analysis, observation, client interviews) but have different purposes (Werner 2004).

Implementation analysis focuses on the start-up period for a new program or a new way of doing things within an existing program. Its primary questions are, is the program up and running? and does it resemble what we thought it would look like? Implementation analysis is particularly important because it tells whether the program was actually put in place more or less as envisioned. If some communities never managed to get the program up and running, or never included many of the partners needed to make it function adequately, there is no point in taking the next evaluation step to ask whether the program is having the expected effects on clients. How could it, when it is not really there?

For the ultimate evaluation purpose of determining program impact, learning from implementation analysis about variations in program structure and design that may make a difference for client outcomes is also important. For instance, if the program is expected to operate as a partnership of welfare, workforce or job training, education, and substance abuse treatment agencies but if many communities were able to integrate only two or three of these potential partners, implementation analysis will reveal the program's gaps and provide the information to incorporate into predictive analyses later in the evaluation.

Process analysis focuses on the ways that programs work once they have reached a steady state of mature functioning. Its key questions are, how are people getting into the program, how are services being delivered, how are people exiting the program, and are these exits appropriate? Process analyses can show whether the intake process is working well or, if not, where it is breaking down and why (e.g., why the program has been able to enroll only a small fraction of the clients it was set up to serve). It can indicate whether certain offices or certain caseworkers are routinely more successful at getting their clients specific services promptly or having clients who go on to succeed. It can show the proportion of clients who leave the program in various ways—for instance, dropping out very soon after enrollment, being sanctioned off, cases being closed for administrative reasons, leaving after completing some program offerings but not others, or leaving "successfully" however the program defines that—and help administrators discover ways to reduce inappropriate exits or reverse exits caused by inappropriate program actions.

Here we look at a couple of examples from programs addressing two issues that have not received a lot of attention earlier in the book—job training and child care.

Example 8: The High Growth Job Training Initiative

The president's High Growth Job Training Initiative (HGJTI) is a major national effort begun in 2002 to encourage the development of market-driven strategies to address critical workforce challenges as defined by business and industry. A first report in a larger study of HGJTI documents the lessons, experiences, and sustainability of 20 of the earliest HGJTI grantees as told by the project administrators (Trutko et al. 2007). Major implementation lessons emerging from the early grantees include the importance of establishing and maintaining partnerships, especially with employers; excellent, frequent, and clear communication with partners; having the right staff, with skills specific to the targeted industries; providing supportive services, such as child care, transportation, and referral for family services for the often disadvantaged trainees to help them sustain employment; and beginning early the process of ensuring that project activities will have the support to continue beyond the HGJTI grant period. Projects that did more of these things, or did them better, were more successful at establishing successful strategies for helping disadvantaged workers move into jobs in high-growth businesses and industries.

Example 9: Shaping Child Care Systems to Meet Family Needs

Child care subsidies help low-income families afford child care for their children as they seek to become or remain employed. Having a subsidy is associated with higher rates of employment and better employment outcomes. Adequate funding is always an issue that excludes some families, but research has documented that even when funds are available, some eligible families that want subsidies do not receive them, families that do receive them often stay on subsidies for relatively short periods, and some families that do not stay in the program appear to remain eligible even after they leave. Process analyses suggest that the subsidy policies and practices of state and local child care agencies can contribute to whether some eligible families receive subsidies in the first place, as well as whether eligible families that receive subsidies are able to retain them over time. These policies and practices pertain to what families must do to apply for subsidies, how to recertify eligibility, and how to report changes in circumstances that may alter eligibility, as well as how often families must take these steps, how easy or difficult their interactions are with the subsidy agency, and how agencies define eligibility when families experience changes in their circumstances.

Process analyses documenting the importance of these issues have led states and localities to focus more on identifying ways to improve their services and design their programs to make it easier for eligible families to get and keep subsidies. In addition to making processes easier for parents, several strategies appear to help administrators meet other critical program goals, such as reducing staff workload, keeping program costs down, and reducing improper payments. Some strategies that better support parents—for example, decreasing paperwork, simplifying interactions with parents, reducing inadvertent terminations or needless churning of clients—can also minimize unnecessary procedures that raise administrative costs (results of numerous studies, summarized in Adams, Snyder, and Banghart 2008).

Special Surveys

When no information is available on what managers most need to know about their programs, a new survey may be the only option. Many special-purpose surveys are conducted in the United States every year to gather important information that answers program managers' questions and helps with decisions about program continuation or improvement.

Example 10: Impact of Health Care Reform in Massachusetts

To assess the impact of health care reform legislation in Massachusetts designed to ensure universal health care coverage within a few years of enactment, the state commissioned a special survey to assess annual progress (Long, Cook, and Stockley 2008). Results showed that the legislation was definitely having an impact—lack of insurance among working-age adults dropped by almost half within one year, from 13 to 7 percent, access to care improved, and the number of people who had trouble paying medical bills dropped. Results helped ensure that the reforms remain in place. By the end of the second year after the legislation passed, only 2.6 percent of the state's population remained uninsured, and the strategy continued to enjoy wide popular support.

Example 11: What Happened when Michigan Cut Back Its General Assistance Program

Great reductions in welfare rolls after public policy change sometimes stimulate special surveys to try to locate people who lost benefits and see how they are faring. Such studies are especially important when the populations of concern are too small to be assessed reliably using the large national databases described earlier in this chapter. Early in the 1990s, Michigan made major changes to its General Assistance (GA) program that revoked eligibility for large numbers of recipients, at least partially based on the rationale that many could work and that the state budget was in crisis. Danziger and Kossoudji (1994–95) drew a sample of terminated clients and interviewed them to discover what had happened to them after losing benefits. They found that only 25 percent of former recipients were able to find enough work to offset the loss of benefits. Most former GA recipients could not find steady jobs because of poor health, disability, age, mental condition, and lack of education. Two-thirds were still on food stamps. Only 10 percent were fully self-sufficient. Results were widely disseminated and showed that eliminating GA gave the state short-term budget gains at the expense of the well-being of a huge group of people who had already been doing everything they could to help themselves.

Example 12: Surveys of State Agencies

State safety net agencies routinely report certain aspects of their activity to their federal counterparts, but many other aspects of their work would remain mysteries in the absence of special surveys conducted by trade associations or private policy researchers. We offer two examples from safety net domains that have not received much attention so far in this book—mental health and child welfare—and one from food stamps.

State mental health agencies. The National Association of State Mental Health Program Directors is the national trade association for state agencies responsible for running or contracting for programs to serve people with serious mental illness, including state hospitals and community-based mental health services. To aid members in their management tasks, the association has a research institute that maintains a State Mental Health Agency Profiles System and Revenue Expenditures Survey database. Every year, member agencies provide their own information to this database and can then access it to learn how other states are addressing particular issues. Users may select from among many organizational characteristics (e.g., which state mental health agencies also have responsibility for substance abuse programs, which have the same number of organizational layers as one's own) and what difference it makes if they do.[4] They can also look at state mental health agency financial sources and expenditure categories. State managers can use these comparisons to consider options that would enable their agency to do its job better and also to document to funders where it stands in relation to similar agencies in other states.

Food stamp modernization. Researchers may also conduct surveys of state agencies for a number of reasons. Sometimes a federal agency contracts for such research because it wants to know how state and local offices are implementing new regulations. For instance, a study funded by the federal Food Stamp Program in 2008 asked Food Stamp offices in every state what they were doing to modernize and simplify application processes to make food stamps more accessible to eligible households. Without such a survey, the federal program administrators have no way of knowing whether newly available flexibility is being used to benefit consumers. Results will give federal program administrators information to help less innovative Food Stamp offices implement the approaches that are working well elsewhere.

Child welfare financing. A final example is a survey of state child welfare agencies that began in 1998 (looking at 1996 data) as part of a larger effort to assess the impact of welfare reform. The survey, which collected data from all 50 states and the District of Columbia on child welfare spending, was able to show for the first time *all* the revenue sources that state child welfare agencies received and what they used them for. The survey's information proved of sufficient value to policymakers that it has been repeated bi-annually since 1996 (Scarcella et al. 2006). The studies are able to attribute year-to-year fluctuations in funding types, levels, and financing strategies to the availability and use of various funding sources for which states have flexibility in how they allocate dollars; how states use various funding sources; legal or political factors; and how the child welfare agency budget fits into the "big picture" of states' overall financing strategies.

Analysis of Caseloads and Information on Clients Served

Chapter 4 presented many examples of the most basic type of caseload analysis, answering the question, is the caseload increasing or decreasing over time? While this information is obviously important to have from a national perspective, program managers will certainly have many more questions for which more detailed analysis of caseload data and client records will be able to supply answers. Some very common managerial questions include the following: Are some of my offices or agencies doing very well while others are not? Why? Do we do better with some people than with others? Which ones? What can I do to increase the performance of the agencies or people that report to me? The same approach to these analyses can be done for outcomes of many different types. The following include common outcome types:

- Speed (days between submitting a food stamp application, being approved for benefits, and receiving benefits; response time for police, fire, or ambulance calls)
- Volume (applications processed per day or per worker, number of counseling hours per week)
- Proportion (proportion with full-time job at exit, proportion satisfied with treatment, proportion receiving child care of those eligible, proportion of SSI applications turned down initially but approved on appeal)

One would look at the outcome first for all clients and perhaps compare the outcome to statewide or national performance or to some performance standard or expectation set at the federal level. Thereafter, one could analyze the outcomes in several ways, depending on what may be affecting them. For instance,

- If program characteristics seem to be an issue, one could look at outcomes separately for clients participating in a long program versus those participating in a short program; intensive programming versus simple programming; those with and without access to supportive services if needed; experimental, special new approach versus business as usual, and so on.
- If client characteristics seem to be an issue, one could look at outcomes separately for males and females, those with and without a high school diploma, those with and without a history of incarceration, young adults (under age 25) versus older adults, those with and without prior work histories, and so on.
- If office characteristics seem to be an issue, one could look at outcomes separately for different offices and then for offices closer to or further from public transportation, offices with and without evening hours, offices with open and appealing waiting rooms versus those with locks and bars, offices with open communication patterns among workers versus those with very hierarchical relationships, and so on.
- If worker characteristics seem to be an issue, one could look at outcomes separately for workers with more and less experience, older and younger workers, workers who themselves experienced the same things that current clients experience versus workers who did not have these experiences, workers with and without particular degrees or training, and so on.

Caseload and client information is only the starting point for performance improvement. Ideally, such information is used to fuel an ongoing process of quality improvement, which is best undertaken in a spirit of offering clients the best possible service and not in an atmosphere of blame or finger-pointing. Armed with the data, managers and staff work together in regularly scheduled meetings to review the findings and discuss what might be responsible for observed differences in performance. Some differences may be acceptable, such as when differences arise because lower-performing offices serve clients with more barriers or difficulties than those served by higher-performing offices. But others may be less acceptable, such as when non-English speakers are consistently less well served than native English speakers. Once differences are identified that management needs to do something about, managers and staff work together to develop approaches to service delivery that bring poor performance up to the standard expected. Repeated measurement and further rounds of data analysis and discussion will reveal how well remedies are working and provide the opportunity for assessing whether something else needs to be tried or everyone can feel a sense of accomplishment in improving inadequate performance.

Cost Questions

There is never enough money to do everything that everyone wants to do. Households make daily trade-offs between what they want and what they can afford; governments do the same. Legislative bodies at every level have budget analysts who estimate the probable cost of public programs and balance them against probable income (taxes collected) for the short and long term. Every major new program proposed to a legislative body undergoes a cost analysis and may ultimately rise or fall on its affordability. We saw earlier in this chapter that states with Medicaid 1915 waivers are required to show that costs to the federal government under the waiver do not exceed projected federal costs under "no waiver" conditions. We use an example from the arena of homelessness to illustrate the way that well-targeted cost and savings analyses may provide the leverage to move otherwise uninterested governments at every level to adopt policies they would never have considered without the cost data.

Example 13: Paradigm Shift in Community Approaches to Homelessness

For about two decades starting in the early 1980s, most communities in the United States that chose to do anything about homelessness concentrated on providing emergency shelter—an ultimate safety net program. They tended to focus the assistance they offered on people who were most ready to help themselves but did little to end the homelessness of people with serious mental illness, addictions, and chronic physical conditions who were not acting to help themselves and were also the most visible local manifestation of homelessness because of their presence on city streets.

In 2002, advocates committed to changing this approach brought together the evidence of three pieces of research to present a convincing case to HUD for turning these practices on their head. Ultimately, they moved many communities to make a commitment to *end* homelessness rather than attempt to manage it. First, they assembled research documenting that an intervention called "permanent supportive housing" (PSH) works to attract and retain chronically homeless disabled people in housing (Shern et al. 1997; Tsemberis and Eisenberg 2000) and reduce street and chronic homelessness (HUD 2008). Second, they pointed to estimates based on the 1996 National Survey of Homeless Assistance Providers and Clients that the probable number of chronically homeless people was small enough to be a feasible policy target (at most, 200,000 to 250,000 people nationally). The clincher for public policy commitment came with the evidence that permanent supportive housing saves cities, counties, and states money.

In a privately funded study, Culhane, Metraux, and Hadley (2002) examined the NY/NY Initiative, a collaboration between New York State and New York City mental health agencies that placed homeless individuals with serious mental illness in a variety of permanent supportive housing arrangements and used supportive services to help them stay there. These tenants were long-term, multiply disabled homeless people who would never have been able to leave homelessness on their own— the very people that most approaches to homelessness ignored. They were also frequent users of city-funded emergency rooms, hospital inpatient beds, jails, ambulances, and shelters. The study examined three issues— changed *use* of public services, changed *costs* resulting from the changed use, and *savings* (whether PSH cost the same or less than pre-PSH use of public services). The results provided powerful evidence that supportive housing produces outcomes that policymakers want—reductions in inappropriate use of emergency public services and their associated costs and cost savings even after accounting for the costs of the supportive housing itself. The NY/NY analysis has galvanized many cities and the country as a whole to adopt the goal of ending chronic homelessness. Subsequent analyses conducted nationally (Rosenheck et al. 2003) and locally (see, for example, Burt 2008, chapter 7) have echoed its findings and kept local commitments high.

This approach has proved so successful that it is generating local spin-offs involving mainstream agencies. Local jails are one such agency type. As many have come to recognize that a significant portion of their population is homeless and also frequently incarcerated, they are taking innovative steps to address the issue as part of two national trends: ending homelessness and prisoner reentry activities designed to reduce recidivism. In Portland, Oregon, for example, the sheriff worked with the homeless system to identify the 15 most frequent users of jail time over a several-year period. All turned out to be homeless when they were not in jail. The homeless system moved these 15 people into permanent supportive housing, which ended their homelessness and also drastically reduced their likelihood of going to jail (half were never in jail the whole year after moving into housing). The sheriff is now an ardent supporter of Portland's push to end homelessness, which has reduced street homelessness by 70 percent in four years.

Questions You Might Ask

We might also apply the analytic approach described through much of this chapter to answer very personal questions, such as, If I need surgery, which hospital should I go to?

Consumers of services often need clear and accurate information at least as much as people who make policy decisions. Unfortunately, they are less likely to get the information they need or to understand the questions they should ask about the information that *is* available to them. We give one brief example of a situation in which a single piece of information is misleading and one needs to push for more clarification. Many similar examples exist in all aspects of daily decisionmaking.

Figure 7.1 makes the decision here look simple—Apollo Hospital is clearly better, one-third fewer people die there. But what else should a person ask before selecting a hospital? As we saw earlier in this chapter, it is always important to know about the challenges and barriers facing the clients of Program A compared to those that face Program B's clients. While Program A may look better on the surface, it may be dealing with clients whose problems are much easier to resolve than those of Program B's clients.

In a second view of the situation in figure 7.2, while Apollo Hospital's overall death rate is significantly lower than that of Mercy Hospital, a far higher proportion of Mercy's patients were in poor condition when they reached the hospital—that is, at the moment they walked in, before the

Figure 7.1. Which Hospital Would You Choose?

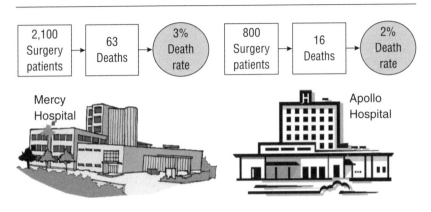

Figure 7.2. Which Hospital Would You Choose?

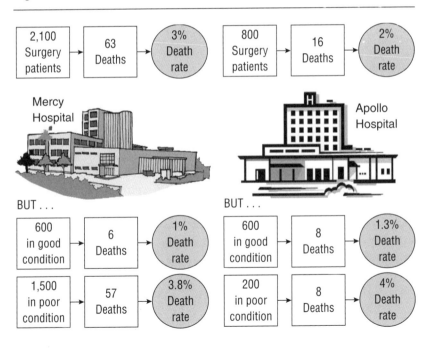

hospital did anything to or for them, they were more likely to die. It turns out that patients are *less* likely to leave Apollo Hospital alive compared to Mercy Hospital patients, whether they are in good condition or poor condition at entry. Mercy Hospital looked less competent initially simply because we did not know that compared to Apollo Hospital, it was treating a much higher proportion of really sick people. So whether a person is really sick or is reasonably healthy, he or she is better off at Mercy. And we should all learn to think critically when someone gives us a little information.

The Ultimate Social Safety Net Question

Since this book is about programs that are considered part of the social safety net in the United States, it is fair to end this chapter on policy analysis and evaluation by asking a very broad question about that safety net, which is, how good is it? One can answer this question only by comparing outcomes for people in need in the United States to similar outcomes in equivalent countries. Most such comparisons use data from other industrialized nations to examine how the United States stands on such basic safety net goals as the proportion of children or elderly living in poverty, the proportion of people without access to health care, the proportion of young children with working parents who receive quality child care, and the like. A variety of institutions gather such data, including the World Bank and United Nations agencies, such as the World Health Organization. In addition, some special studies, such as the Luxembourg Income Study, have collected poverty, income, inequality, employment, and similar measures for many of the more developed nations for many years. One can query these databases about specific countries, specific indicators, and specific years to learn how a given country compares on very basic indicators of well-being.

Here we look at just three indicators—the proportion of children in poverty, the proportion of elderly in poverty, and infant mortality (deaths within 12 months per 1,000 live births)—for 22 industrialized countries (Australia, Austria, Belgium, Canada, the Czech Republic, Denmark, Finland, France, Germany, Greece, Ireland, Israel, Italy, Luxembourg, the Netherlands, Norway, the Russian Federation, Spain, Sweden, Switzerland, the United Kingdom, and the United States); we include Mexico as an example of a medium-income country. We select these measures because they correspond roughly to safety net features meant to increase income, such as TANF, and features meant to affect health, such as Medicaid and SCHIP, which provide health care and thus affect health outcomes. (Unfortunately, there is no simple indicator of "adequate food" or "adequate nutrition" available to represent the Food Stamp Program.) Poverty information comes from the Luxembourg Income Study (LIS) and reflects the year 2000.[5] To provide a metric for "poverty" that has a common meaning across countries with very different economies, the LIS calculates relative measures, the proportion of a population or subpopulation living in a household whose income is 40 (or 50 or 60) percent or less of the national median household income. Here we show comparisons using 40 percent of national median income:

- *Child poverty:* The United States ranks 21st of the 23 countries examined, at 14.1 percent of children living in households at or below 40 percent of the median national income in 2000. Proportions ranged from 1.2 percent of all children in Denmark to 19.7 percent in Mexico. Only Russia at 16.6 percent and Mexico at 19.7 percent had higher proportions of poor children than the United States.
- *Elderly poverty:* The United States ranks 20th of the 23 countries examined, at 15.1 percent of the elderly living in households at or below 40 percent of the median national income in 2000. Proportions ranged from 0.8 percent of all elderly in Denmark to 21.9 percent in Mexico. Only Ireland at 15.2 percent, Greece at 17.0 percent, and Mexico at 21.9 percent had higher proportions of poor elderly than the United States.
- *Infant mortality:* The United States ranks 21st of the 23 countries examined, at 6.45 deaths per 1,000 live births in 2006 (the latest year available). Rates ranged from 2.9 in Finland and Sweden to 29.1 in Mexico. Only Russia at 13.7 and Mexico at 29.1 had higher rates of infant mortality than the United States. Information about infant mortality comes from the World Health Organization's data.[6]

Looking at this information, one is hard pressed not to conclude that the U.S. social safety net does not do a very good job of meeting the three goals we attributed to it in chapter 1: providing basic economic security, protecting vulnerable populations, and promoting equality of opportunity. Although TANF and the EITC are supposed to protect children from the extremes of poverty, child poverty is still much higher here than in most similar countries. In the 1960s, changes in Social Security halved the number of elderly people living in poverty, but the proportion of elderly in the United States with incomes below 40 percent of the median national income is still much higher than that in most other industrialized countries. And our health care system still leaves about 15 percent of Americans (45.7 million people in 2007 according to U.S. Census Bureau 2008) without health insurance and thus without access to adequate care. A policymaker might look at these and similar indicators and ask: Is this the way we want to be? Is this the way to give our population the supports it needs to take on the challenges of a new century? The answers will depend at least as much or more on values as they will on data, as we discuss in the next chapter.

Conclusions

There is no single "right" research design for every policy question. Gathering and analyzing information to inform policy decisions cost money, so the choice of a research design should be approached sensibly, by asking what level and type of information are really *needed?* in each specific case. The question of what is *possible* also arises, and sometimes the question of what is *ethical.*

We saw in this chapter that sometimes all we need to do after implementing a policy is to wait a year and look at caseloads to see the answer. TANF caseloads went down. We can also see unintended effects (Medicaid and Food Stamp caseloads went down when TANF started) and the impact of taking steps to rectify them (after outreach efforts and relaxation of some rules, Medicaid and Food Stamp caseloads went back up).

Caseload data can also tell us that a program is not responsive to changing need levels, as when TANF caseloads continued to fall in the face of the worsening economic conditions and job losses of 2008. Or we can do a simple population survey if the focus of a change will not be reflected in the caseloads of public agencies. Such surveys showed that one year after enacting several health insurance reforms, health insurance coverage in Massachusetts went up and the number of uninsured people went down by half, to about 7 percent, and that by the end of the second year only 2.6 percent of the state's population was uninsured (Long et al. 2008). These results are certainly good enough for policy decisionmaking.

It is important to note that even with experiments using random assignment, which are considered the best for assessing policy impact, analyses almost always use participants' initial conditions and characteristics as controls before assessing the experimental effects; they rarely just compare treatment to control groups and leave it at that. The concept of control derived from laboratory experiments, clinical drug trials, and the like hardly ever exists in social experiments. Because the world does not stand still, no social experiment carried out over several years in communities of different structures and interaction patterns is ever really "under control," even if initial randomization is carried out perfectly.

By the same token, just because something has worked well in a reasonably controlled, reasonably funded pilot study in one or a few communities does not mean that thousands of other communities will be able to "buy" it and put it in place as if it were a jar of pickles. As we discussed at the end of chapter 5, every community is different, and every new approach to service delivery will need to be adapted to how particular communities do business. This reality of program operations "on the ground" is such that new programs will always need a reasonable amount of time to start up and reach a steady state—less time for relatively simple programs and more for very complex innovations. For instance, when several states (Hawaii, Rhode Island, and Tennessee) set out to revamp their entire state system for people with no health insurance, it took several years for them to get anywhere close to a steady state (Ku et al. 2000).

A final aspect of policy research worth noting is how much one can usually expect any study, or even a whole body of research, to affect policy decisions. The answer is probably more for managers, less for legislators. The more a policy decision is affected by politics—that is, things other than evidence of what works—the less policy research will play a role in tipping the decision one way or the other. It is very rare to be able to cite a situation, such as example 13 above, where it is very clear that research results made a big difference and essentially produced a policy turnaround—and that only happened as a consequence of determined advocacy using research results as the basis for convincing decisionmakers to change course, not because the data "spoke for themselves." Data never speak for themselves; they always need interpretation and packaging for different audiences. Mostly, what research results do is increase the confidence of decisionmakers that their choices are the right ones. They would have made the choice anyway—after all, if they are legislators they have to vote. But it is better that they feel they can defend the choice, that research evidence backs them up. The worst case, for public policy, is when decisions are made and policies are set strictly on the basis of politics. The consequences in such cases are often indefensible rules, unworkable programs, and wasted time, energy, and resources.

At the program manager level, decisions have a greater chance of being based on solid information. Here a manager can really use good data and good analysis. Good program managers intent on providing the best possible programs will use performance data regularly to determine how to make their programs serve clients better.

In between these two levels of data use are many other circumstances in which policy analysis can be used to good purpose. Advocates for new policies are always looking for good data that can help them make their case and are often far more expert than the researchers themselves at translating research findings into bite-size pieces that policymakers can absorb. Planning and evaluation divisions of federal and state agencies commission studies to provide information for decisionmaking within their agencies, expecting the information to influence decisions about particular programs when they are up for legislative reauthorization. Thus, the enterprise of policy research and analysis remains alive and well.

We end this chapter with a reminder that even the best information can take us only so far in the policy arena. It cannot help us with the decisions of *what we are trying to accomplish;* it can tell us only how well we are progressing toward program goals that have been established by processes related to value decisions rather than pragmatic ones. As we have discussed at various points throughout this book, the ultimate policy decisions come down to the matter of values. We as a nation make choices about how to reconcile our sometimes conflicting values as we create safety net programs and hope that by doing so we have created a functioning safety net. These are the issues with which we began this book and to which we return in its last chapter.

8

Implications for the Future

The United States has woven its social safety net over the course of more than two centuries. Today, it reflects the accumulation of programs and approaches created in different eras, each with its own national values, mores, priorities, economic conditions, and political will. The result is a complex mix of governmental and nongovernmental programs, paid for by a blend of federal, state, local, and private funding.

Chapter 1 described three goals of the public social safety net: providing economic security, protecting vulnerable populations, and promoting equality of opportunity. At one time or another in this country's history, the balance has shifted among these three goals, but rarely, if ever, has any one of them been completely off the table. These goals encompass many objectives, which again shift in priority from era to era. Among them are protecting vulnerable individuals against abuse and neglect, ensuring access to health care, providing insurance against economic hardships, and developing timely systems of benefits and services to help people who are unemployed, destitute, homeless, or otherwise at risk socially and economically.

Whereas any of us, regardless of income or position in society, could find ourselves in situations that place us at risk of hardship, in reality poor people face greater risks. Many poor children grow up to become successful and prosperous adults, but too many children born into vulnerable situations find it extremely difficult to escape them. Every modern nation recognizes that, to varying degrees, one legitimate task of government is to protect those who are in crisis or otherwise vulnerable and to alleviate hardships, including those resulting from poverty. A social safety net has to do more than provide emergency services or a minimal level of subsistence: it must also address the underlying causes of poverty and inequality.

How Are We Doing?

At the end of chapter 7, we posed two questions: How good is the U.S. safety net? How well does it accomplish the three goals of providing economic security, protecting vulnerable populations, and providing equality of opportunity? We saw that the United States does quite poorly when compared to other industrialized nations with respect to child poverty and poverty among senior citizens, highlighting those groups because they are usually perceived to be "deserving" and not able to do anything about their situation for themselves. The story is no different for overall poverty; the U.S. poverty rate is higher than that in all the countries we compared it to other than Russia and Mexico. This country, then, probably gets a C⁻ at best on providing economic security, especially given our resources.

Nor do we shine with respect to protecting vulnerable populations. We do quite badly compared to other industrialized nations on infant mortality, largely because too many poor mothers do not get good prenatal health care and nutrition. After decades of social and behavioral policies, the combined results of poverty and income inequality are sobering. The U.S. Census Bureau (2008) reports that nearly 38 million people were poor in 2007, based on the official federal poverty threshold, including 13.3 million children. Over 45 million people had no private or public health insurance coverage, including 21 million full-time workers and 8.1 million children. Eight in 10 of these uninsured people are members of low- or moderate-income working families who are not eligible for Medicaid and whose employers do not offer health insurance. Many poor people in this country are vulnerable to homelessness because housing costs have far outstripped the earning power of low-wage jobs (the federal minimum wage saw its first increase in 2007 after 10 years of no change and losing ground to inflation). Severely inadequate state budgets for mental health leave millions of extremely disabled people without consistently available basic needs, including housing and medical care. Between 2 and 3 million Americans experience homelessness in the course of a year, with between

650,000 and 700,000 homeless at any given time; between 150,000 and 200,000 are chronically homeless (HUD 2008; Burt, Aron, and Lee 2001). Virtually all these people come from poverty and go back to it; at least 1 poor person of every 14—including 1 poor child in 14—will experience some homelessness *every year*. This track record would probably earn us no better than a D on protecting vulnerable populations, compared with other industrialized countries.

Finally, let's look at how we do on ensuring equality of opportunity. Free public education has historically been the route to leaving poverty and securing the American dream of a middle-class life. Millions of immigrants over a century and a half have taken this route to opportunity. When we look at how the public schools of today are doing at giving youth, especially poor youth, the foundation they need to thrive in the 21st century, we find that we are doing quite badly. With receipt of a high school diploma as the measure, American high schools are failing about 25 percent of children—a figure that has not changed appreciably for at least three decades (Heckman and LaFontaine 2008).[1] For minority students, that rate goes up to 35 percent. Thus, schools serving the very people who need the most help to start their lives on an equal footing usually fail to deliver.

Most people in this country, though, believe not that the schools failed but that the students did. That attitude, entirely in keeping with the fundamental American approach, attributes all responsibility to individuals and none, or very little, to the conditions of their lives. But we know from extensive research that schools in even the poorest neighborhoods, with the most disadvantaged student body, *can* succeed if they start early, persist, and do it right (see, e.g., Success for All Foundation 2006). Improvement is not necessarily a matter of funding, although funding helps. It is a matter of organization, school and community involvement, proven strategy, and, above all, institutional commitment. The problem is not that millions of individual school children make the same decision to drop out but that the systems fail those children and have done so for a very long time.

Meanwhile, many disadvantaged youth are not prepared to rise above poverty as adults, especially minority men, many of whom spend some portion of their lives incarcerated. The U.S. prison population nearly tripled between 1987 and 2007, the year when this nation reached its highest rate of incarceration ever, 1 in every 99 adults. This is a higher rate than in any other country in the world; Germany, for instance, incarcerates 93 of every 100,000 people (adults and children); we incarcerate eight times as many—750 per 100,000. We have 1.6 million adults in prisons and about 700,000 more in jails on any given day. Furthermore, racial and gender discrepancies abound. One in every 106 white men is incarcerated, which is bad enough, but the statistics are truly intimidating for minority males—1 in every 15 African-American and 1 in every 36 Hispanic men are incarcerated. If we add age to that mix, 1 in every 9 African-American men between the ages of 20 and 34 are incarcerated, compared with 1 in 30 of all men in that age range (Pew Center on the States 2008).

Why Should We Care?

Should we care about the high school dropout rate among poor and minority youth? About the incarceration rate? About the number of babies born to poor mothers whose risk of living to see their first birthday is lower here than in almost all industrialized countries and some developing ones?

The question of *values* is one we must leave to readers to decide for themselves. But what about *practicality*—can we afford *not to care,* not to rethink our national attitude toward conditions that contribute to poverty and to how we maintain the social safety net for the poor and vulnerable among us? We think not.

Each prisoner, for example, costs about $25,000 a year to keep in prison. States spent $44 billion a year in 2007 to keep people in prison, up from $10.6 billion in 1987.[2] This 315 percent increase (127 percent in inflation-adjusted dollars) has made prisons one of the four most expensive items in state budgets along with Medicaid, schools, and transportation. In many states, prison costs exceed those of schools and Medicaid and have started to squeeze out spending on those vital items (Pew Center on the States 2008). If we had used these resources instead to make sure that those incarcerated men had received a good education as children and to help them use their energies and talents in the legitimate economy, we would probably not be paying to keep them in prison now. And they might very well be contributing substantially to their families and raising their own children to move further beyond poverty.

These are the same poorly educated people who drop out of high school, and by so doing, they doom themselves to a life of low-wage work or to making money only in the underground or illegal economy. Of course, chaining youth to high school desks until they can get a diploma is not the answer: the dropouts have usually been failing in school long before the schools count them as actual dropouts at age 16. The answer lies far deeper than that; it lies in doing whatever it takes to ensure that every child *likes* school, *likes* reading, *likes* math and science and can do them all at least at grade level by third grade or earlier. Despite the tested strategies for doing just that, at every level of school from prekindergarten through high school, most schools do not use them.

In 2008, there were about 14,000 public school districts in the United States, operating about 97,000 schools, serving about 50 million students, and spending about $489 billion (National Center for Educational Statistics 2008). And with all that, one in four of those students will drop out, *on average.* Some of the worst schools in the poorest neighborhoods throughout the nation fail to graduate at least three times that proportion of students. These are the youth of greatest concern; many remain poor or have difficulty engaging with the social and economic mainstream their whole lives. They and their children are likely to require the social safety net. This country cannot afford to "throw away" a quarter of each generation. To remain competitive in the world of the 21st century, we need the talents and creativity of every one of our citizens. We do not have them. Instead, we are in a vicious cycle of increasing inequality. Jobs in the low-wage market are "dumbed down" to accommodate the inabilities of poorly educated people—people our schools have failed—while jobs created in fields that offer opportunity for advancement often require a college education. High school graduates go to college, not high school dropouts.

From economists such as Heckman and LaFontaine, worried about the future earning power of high school dropouts, to business leaders worried about where good workers are going to come from, to pundits in newspaper columns and blogs throughout the country, many are deeply anxious about American competitiveness. More and more ordinary Americans recognize that this nation is at a crossroads on many fronts, from employment to education to energy. At present, just as we do with oil, we *import* a great deal of the talent currently going into our most innovative products; the best minds of many nations come here for training and schooling, and then stay. We need to do better at growing our own, rather than wasting a good part of each of our generations or, worse, spending resources to keep them incarcerated—resources that would have been better spent on proven educational strategies.

Here is where federalism comes in. Even if the federal government or any state government appropriated the resources to fully fund approaches that can improve economic opportunity and have strong research evidence of success—for example, in ensuring reading and math competence—the approaches cannot be imposed. *Testing* can be and has been imposed, but not successful educational methods. Each school district makes its own decision on how to use the federal or state funds and on which approaches to adopt. Schools and local officials need to be convinced. The same decisionmaking autonomy at the state or local level prevails with respect to the way we currently offer almost every reform option for every safety net program.

The need for major reforms in public education is just one example, albeit a very important one, of why we think the time has come to build a new national consensus to fight poverty. In addition to our fighting for economic well-being—that is, helping people develop the skills to get well-paying jobs rather than just consigning them to welfare or the secondary low-wage job market—we also need to make major changes in the ways that poor people are channeled to the worst schools, the worst streets, the worst park and recreational facilities, the worst housing, the most toxic environments, and so on. If we do not, every new cohort of poor children will start life already behind and fall farther behind as it grows up. And we as a nation will lose. Furthermore, a failure to address the problems early on will only increase stress on the last-resort safety net programs.

What Should We Do?

Before anything will really change, before we commit to doing what it will really take to bring about a significant reduction in poverty and its effects, the nation as a whole will have to see that investment as critical to our national interest. We must undertake a public examination of national priorities on the order of what occurred during the New Deal in the 1930s and the War on Poverty in the late 1960s and early 1970s. Change will not happen without strong and committed leadership. Those earlier eras made some progress, particularly in reducing poverty among the elderly and in enacting programs intended to improve the social conditions and opportunity structures that limit economic options. By the mid-1980s, though, the public dialogue had shifted away from public policies for addressing poverty and toward encouraging or requiring more individual responsibility for changing one's own condition, at least among those considered employable.

It is time again for a national commitment to eliminating poverty. While many changes could smooth, streamline, and increase the efficiency and effectiveness of particular programs or funding streams, an overarching vision and strategy are needed first. The United Kingdom's public policy commitment to end childhood poverty by 2020 placed high priority on the issue and set clear annual targets that have to be reached to meet that goal. Political leadership ensures that the issue remains high on the public agenda. We believe that the vision is primary: only with a powerful commitment to creating and communicating the vision will the United States be able to engage in the profound national dialogue necessary to reconfigure our often-conflicting values in ways that will help us shape the future. As a nation, we need to decide who should get public services and how to provide them without discouraging work and the work ethic and without hurting economic growth. Although that dilemma—the right balance between public supports and individual initiative—has been at the center of social policy deliberations over the past century, the United States has gone about it in ways that have allowed us to sidestep basic questions about the appropriate modern social contract.[3]

We see that social contract and the social safety net that should accompany it broadly and in parallel to what much of the world considers legitimate government policies to increase social inclusion. We offer three premises for the framework around which to stage this national dialogue, corresponding roughly to the goals articulated earlier of protecting vulnerable populations, reducing poverty, and providing equal opportunity:

- *People with major vulnerabilities:* Develop or expand supports for those who cannot work and do not have adequate personal or familial resources—children, medically and mentally incapacitated or disabled people, low-income senior citizens, and others with complex issues and needs that put them at the greatest risk of hunger, victimization, destitution, and homelessness. *Supports* need to include health and mental health care, housing, nutrition, and service connections to ensure people get what they need. *Eligibility* needs to be broad enough to encompass everyone in need, for shorter or longer periods depending on circumstances (i.e., not just the absolutely most needy, as is now the case in too many programs that keep caseloads and expenditures under control by tightening eligibility requirements to limit access only to those with the most severe circumstances).

- *People who can work:* If working is to be the main route out of poverty, then we need to have policies that encourage or require adequate wages and benefits, and we need to provide more and better supports for workers. Lowering the costs of health insurance and health care would be one way to increase the disposable income of workers. *Supports* need to include tuition assistance for life-long education and skills development to allow workers to refresh their skills continuously with a focus on upward mobility, guaranteed health care for workers and their families, adequate medical leave, child care and supports for preschool and school-age children, better wages, nutrition and housing subsidies, earned income tax credits, and the like. *Eligibility* should extend up to at least 200 percent of the poverty line as currently measured, since ample evidence indicates that households are still not able to meet even basic needs for food and shelter below that income level. Higher would be better, approximating the level of support for working families found in many European countries. Even better would be to make these work supports universal and then use the tax system to recover resources from high-income households, as we do with Social Security.

- *Equality of opportunity:* This is the most important part of the framework but the hardest to achieve. The first two components could probably be accomplished with an adequate investment of resources and better-run programs. But increasing equality of opportunity means making significant long-term investments in changing neighborhoods, changing schools, changing perceptions and expectations for the future, and changing lives. Social experiments in welfare and work supports, such as the Minnesota Family Investment Program and New Hope, and school changes, such as Success for All, show it can be done. If we succeed at this goal, fewer people will need safety net programs to support and protect them.

Strengthen and Improve Services for Vulnerable Populations

The first elements of an adequate social safety net involve sufficient and appropriate services to protect people with significant vulnerabilities and remove the conditions that make them vulnerable. People who are homeless, abused, neglected, abandoned, victimized, or disabled by medical or mental health problems need the basics—food, housing, and a meaningful and long-lasting support system. It is essential that enough of the right kinds of services be readily available for those in need and that programs be well-managed and adopt proven and effective strategies for delivering services. To bring the safety net up to this level of performance will require both program expansions and improved practices.

The greatest service challenges involve individuals with complex multiple needs, as we discussed in chapter 5. But funding and eligibility silos impede the ability of service agencies to help those with multiple and complexly interacting issues. While the federal government can simplify cross-program collaboration and integration of essential services by breaking down the separate funding and regulatory silos, the commitment to serving each population must be clear.

Integrated services are good for clients with complex needs, because people are more likely to get what they need in a timely manner and with due regard for all the issues they are trying to handle. But integrated services may not be necessary for all clients. Having a coordinator of services on staff will help maintain the philosophy of integration and make sure that staff understand when, and for whom, integration is important. No one simple sequence of services will be able to address the complexity of needs presented by different people, nor will a single structure of service delivery work in every community. The motivation of any community to develop integrated service mechanisms or to integrate systems will depend on the scope of the problems being addressed and the resources available to address them. Each community has to evolve its structure for itself, paying attention to the location of talent, interest, leadership, and resources. Federal programs must allow communities the flexibility to decide how to blend funds for different purposes and how to set priorities to meet the needs of their vulnerable and poor residents, regardless of the label attached to the funding coming from the federal government.

Support Working People

Peoples who work should be able to earn enough to support a decent standard of living. Welfare reform presumes that earnings from employment should be the main family resource and that working will make families self-sufficient. This clearly is not happening, if by self-sufficient we mean that families leaving welfare for work can earn enough to pay for adequate food, housing, health care, transportation to work, and child care. Even low-income working families that have never been on welfare have trouble paying for these essentials.

Working families should not be poor, regardless of the structure of the household. The welfare reforms after 1996 placed special emphasis on parental responsibility for supporting children. Language in legislation and regulations specifically supported the formation and maintenance of two-parent families, reflecting considerable research showing the importance of both parents in child development. While policies that support marriage may be useful, they cannot be a substitute for income and wage policies that give all working mothers and fathers the ability to support their children regardless of marital status. Moreover, nontraditional family structures and single parenthood cannot be equated with dysfunction; most single-parent households, like most two-parent households, are stable and functional. Parents who live apart from their children are often very much involved, nurturing and providing financially for their families. The income of single-parent families is lower primarily because they have only one wage earner and the structure of the postindustrial American economy and labor market has made it very difficult to maintain an adequate family income on a single salary. Social and economic policies should be designed to support all working parents, and this support may entail substantially raising the minimum wage and incorporating automatic inflation adjustments. Expanding the EITC to all workers and increasing the availability of job training and work supports for all low-wage workers, including noncustodial parents, would also help raise incomes for working families.

Although welfare reform included some complementary provisions to ensure that work could be each family's personal economic safety net, they were and are not enough and are short rather than long term. More needs to be done. Expanding the EITC to more workers without dependent children and raising the income level for receiving the credit could provide incentives for more workers to join—or rejoin—the formal labor market. Many low-income workers are in contingent situations, working on contract, for example, rather than as permanent employees. They are subject to federal self-employment (Social Security) taxes, even though they are not business owners. Lowering the self-employment tax for low-income contingent workers would raise their incomes. Low-income workers can work more if they have supports, such as child care and transportation assistance, to offset the costs of working. Health care and assistance with the cost of housing are other vital supports that need to be made available to far more families than currently receive them.

Reduce Inequality

As many have noted before us, income inequality in the United States has increased substantially in the past two decades, and there does not appear to be an end in sight. Much of this increasing income inequality has its roots in substantial inequalities of opportunity for poor compared to middle- and upper-income households. Some basic economic theories tend to restrain American policymakers from actively addressing poverty and inequality, reflecting concerns that spending public resources to increase income equality will hamper economic growth. Economic theories about development suggest that as a nation industrializes, it may first experience an increase in inequality caused by tighter wages that result from technological change, increased market competition, and other factors. Once markets stabilize, though, inequality usually decreases (Lindert and Williamson 1985; Burtless 1985). The pattern holds today, although the United States and many other nations are now seeing a rise in income inequality. While economists continue to analyze the causes of the newest trends, policy strategies should be pursued to bring income inequality within reasonable bounds, recognizing the trade-offs between economic growth (or efficiency) and economic equality.

Lindert (2006) makes our general point in the context of analyzing the effects of welfare state policies on economic growth. He notes the obvious, that the United States is a wealthy, stable country well able to afford to support its population should it choose to do so. At various times in our history, we have made critical policy decisions to benefit various groups even when those policies might run counter to economic theory and might bring our economic growth down slightly from the absolutely highest level it might have achieved. These policies include agricultural and other business subsidies, tax breaks for oil companies, government jobs during the Great Depression, and Social Security (which despite being considered "earned," actually costs taxpayers about $2 for every $1 contributed by retirees), to name a few.

With a national and political commitment to eradicate poverty and protect and help the vulnerable among us, we can do better than we have to date. We can choose policies that balance economic growth and equality. In describing the trade-offs among policies that can reduce inequality,

Lindert (2006) presents a policy fingerprint that delineates strategies adopted by many countries to favor the well-off, even though they may have had a negative effect on efficiency. His model, which is the basis for table 8.1, offers an interesting way to consider alternatives that would reduce inequality rather than increase it, recognizing that such choices might entail somewhat lower economic growth but would be balanced by spreading well-being more broadly among the whole population.

Since this country has implemented policies for the nonpoor even when they were likely to have a negative effect on economic growth, perhaps

Table 8.1. Policy Levers That Might Negatively Affect Economic Growth but Benefit Individuals

Policies that benefit middle- and upper-income households and increase income disparity	Policies that benefit low-income and poor households and help equalize income
Deny government funding that would make primary education affordable for the poor	Provide government funding that improves primary education for all children
Deny government funding that would give equal education to girls	Provide government funding that requires equal education to girls
Bias education subsidies in favor of university students at the expense of primary school students	Equalize education subsidies to university students and to primary school students
Bias health subsidies toward high-budget care for the elderly and well-off, at the expense of preventive and out-patient care for the young and the poor	Equalize health subsidies for the elderly and well-off with subsidies for preventive care for the young and nonelderly
Protect agriculture against competition, with the gains inevitably going to landowners	Allow agricultural markets to operate freely, lifting credit constraints and subsidizing small farmers
Protect an industrial sector against competition, creating industry rents that accrue to the privileged	Allow free market industrial markets to operate, lifting credit constraints and subsidizing new small businesses
Overprotect senior workers against dismissals, leading to lower hiring of new workers	Provide subsidies for hiring new workers and expanding their presence in the workforce

Source: The left panel is taken from Lindert (2006); the right panel applies Lindert's logic to identify alternatives that could reduce income inequality.

similar approaches could also be taken or expanded to alleviate poverty. Some hard decisions might be required about government spending, but with the political will to do so, the United States could substantially reduce economic inequality. Careful consideration of which trade-offs work best could minimize any negative effects.

Making the Commitment

At certain times, the inadequacies of the social safety net become all too apparent. In times of severe crisis, such as the September 11th attacks in 2001 or the disaster following Hurricanes Katrina and Rita in 2005, the nation willingly jumps into crisis mode. Massive special action is needed from both the private sector and the government, in part because the ongoing safety net (and emergency preparedness) is not sufficient. In true American fashion, the nation does address emergencies, even if not always as quickly or as completely as one might wish.

During a major crisis, however, or when a particularly egregious case of abuse or neglect occurs, the weaknesses of government programs that otherwise might not be as visible become apparent: unwieldy bureaucratic red tape, lack of coordination, procedural delays, lack of accountability, needy people who "fall through the cracks," and inefficient management and service delivery. The public may be outraged for a while and call for policy reform, but typically once the immediate crisis passes, the system settles back to the status quo. Thus far, crises have not catalyzed any serious commitment to shoring up the basic social safety net. Nor have we done much to address the underlying causes of poverty that exacerbate social hardship, although the recent lessons of Katrina and Rita may have had some effect on strengthening the nation's ability to respond to natural disasters.

Meanwhile, the U.S. social safety net is periodically mended, adding a few new important strings, mainly for those considered deserving of public help. Examples include Social Security retirement income for the aged, EITC for working families, and health insurance for low-income children. Instead of making major policy changes to address social problems, we have adopted incremental reforms program by program, with some reforms counteracting others (chapter 3). The basic dimensions of the safety net remain, however: work has become the core of personal security, family and private charity is assumed, public benefits are kept low to avoid disincentives to individual initiative, and services are mainly reserved for those considered deserving.

Poverty is the common thread associated with hardships that require a safety net; therefore, eliminating or reducing poverty should be a major goal of the safety net as a whole. Once we have general agreement that poverty and economic inequality are bad for this country and that reducing them is an important national priority, then we can select strategies to do what needs to be done.

As we contemplate such a commitment, we will inevitably question whether we can afford it. We counter that question with another—can we afford *not* to make the commitment if we want to remain competitive in the global economy? In an economy the size of ours and with the wealth we have, how can we argue that we could not find the money if we wanted to? If we *want* to, we *can* pay for an adequate safety net. The examples below illustrate creative ways to find the necessary funds:

- Simply limiting the mortgage interest deduction on second and third homes to interest on only the first $200,000 would leave enough money in the Treasury to pay for housing subsidies for *every household* with a worst-case housing need.
- Spending half the $49 billion currently going to prisons every year on schools would increase school budgets by 5 percent. Concentrating those resources on schools in the neighborhoods that send the highest proportion of their youth to prison and using the money to provide prekindergarten through 12th grade programs that raise children to grade level in reading and math and keep them there would substantially increase the odds that they would become law-abiding and self-sufficient adults.
- Each F-22A Stealth fighter jet costs $361 million (GAO 2006). The Air Force plans to procure more than 100 of these planes. If the Air Force got one fewer F-22A and the money were applied to child care instead, it would increase the funding in the Child Care and Development Block Grant for a year by about 12 percent— enough to serve about 120,000 more children while their parents work. Nine fewer F-22As would pay for child care for all children of low-income working families estimated to need it (Long and Clark 1997).
- In California, voters passed Proposition 63 in 2004 to raise money to serve people with mental illness. Proposition 63 imposed an

additional tax on all income of over $1 million reported on annual state income tax returns. The tax affects very few California taxpayers and only those who can well afford it; it benefits tens of thousands of mentally ill people who would not otherwise have received appropriate services or housing. Congress could do the same.

Even with a greater commitment of permanent funding and the political will to address poverty, economic problems, and inequality, programs must still be improved. The integration of services both to meet complex needs and to prevent them in the first place requires improved program practices. The social safety net is administered by a cadre of professionals and a combination of public and nongovernmental institutions. As highlighted throughout previous chapters, many effective, innovative, and forward-thinking programs have developed proven approaches to ensuring efficient and equitable access to services and to coordinating seamless provision of quality services to those in need. In addition to making sure that all the pieces of the net are intact and all the appropriate programs exist, the national government should facilitate the transfer of knowledge about effective practices among programs and service providers (chapter 7). The decades of program experience in states and communities across the nation provide many lessons. Unless policymakers and program administrators heed those lessons, though, the problems of accessing, coordinating, and maintaining services will repeat themselves, as subsequent generations of caring staff and officials grapple with the long lines of adults, children, and families in need.

Finally, it is essential that we include ongoing monitoring and continuous evaluation as an integral part of social safety net policy. Policymakers must take care not to make this function a separate activity viewed as an additional federal requirement. Instead, program monitoring, performance management systems, and program evaluations should be designed to meet both management and evaluative purposes. Administrators, elected officials, and the general public must know whether programs are accomplishing their intended purposes, whether the needs of vulnerable people are being met, and whether the nation's poverty is being reduced. Having such information on a routine basis allows administrators and policymakers to plan and make necessary adjustments to improve programs. It also facilitates transfer of knowledge about promising practices across programs and allows the nation the flexibility to adapt as new priorities or problems arise, making reasoned and rational decisions.

History has shown that the problems of poverty and hardship are constants in any society or nation. It would be naïve and simplistic to think that any nation, state, or community can totally and permanently eliminate all poverty—although some European countries come close, with relative poverty rates below 3 percent. With careful planning and program design, the U.S. safety net can be strengthened. The programs constituting its foundation exist, although many of the strings need to be retied and made broader and stronger. What we need now is to make reducing, if not eliminating, poverty a national priority and to commit to providing the resources to prevent hardship and ensure the availability and adequacy of all supports vulnerable and at-risk persons need.

Notes

Chapter 1. U.S. Social Policy and the Social Safety Net in Historical Perspective

1. The United States has signed the convention, signaling support, but has not yet ratified this international treaty. According to the United Nations, the only other country that has not ratified the convention is Somalia (Unite for Children 2009).

2. The historical trends and themes briefly noted in this chapter are treated in detail in DiNitto (2000), Katz (1989), Patterson (2000), Scokpol (1995), and Trattner (1998).

Chapter 2. Poverty

1. For example, eligibility for food stamps is set by the Department of Agriculture. It requires an income no higher than the poverty threshold *after exemptions*, but exemptions allow households to qualify with gross incomes as high as 130 percent of poverty. In contrast, eligibility for TANF is set by the states. In 2006, two states had income eligibility cutoffs higher than poverty thresholds, 13 states used the federal poverty level, and the rest had lower income cutoffs, with the least inclusive cutting off eligibility for households with incomes exceeding 16 or 18 percent of the federal poverty line.

2. The basic CPI is designated CPI-U. A consistent retrospective time series of inflation rates based on the new way of calculating housing values is known as the CPI-U-X1.

3. A poverty spell was defined as a period of at least two months in which household income fell below the federal poverty level for a household of a specific composition and size, followed by a period of at least two months in which the household was not poor.

4. "State and County Quick Facts," http://quickfacts.census.gov/qfd/states/00000.html.

5. Figure 2.6 displays findings only for metropolitan areas, because the Census Bureau did not release breakouts by census tract for nonmetropolitan areas until the 1990 census.

6. http://www.dol.gov/esa/minwage/america.htm.

Chapter 3. Recent Changes to U.S. Social Safety Net Policies

1. Employment is not the only objective of TANF programs. The purpose of TANF as stated in the 1996 law is to "increase the flexibility of states in operating a program designed to (1) provide assistance to needy families so that children may be cared for in their own homes or in the homes of relatives; (2) end the dependence of needy parents on government benefits by promoting job preparation, work, and marriage; (3) prevent and reduce the incidence of out-of-wedlock pregnancies and establish annual numerical goals for preventing and reducing the incidence of these pregnancies; and (4) encourage the formation and maintenance of two-parent families."

2. The Food Stamp Program was renamed the Supplemental Nutrition Assistance Program in 2008, as discussed in the next section of this chapter.

3. Under a few circumstances, such as when a tenant has very little income, different rules may apply. Most housing authorities require at least a minimum payment of $25 per month.

Chapter 4. Getting onto the Rolls

1. Erik Eckholm, "As Jobs Vanish and Prices Rise, Food Stamps Use Nears Record," *New York Times*, March 31, 2008.

2. Data in figure 4.4 are based on state Medicaid enrollment reports for December of each year, compiled for the Kaiser Commission on Medicaid and the Uninsured.

3. Except for immigrants, whose situation we discuss below.

4. http://facts.kff.org/chart.aspx?ch+477. Analyses done by Urban Institute researchers used simulations based on data from the Current Population Survey.

5. Another group,"able-bodied adults without disabilities," was restricted to three months of eligibility unless they participated in work search or employment. Those restrictions still apply, contributing to the overall drop in Food Stamp participation.

Chapter 5. Service Delivery Mechanisms and Innovations

1. We use this example, although it is old, because it is a very carefully done evaluation of a type that has not been funded during at least the past decade. Its findings still provide important lessons for practitioners, managers, and decisionmakers.

2. Material for example 1 draws heavily from Mitchell et al. (1979).

3. See chapters 1 and 3 for more detail on the differences between AFDC and TANF.

4. The material in example 2 owes much to the analyses presented in Martinson and Holcomb (2002) and Pindus et al. (2000).

5. Example 3 draws heavily on Nightingale, Pindus, and Trutko (2002), and Pindus et al. (2000).

6. Example 4 is based on Burt, Geen, and Duke (1998); Gennetian, Miller, and Smith (2005); Knox, Miller, and Gennetian (2000); and Martinson et al. (2007).

7. Our description of the New Hope project and its outcomes relies heavily on Hurston et al. (2003).

8. Information for Example 6 comes from Burt, Resnick, and Novick (1998) and the YouthZone web site, http://www.youthzone.com.

9. Material for example 7 is drawn from Burt et al. (2002); Burt et al. (2004); Burt, Pearson, and Montgomery (2005); Burt and Anderson (2006); Burt (2007, 2008); Padgett, Gulcar, and Tsemberis (2006); and current work by Burt.

10. Here is how Wikipedia describes him: "William Edwards Deming was an American statistician, college professor, author, lecturer, and consultant. Deming is widely credited with improving production in the United States during World War II, although he is perhaps best known for his work in Japan. There, from 1950 onward, he taught top management how to improve design (and thus service), product quality, testing and sales (the latter through global markets). Deming made a significant contribution to Japan's becoming renowned for producing innovative high-quality products."

Chapter 7. Policy Analysis, Evaluation, and Performance Monitoring

1. There are many good academic textbooks on evaluation. One written specifically for program administrators and managers is Wholey, Hatry, and Newcomer (2004).

2. The National Survey of America's Families was a special survey conducted in conjunction with a major project of the Urban Institute called Assessing the New Federalism, which began shortly after the passage of PRWORA in 1996 and was intended to assess the impacts of welfare reform. Three waves of the survey were done, in 1997, 1999, and 2001. Over 45,000 families were interviewed for each wave. In addition to being able to produce national estimates, samples were large enough in 13 states to produce results at the state level. This is the only national survey that combines all the many topics and issues of concern for low-income families into one, which was needed to assess the full effects of welfare reform. Topics covered include employment, education, income levels and sources, household composition, child care, child support, foster care and children living elsewhere, health and health insurance, housing, housing hardship and food insecurity, and mothers' and children's mental health.

3. The Welfare Rules Database was originally developed by the Urban Institute as part of its foundation-funded project, Assessing the New Federalism, which began in 1996, the year TANF was enacted. DHHS assumed funding for the database to ensure its continuance as a valuable policy tool.

4. This database can be accessed at http://www.nri-inc.org/projects/profiles, where one can see the many questions this database is able to answer for a state program manager and other interested parties.

5. 2000 was the year most consistently available for the 23 countries. Only the United Kingdom is represented by 1999 data. Luxemburg Income Study Database, http://www.lisproject.org/keyfigures (multiple countries, 1999–2000). In the United States, the federal poverty line generally comes in at about 30 percent of median income.

6. Table 2 at http://www.who.int/healthinfo/morttables/en/index.

Chapter 8. Implications for the Future

1. The U.S. Department of Education puts the high school graduation rate at about 88 percent, but this includes about 20 percent of youth who drop out of high school but at some later point complete a general equivalency diploma (GED) by taking a test. Research summarized by Heckman and LaFontaine (2008) shows that people with only a GED—that is, without a high school diploma—do as poorly in the labor market as high school dropouts, so we follow their lead in focusing only on people with a high school diploma.

2. Add federal outlays to the mix and the total reached $49 billion in 2007.

3. See, for instance, Eisinger (1998) for a detailed description of how our conflicting value premises have affected government actions to address hunger over more than a century.

References

Acs, Gregory, and Pamela Loprest. 2007a. "TANF Caseload Composition and Leavers Synthesis Report." Washington, DC: The Urban Institute.

———. 2007b. "Helping Women Stay Off Welfare." Washington, DC: The Urban Institute.

Adams, Gina, Kathleen Snyder, and Patti Banghart. 2008. "Designing Subsidy Systems to Meet the Needs of Families: An Overview of Policy Research Findings." Washington, DC: The Urban Institute. http://www.urban.org/url.cfm?ID=411611.

Barnow, Burt S., and Christopher T. King. 2000. "Publicly Funded Training in a Changing Labor Market." In *Improving the Odds: Increasing the Effectiveness of Publicly Funded Training,* edited by Burt S. Barnow and Christopher T. King (1–18). Washington, DC: Urban Institute Press.

Barnow, Burt S., and Demetra Smith Nightingale. 2007. "An Overview of U.S. Workforce Development Policy in 2005." In *Reshaping the American Workforce in a Changing Economy,* edited by Harry Holzer and Demetra Smith Nightingale (25–37). Washington, DC: Urban Institute Press.

Bawden, D. Lee, ed. 1989. *The Social Contract Revisited.* Washington, DC: Urban Institute Press.

Berman, Eli, John Bound, and Zvi Griliches. 1994. "Changes in the Demand for Skilled Labor within U.S. Manufacturing: Evidence from the Annual Survey of Manufacturers." *Quarterly Journal of Economics* 109: 367–97.

Bernstein, Jared, and Isaac Shapiro. 2005. "Unhappy Anniversary: Federal Minimum Wage Remains Unchanged for Eighth Straight Year, Falls to 56-year Low Relative to the Average Wage." Washington, DC: Center on Budget and Policy Priorities, Economic Policy Institute.

Blackburn, McKinley L., David E. Bloom, and Richard B. Freeman. 1990. "The Declining Economic Position of Less Skilled American Men." In *A Future of Lousy Jobs*, edited by Gary Burtless (31–76). Washington, DC: Brookings Institution Press.

Blank, Rebecca. 1989. "The Effect of Medical Need on Medicaid and AFDC Participation." *Journal of Human Resources* 24(1): 55–87.

———. 2008. "Presidential Address: How to Improve Poverty Measurement in the United States." *Journal of Policy Analysis and Management* 27(2): 233–54.

Boris, Elizabeth T. 1999. "Nonprofit Organizations in a Democracy: Varied Roles and Responsibilities." In *Nonprofits and Government: Collaboration and Conflict*, edited by Elizabeth T. Boris and C. Eugene Steuerle (1–35). Washington, DC: Urban Institute Press.

Borjas, George. 2007. "Immigration Policy and Human Capital." In *Reshaping the American Workforce in a Changing Economy*, edited by Harry J. Holzer and Demetra Smith Nightingale (183–200). Washington, DC: Urban Institute Press.

Burke, Vincent, and Vee Burke. 1974. *Nixon's Good Deed: Welfare Reform*. New York: Columbia University Press.

Burt, Martha R. 2002. "The Hard-to-Serve: Definitions and Implications." In *Welfare Reform: The Next Act*, edited by Alan Weil and Kenneth Finegold (163–78). Washington, DC: Urban Institute Press.

———. 2007. "System Change Efforts and Their Results, Los Angeles, 2005–2006: Hilton Foundation Project to End Homelessness among People with Serious Mental Illness." Washington, DC: The Urban Institute.

———. 2008. "Pushing the Envelope: Broadening and Deepening Involvement in THCH Communities as Projects End." Oakland, CA: Corporation for Supportive Housing.

Burt, Martha R., and Jacquelyn Anderson. 2006. "Taking Health Care Home: Impact of System Change Efforts at the Two-Year Mark." Oakland, CA: Corporation for Supportive Housing.

Burt, Martha R., and Karen J. Pittman. 1985. *Testing the Social Safety Net: The Impact of Changes in Support Programs during the Reagan Administration*. Washington, DC: Urban Institute Press.

Burt, Martha R., Laudan Y. Aron, and Edgar Lee. 2001. *Helping America's Homeless: Emergency Shelter or Affordable Housing?* Washington, DC: Urban Institute Press.

Burt, Martha R., Rob Geen, and Amy Ellen Duke. 1998. "Income Support and Social Services for Low-Income People in Minnesota." Washington, DC: The Urban Institute.

Burt, Martha R., Carol Pearson, and Ann Elizabeth Montgomery. 2005. *Strategies for Preventing Homelessness*. Washington, DC: Department of Housing and Urban Development.

Burt, Martha R., Gary Resnick, and Emily Novick. 1998. *Building Supportive Communities for At-Risk Adolescents: It Takes More than Services*. Washington, DC: American Psychological Association.

Burt, Martha R., John Hedderson, Janine Zweig, Mary Jo Ortiz, Laudan Y. Aron-Turnham, and Sabina Johnson. 2004. *Strategies for Reducing Chronic Street Homelessness*. Washington, DC: Department of Housing and Urban Development.

Burt, Martha R., David Pollack, Amy Sosland, Kelly S. Mikelson, Elizabeth Drapa, Kristi Greenwalt, and Patrick Sharkey. 2002. *Evaluation of Continuums of Care for Homeless People.* Washington, DC: Department of Housing and Urban Development.

Burtless, Gary, ed. 1990. *A Future of Lousy Jobs.* Washington, DC: Brookings Institution Press.

Cancian, Maria, Daniel R. Meyer, and Chi-Fang Wu. 2006. "Welfare Patterns after the Welfare Revolution." *La Follette Policy Report* 15(2): 1–2, 10–15.

Capps, Randy, Everett J. Henderson, and Kenneth Finegold. 2006. "Food Stamp Use by Legal Immigrants before and after the 2003 Restorations: Report for 2001–02 Results and 1999–2000 through 2001–02 Trends." Washington, DC: The Urban Institute.

Capps, Randy, Michael Fix, Jeffrey S. Passel, Jason Ost, and Dan Perez-Lopez. 2003. "A Profile of the Low-Wage Immigrant Workforce." *Immigrant Families and Workers* Policy Brief 4. Washington, DC: The Urban Institute.

Capps, Randy, Robin Koralek, Katherine Lotspeich, Michael Fix, Pamela Holcomb, and Jane Reardon Anderson. 2004. "Assessing Implementation of the 2002 Farm Bill's Legal Immigrant Food Stamp Restorations." Washington, DC: The Urban Institute.

Castner, Laura. 2000. "Trends in FSP Participation Rates: Focus on 1994 to 1998." Washington, DC: Mathematica Policy Research.

Cellini, Stephanie Riegg, Signe-Mary McKernan, and Caroline Ratcliffe. 2008. "The Dynamics of Poverty in the United States: A Review of Data, Methods, and Findings." *Journal of Policy Analysis and Management* 27(3): 577–605.

Center for American Progress. 2007. *From Poverty to Prosperity: A National Strategy to Cut Poverty in Half.* Washington, DC: Center for American Progress.

Center on Budget and Program Priorities. 2006. "TANF at 10: Program Results Are More Mixed Than Often Understood." Washington, DC: Center on Budget and Program Priorities. http://www.cbpp.org/8-17-06tanf.htm.

Chevan, Albert, and Randall Stokes. 2000. "Growth in Family Income Inequality, 1970–1990: Industrial Restructuring and Demographic Change." *Demography* 37(3): 365–80.

Child Trends. 2007. "Welfare Receipt (AFDC/TANF)." Washington, DC: Child Trends. http://www.childtrendsdatabank.org/indicators/50AFDCTANF.cfm.

Citro, Constance, and Robert Michaels. 1995. *Measuring Poverty: A New Approach.* Washington, DC: National Academy Press.

Congressional Budget Office. 2004. "What Accounts for the Decline in Manufacturing Employment?" Washington, DC: Congressional Budget Office.

Cottingham, Phoebe H., and David T. Ellwood, eds. 1989. *Welfare Policy for the 1990s.* Cambridge, MA: Harvard University Press.

Culhane, Dennis P., Stephen Metraux, and Trevor Hadley. 2002. "Public Service Reductions Associated with Placement of Homeless Persons with Severe Mental Illness in Supportive Housing." *Housing Policy Debate* 13(1): 107–63.

Cunnyngham, Karen. 2003. "Food Stamp Participation Rates: 2003." Washington, DC: Mathematica Policy Research.

Currie, Janet M., and Jeffrey Grogger. 2001. "Explaining Recent Declines in Food Stamp Program Participation." In *Brookings-Wharton Papers on Urban Affairs* (203–29). Washington, DC: Brookings Institution Press.

Danziger, Sandra, and Sherrie Kossoudji. 1994–95. "What Happened to General Assistance Recipients in Michigan?" *Focus* 16 (winter): 32–34.

Danziger, Sandra, and Kristin S. Seefeldt. 2002. "Barriers to Employment and the 'Hard to Serve': Implications for Services, Sanctions, and Time Limits." *Focus* 22(1): 76–81.

Dean, Stacy, Colleen Pawling, and Dorothy Rosenbaum. 2008. "Implementing New Changes to the Food Stamp Program: A Provision by Provision Analysis of the 2008 Farm Bill." Washington, DC: Center on Budget and Policy Priorities. http://www. cbpp.org/7-1-08fa.pdf.

DeNavas-Walt, Carmen, Bernadette D. Proctor, and Jessica C. Smith. 2007. "Income, Poverty, and Health Insurance Coverage in the United States: 2006." Suitland, MD: U.S. Census Bureau. http://www.census.gov/prod/2007pubs/p60-233.pdf.

Derr, Michelle, Heather Hill, and LaDonna Pavetti. 2000. "Addressing Mental Health Problems among TANF Recipients: A Guide for Program Administrators." Washington, DC: Mathematica Policy Research.

De Vita, Carol J., and Cory Fleming. 2001. "Building Capacity in Nonprofit Organizations." Washington, DC: The Urban Institute. http://www.urban.org/url.cfm? ID=410093.

DiNitto, Diana M. 2000. *Social Welfare: Politics and Public Policy,* 5th ed. Boston: Allyn and Bacon.

Dolbeare, Cushing N. 2002. "Changing Priorities: The Federal Budget and Housing Assistance, 1976–2007." Washington, DC: National Low Income Housing Coalition. http://www.nlihc.org/pubs/index.htm#6.

Dubay, Lisa, John Holahan, and Allison Cook. 2007. "The Uninsured and the Affordability of Health Insurance Coverage." *Health Affairs* 26(1): 22–80.

Eisinger, Peter. 1998. *Toward an End to Hunger in America.* Washington, DC: Brookings Institution Press.

Ellis, Eileen R., Dennis Roberts, David M. Rousseau, and Karyn Schwartz. 2008. "Medicaid Enrollment in 50 States: June 2006 Data Update." Washington, DC: Kaiser Commission on Medicaid and the Uninsured.

Ellwood, David T. 1989. *Poor Support: Poverty in the American Family.* Boston: Harvard University Press.

"Facts at a Glance." 2005. Washington, DC: Child Trends, Inc.

Fisher, Gordon M. 1996. "Relative or Absolute—New Light on the Behavior of Poverty Lines Over Time." *Newsletter of the Government Statistics Section and the Social Statistics Section of the American Statistical Association* (summer): 10–12. http://aspe. hhs.gov/poverty/papers/relabs.htm.

———. 1997. "The Development of the Orshansky Poverty Thresholds and Their Subsequent History as the Official U.S. Poverty Measure." Washington, DC: Bureau of the Census. *Poverty Measurement Working Papers.* Originally published as "The Development and History of the Poverty Thresholds." 1992. *Social Security Bulletin* 55(5): 3–14. http://www.census.gov/hhes/poverty/povmeas/papers/orshansky.html.

Forbes, Kristin J. 2004. "U.S. Manufacturing: Challenges and Recommendations." Comments at the National Association for Business Economic's 2004 Washington Economic Policy Conference. Washington, DC: Council of Economic Advisors.

Furner, Mary O. 1996. "Downsizing Government: An Historic Perspective." *Future of the Public Sector* Policy Brief 9. Washington, DC: The Urban Institute.

Gais, Thomas L, Richard P. Nathan, Irene Lurie, and Thomas Kaplan. 2001. "Implementation of the Personal Responsibility Act of 1996." In *The New World of Welfare,* edited by Ron Haskins and Rebecca M. Blank (35–69). Washington, DC: Brookings Institution Press.

GAO. See U.S. General Accounting Office and U.S. Government Accountability Office.

Gennetian, Lisa A., Cynthia Miller, and Jared Smith. 2005. "Turning Welfare into a Work Support: Six-Year Impacts on Parents and Children from the Minnesota Family Investment Program." New York: Manpower Demonstration Research Corporation.

Giannarelli, Linda, Paul Johnson, Sandi Nelson, and Meghan Williamson. 2005. "TRIM3's 2001 Baseline Simulation of Medicaid and SCHIP Eligibility and Enrollment: Methods and Results." Washington, DC: The Urban Institute. http://aspe.hhs.gov/health/reports/05/medicaid-schip-simulation/index.htm.

Gill, Emily R. 2004. "Religious Organizations, Charitable Choice, and the Limits of Freedom of Conscience." *Perspectives on Politics* 2(4): 741–55.

Gleason, Philip, Carole Trippe, Scott Cody, and Jacquelyn Anderson. 2001. "The Effects of Welfare Reform on the Characteristics of the Food Stamp Population." Washington, DC: Mathematica Policy Research, Inc.

Golden, Olivia. 2005. *Eight Years of Welfare Reform.* Washington, DC: The Urban Institute. http://www.urban.org/url.cfm?ID=311198.

Graves, John, and Sharon Long. 2006. "Why Do People Lack Health Insurance?" *Health Policy Online* Brief 14. Washington, DC: The Urban Institute. http://www.urban.org/url.cfm?ID=411317.

Greenstein, Robert. 2005. "The Earned Income Tax Credit: Boosting Employment, Aiding the Working Poor." Washington, DC: Center for Budget and Policy Priorities.

Greenstein, Robert, and Jocelyn Guyer. 2001. "Supporting Work through Medicaid and Food Stamps." In *The New World of Welfare,* edited by Ron Haskins and Rebecca M. Blank (346–60). Washington, DC: Brookings Institution Press.

Grogger, Jeffrey, Lynn A. Karoly, and Jacob A. Klerman. 2002. *Consequences of Welfare Report: A Research Synthesis.* Santa Monica, CA: RAND Institute. http://www.rand.org/pubs/drafts/DRU2676/.

Hanratty, Maria J. 2006. "Has the Food Stamp Program Become More Accessible? Impacts of Recent Changes in Reporting Requirements and Asset Eligibility Limits." *Journal of Policy Analysis and Management* 25(3): 603–21.

Harrison, Bennett, and Barry Bluestone. 1988. *The Great U-Turn: Corporate Restructuring and the Polarizing of America.* New York: Basic Books.

Harvey, Carol, Michael J. Camasso, and Radha Jagannathan. 2000. "Evaluating Welfare Reform Waivers under Section 1115." *Journal of Economic Perspectives* 14(4): 165–88.

Haskins, Ron, and Rebecca M. Blank. 2001. "Welfare Reform: An Agenda for Reauthorization." In *The New World of Welfare,* edited by Ron Haskins and Rebecca M. Blank (3–32). Washington, DC: Brookings Institution Press.

Heckman, James J., and Paul A. LaFontaine. 2008. "The Declining American High School Graduation Rate: Evidence, Sources, and Consequences." *NBER Reporter: Research Summary 2008* no. 1. Cambridge, MA: National Bureau of Economics Research.

Holahan, John, and Mary Beth Pohl. 2003. "Leaders and Laggards in State Coverage Expansions." In *Federalism and Health Policy,* edited by John Holahan, Alan Weil, and Joshua Wiener (179–214). Washington, DC: Urban Institute Press.

Holahan, John F., and Alan Weil. 2002. "Health Insurance, Welfare, and Work." In *Welfare Reform: The Next Act,* edited by Alan Weil and Kenneth Finegold (143–61). Washington, DC: Urban Institute Press.

Holahan, John, Brian Bruen, and David Liska. 1998. "The Decline in Medicaid Spending Growth in 1996: Why Did It Happen?" Washington, DC: Urban Institute.

Holcomb, Pamela A., and Karin Martinson. 2002. "Putting Policy into Practice: Five Years of Welfare Reform." In *Welfare Reform: The Next Act,* edited by Alan Weil and Kenneth Finegold (1–15). Washington, DC: Urban Institute Press.

Holcomb, Pamela A., and Demetra Smith Nightingale. 1997. "Alternative Strategies for Increasing Employment." *The Future of Children* 7(1): 52–64.

Holtz, V. Joseph, and John Karl Scholz. 2003. "The Earned Income Tax Credit." In *Means-Tested Transfer Programs in the United States,* edited by Robert A. Moffitt (141–98). Chicago: University of Chicago Press.

Holzer, Harry, and Paul Offner. 2006. "Trends in the Employment Outcomes of Young Black Men, 1979–2000." In *Black Males Left Behind,* edited by Ronald B. Mincy (1–37). Washington, DC: Urban Institute Press.

HUD. See U.S. Department of Housing and Urban Development.

Huston, Althea C., Cynthia Miller, Lashawn Richburg-Hayes, Greg J. Duncan, Carolyn A. Eldred, Thomas S. Weisner, Edward Lowe, Vonnie C. McLoyd, Danielle A. Crosby, Marika N. Ripke, and Cindy Redcross. 2003. *New Hope for Families and Children: Five-Year Results of a Program to Reduce Poverty and Reform Welfare.* New York: Manpower Demonstration Research Corporation.

Iceland, John. 2003. "Dynamics of Economic Well-Being: Poverty 1996–1999." *Current Population Reports, Household Economic Studies* Series P70-91. Washington, DC: U.S. Bureau of the Census.

Jargowsky, Paul A. 2003. "Stunning Progress, Hidden Problems: The Dramatic Decline of Concentrated Poverty in the 1990s." Washington, DC: The Brookings Institution.

Jargowsky, Paul A., and Isabel V. Sawhill. 2006. "The Decline of the Underclass." Center on Children and Families Brief 36. Washington, DC: The Brookings Institution.

Kabbani, Nadar, and Parke E. Wilde. 2003. "Short Recertification Periods in the U.S. Food Stamp Program." *Journal of Human Resources* 38(Supplement): 1051–79.

Kaiser Commission on Medicaid and the Uninsured. 2008. *State Children's Health Insurance Program: Reauthorization History.* Washington, DC: Kaiser Commission on Medicaid and the Uninsured.

Katz, Michael B. 1989. *The Undeserving Poor: From the War on Poverty to the War on Welfare.* New York: Pantheon.

Kennedy, Sheila Suess, and Wolfgang Bielefeld. 2002. "Government Shekels without Shackles? The Administrative Challenges of Charitable Choice." *Public Administration Review* 62(1): 4–11.

Kenney, Genevieve M. 2008. "The Failure of SCHIP Reauthorization: What's Next?" Washington, DC: The Urban Institute. http://www.urban.org/url.cfm?ID=411628.

Kenney, Genevieve M., Jennifer M. Haley, and Alexandra Tebay. 2003. "Children's Insurance Coverage and Service Use Improve." *Snapshots of America's Families III* 1. Washington, DC: The Urban Institute. http://www.urban.org/url.cfm?ID=310816.

Kirby, Gretchen, and Jacquelyn Anderson. 2000. "Addressing Substance Abuse Problems among TANF Recipients: A Guide for Program Administrators. Final Report." Washington, DC: Mathematica Policy Research.

Knox, Virginia, Cynthia Miller, and Lisa A. Gennetian. 2000. "Reforming Welfare and Rewarding Work: A Summary of the Final Report on the Minnesota Family Investment Program." New York: Manpower Demonstration Research Corporation.

Kornfeld, Robert. 2002. "Explaining Recent Trends in Food Stamp Program Caseloads: Final Report." Washington, DC: USDA, Food and Nutrition Service, Economic Research Service. http://www.ers.usda.gov/publications/efan02008.

Kramer, Fredrica D., Kenneth Finegold, Carol J. De Vita, and Laura Wherry. 2005. "Implementing the Federal Faith-Based Agenda: Charitable Choice and Compassion Capital Initiatives." *New Federalism Issues and Options for States,* Series A, No. 69. Washington, DC: The Urban Institute.

Kreider, Rose. 2005. "Number, Timing, and Duration of Marriages and Divorces: 2001." *Current Population Reports, Household Economic Studies,* Series P70-97. Suitland, MD: U.S. Bureau of the Census.

Ku, Leighton, Marilyn Ellwood, Sheila Hoag, Barbara Ormond, and Judith Wooldridge. 2000. "Evolution of Medicaid Managed Care Systems and Eligibility Expansions." *Health Care Financing Review* 22(2): 7–27.

Lapham, Susan J., Patricia Montgomery, and Debra Niner. 1993. "We, the American Foreign Born." Suitland, MD: U.S. Bureau of the Census, Ethnic and Hispanic Branch, Population Division.

Lennon, Mary Clare, and Thomas Corbett, eds. 2003. *Policy into Action: Implementation Research and Welfare Reform.* Washington, DC: Urban Institute Press.

Lindert, Peter. 2006. "Equality and Efficiency: What History Teaches Us about Tradeoffs." Washington, DC: World Bank Institute.

Lindert, Peter, and Jeffrey G. Williamson. 1985. "Growth, Equality, and History." *Explorations in Economic History* 22(4): 341–77.

Long, Sharon K., and Sandra J. Clark. 1997. *The New Child Care Block Grant: State Funding Choices and Their Implications.* Washington, DC: Urban Institute. *Assessing the New Federalism* Policy Brief A-12.

Long, Sharon K., Allison Cook, and Karen Stockley. 2008. "Health Insurance Coverage in Massachusetts: Estimates from the 2008 Massachusetts Health Insurance Survey." Washington, DC: The Urban Institute. http://www.urban.org/url.cfm?ID=411815.

Long, Sharon K., Demetra Smith Nightingale, and Douglas Wissoker. 1994. "Evaluation of the Washington State Family Independence Program." Washington, DC: The Urban Institute.

Martinson, Karin, and Pamela A. Holcomb. 2002. "Reforming Welfare: Institutional Change and Challenges." *Assessing the New Federalism,* Occasional Paper No. 60. Washington, DC: The Urban Institute.

Martinson, Karin, Caroline Ratcliffe, Elizabeth Harbison, and Joanna Parnes. 2007. "Minnesota Integrated Services Project: Participant Characteristics and Program Implementation." Washington, DC: The Urban Institute.

McKernan, Signe-Mary, and Caroline Ratcliffe. 2003. "Employment Factors Influencing Food Stamp Participation." Washington, DC: The Urban Institute. http://www.urban. org/url.cfm?ID=410800.

———. 2006. "The Effect of Specific Welfare Policies on Poverty." Washington, DC: Urban Institute. http://www.urban.org/url.cfm?ID=411334.

McLaughlin, Catherine G., Sarah E. Crow, Mary Harrington, and Hanns Kuttner. 2004. "Causes and Consequences of Lack of Health Insurance: Gaps in Our Knowledge." In *Health Policy and the Uninsured,* edited by Catherine G. McLaughlin (xiii–xxv). Washington, DC: Urban Institute Press.

Mead, Lawrence M. 1997. "Citizenship and Social Policy: T. H. Marshall and Poverty." *Social Philosophy and Policy* 14(summer): 197–230.

Meyers, Marcia K., Bonnie Glaser, and Karin MacDonald. 1998. "On the Front Lines of Welfare Delivery: Are Workers Implementing Policy Reforms?" *Journal of Policy Analysis and Management* 17(1): 1–22.

Millennial Housing Commission. 2002. "Executive Summary: The Millennial Housing Commission Report." Washington, DC: Millennial Housing Commission. http:// www.mhc.gov/MHCReport.pdf.

Mills, Bradford, Dorai-Raj Sundar, Everett Peterson, and Jeffrey Alwang. 2001. "Determinants of Food Stamp Program Exits." *Social Service Review* 75(4): 539–60.

Mincy, Ronald. B. 1994. "The Underclass: Concept, Controversy, and Evidence." In *Confronting Poverty: Prescriptions for Change,* edited by Sheldon H. Danziger, G. D. Sandefur, and D. H. Weinberg (109–46). Cambridge: Harvard University Press.

Mincy, Ronald B., Charles Lewis, and Wen-Jui Han. 2006. "Less-Educated Young Black Men in the Economic Boom of the 1990s." In *Black Males Left Behind,* edited by Ronald B. Mincy (1–10). Washington, DC: Urban Institute Press.

Mitchell, John J., Mark Lincoln Chadwin, and Demetra Smith Nightingale. 1979. *Implementing Welfare-Employment Programs: An Institutional Analysis of the Work Incentive (WIN) Program.* Washington, DC: The Urban Institute.

Mitchell, Glenn, Jennifer R. Salmon, Hongbin Chen, and Scott Hinton. 2003. "An Evaluation of Florida's Medicaid Home and Community Based Programs Serving Frail Elders: A Look at Five Outcomes." Tallahassee: Florida Policy Exchange Center.

Moffitt, Robert, and Barbara Wolfe. 1993. "Medicaid, Welfare Dependency, and Work: Is There a Causal Link?" *Health Care Financing Review* 15(1): 123–33.

Mosisa, Abraham, and Steven Hipple. 2006. "Trends in Labor Force Participation in the United States." *Monthly Labor Review,* October, 35–57.

National Center for Educational Statistics. 2008. http://nces.ed.gof/fastfacts.

National Coalition on Health Care. 2007. "Health Insurance Coverage." Washington, DC: National Coalition on Health Care. http://www.nchc.org/facts/coverage.

Nelson, Sandi. 2004. "Trends in Parents' Economic Hardship." *Snapshots of America's Families III* No. 21. Washington, DC: Urban Institute. http://www.urban.org/ url.cfm?ID=310970.

Nightingale, Demetra Smith. 1998. "Who Does What? The Changing Shape of U.S. Federalism." Appendix to *The Government We Deserve: Responsive Democracy and Changing Expectations,* edited by C. Eugene Steuerle, Edward M. Gramlich,

Hugh Heclo, and Demetra Smith Nightingale (174–85). Washington, DC: Urban Institute Press.

Nightingale, Demetra Smith, and Nancy M. Pindus. 1997. "Privatization of Public Social Services: A Background Paper." Washington, DC: The Urban Institute.

Nightingale, Demetra Smith, Nancy Pindus, and John Trutko, with Michael Egner. 2002. "The Implementation of the Welfare-to-Work Grants Program." Washington, DC: The Urban Institute.

Office of Family Assistance. 2007. *Seventh Annual Report to Congress on the Temporary Assistance to Needy Families Program.* Washington, DC: Department of Health and Human Services.

Office of Management and Budget. 2002. *The President's Management Agenda, Fiscal Year 2002.* http://www.whitehouse.gov/omb/budintegration/pma_index.html.

————. 2008. *The President's Budget for FY2009.* Washington, DC: U.S. Government Printing Office.

Osborne, David, and Ted Gaebler. 1992. *Reinventing Government.* New York: Addison-Wesley Publishing.

Padgett, Deborah K., Leyla Gulcar, and Sam Tsemberis. 2006. "Housing First Services for People Who Are Homeless with Co-Occurring Serious Mental Illness and Substance Abuse." *Research on Social Work Practice* 16(1): 74–83.

Page, Marianne E., Joanne Spetz, and Jane Millar. 2006. "Does the Minimum Wage Affect Welfare Caseloads?" *Journal of Policy Analysis and Management* 24(2): 273–95.

Patterson, James T. 2000. *America's Struggle against Poverty in the Twentieth Century.* Cambridge, MA: Harvard University Press.

Pavetti, LaDonna, Kathleen Maloy, and Liz Schott. 2002. "Promoting Medicaid and Food Stamp Participation: Establishing Procedures That Support Participation and Meet Families' Needs." Washington, DC: Mathematica Policy Research. http://www.mathematica-mpr.com/PDFs/promotemedicaid.pdf.

Pawasarat, John, and Lois M. Quinn. 1993. "Wisconsin Welfare Employment Experiments: An Evaluation of the WEJT and CWEP Programs." Milwaukee: Employment and Training Institute, University of Wisconsin-Milwaukee.

Peterson, George E., and Demetra Smith Nightingale. 1995. "What Do We Know about Block Grants?" Washington, DC: The Urban Institute. http://www.urban.org/url.cfm?ID=405512.

Peterson, Paul E. 2005. *The Price of Federalism.* Washington, DC: Brookings Institution Press.

Pew Center on the States. 2008. *One in 100: Behind Bars in America 2008.* Washington, DC: Pew Center on the States.

Pindus, Nancy, Robin Koralek, Karin Martinson, and John Trutko. 2000. "Coordination and Integration of Welfare and Workforce Development Systems." Washington, DC: The Urban Institute.

Pirog, Maureen A., Anne L. Buffardi, Colleen K. Chrisinger, Pradeep Singh, and John Briney. 2008. "Are the Alternatives to Randomized Assignment Nearly as Good? Statistical Corrections to Nonrandomized Evaluations." *Journal of Policy Analysis and Management* 28(1): 169–72.

Popkin, Susan J., Bruce Katz, Mary K. Cunningham, Karen D. Brown, Jeremy Gustafson, and Margery Austin Turner. 2004. "A Decade of HOPE VI: Research Findings and Policy Challenges." Washington, DC: The Urban Institute. http://www.urban.org/url.cfm?ID=411002.

Porter, Kathryn, and Allen Dupree. 2001. "Poverty Trends for Families Headed by Working Single Mothers, 1993 to 1999." Washington, DC: Center for Budget and Policy Priorities.

Radin, Beryl. 2000. "The Government Performance and Results Act and the Tradition of Federal Management Reform: Square Pegs in Round Holes?" *Journal of Policy Analysis and Management* 10(1): 111–35.

Rank, Mark R., and Thomas A. Hirschl. 2001. "Rags or Riches? Estimating the Probabilities of Poverty and Affluence across the Adult American Life Span." *Social Science Quarterly* 82(4): 651–69.

Ricketts, Erol, and Isabel Sawhill. 1988. "Defining and Measuring the Underclass." *Journal of Policy Analysis and Management* 7(2): 316–25.

Rosenheck, Robert, Wesley Kasprow, Linda Frisman, and Wen Liu-Mares. 2003. "Cost-Effectiveness of Supportive Housing for Homeless Persons with Mental Illness." *Archive of General Psychiatry* 60: 940–51.

Rowe, Gretchen, and Linda Giannarelli. 2006. "Getting on, Staying on, and Getting off Welfare: The Complexity of State-by-State Policy Choices." *New Federalism: Issues and Options for States* A-70. Washington, DC: The Urban Institute.

Ruggles, Patricia 1990. *Drawing the Line: Alternative Poverty Measures and Their Implications for Public Policy*. Washington, DC: Urban Institute Press.

Ruggles, Patricia, and R. Williams. n.d. "Measuring the Duration of Poverty Spells." Survey of Income and Program Participation Working Paper 86. Washington, DC: U.S. Bureau of the Census.

Salamon, Lester M. 2002. *The Tools of Government: A Guide to the New Governance*. New York: Oxford University Press.

Salamon, Lester M., Leslie C. Hems, and Kathryn Chinnock. 2000. "The Nonprofit Sector: For What and for Whom?" Baltimore, MD: Johns Hopkins University. http://www.jhu.edu/~ccss/pubs/pdf/f.

Scarcella, Cynthia Andrews, Roseana Bess, Erica H. Zielewski, and Rob Geen. 2006. "The Cost of Protecting Vulnerable Children V: Understanding State Variation in Child Welfare Financing." Washington, DC: The Urban Institute. http://www.urban.org/url.cfm?ID=311314.

Schoeni, Robert F., and Rebecca M. Blank. 2000. "What Has Welfare Reform Accomplished? Impacts on Welfare Participation, Employment, Income, Poverty, and Family Structure." Working Paper 7627. Cambridge, MA: National Bureau of Economic Research. http://www.nber.org/papers/w7627.

Shern, David L., Chip J. Felton, Richard L. Hough, Anthony F. Lehman, Steven M. Goldfinger, Elie Valencia, Deborah Dennis, Roger Straw, and Patricia A. Wood. 1997. "Housing Outcomes for Homeless Adults with Mental Illness: Results from the Second-Round McKinney Program." *Psychiatric Services* 48(2): 239–41.

Scokpol, Theda. 1995. *Social Policy in the United States: Future Possibilities in Historical Perspective*. Princeton, NJ: Princeton University Press.

Smith, Karen E., and Eric Toder. 2005. *Changing Demographics of the Retired Population.* Washington, DC: The Urban Institute.

Smith, Steven Rathgeb. 1999. "Government Financing of Nonprofit Activity." In *Nonprofits and Government: Collaboration and Conflict,* edited by Elizabeth T. Boris and C. Eugene Steuerle (219–56). Washington, DC: Urban Institute Press.

Smith, Vernon K., Kathleen Gifford, Eileen Ellis, Robin Rudowitz, Molly O'Malley, and Caryn Marks. 2007. "As Tough Times Wane, States Act to Improve Medicaid Coverage and Quality: Results from a 50-State Medicaid Budget Survey for State Fiscal Years 2007 and 2008." Washington, DC: Kaiser Commission on Medicaid and the Uninsured.

Smith, Vernon K., Jason Cooke, David M. Rousseau, Robin Rudowitz, and Caryn Marks. 2007. "SCHIP Turns 10: An Update on Enrollment and the Outlook on Reauthorization from the Program's Directors." Washington, DC: Kaiser Commission on Medicaid and the Uninsured.

———. 2008. "Headed for a Crunch: An Update on Medicaid Spending, Coverage, and Policy Heading into an Economic Downturn: Results from a 50-State Medicaid Budget Survey for State Fiscal Years 2008 and 2009." Washington, DC: Kaiser Commission on Medicaid and the Uninsured.

Steuerle, C. Eugene, Edward M. Gramlich, Hugh Heclo, and Demetra Smith Nightingale, eds. 1998. *The Government We Deserve: Responsive Democracy and Changing Expectations* Washington, DC: Urban Institute Press

Stuber, Jennifer, and Karl Kronebusch. 2004. "Stigma and Other Determinants of Participation in TANF and Medicaid." *Journal of Policy Analysis and Management* 23(3): 509–30.

Success for All Foundation. 2006. *Independent Reviews Support Achievement Effects of Success for All.* Baltimore, MD: Success for All Foundation.

Trattner, Walter I. 1999. *From Poor Law to Welfare State: A History of Social Welfare in America.* New York: Simon and Schuster.

Trutko, John, Carolyn T. O'Brien, Pamela A. Holcomb, and Demetra Smith Nightingale. 2007. "Implementation and Sustainability: Emerging Lessons from the Early High Growth Job Training Initiative (HGJTI) Grants." Washington, DC: The Urban Institute. http://www.urban.org/url.cfm?ID=411556.

Tsemberis, Sam, and Ruth F. Eisenberg. 2000. "Pathways to Housing: Supported Housing for Street-Dwelling Homeless Individuals with Psychiatric Disabilities." *Psychiatric Services* 51(4): 487–93.

Unite for Children/UNICEF. 2009. *Convention on the Rights of the Child.* New York: UNICEF. http://www.unicef.org/crc.

U.S. Bureau of the Census. 2004. "Table CH-1. Living Arrangements of Children under 18 Years Old: 1960 to Present" Lanham, MD: U.S. Bureau of the Census. http://www.census.gov/population/socdemo/hh-fam/tabCH-1.pdf.

———. 2008a. *Income, Poverty, and Health Insurance Coverage in the United States: 2007.* P60-235. Washington, DC: U.S. Bureau of the Census.

———. 2008b. *Statistical Abstracts of the United States.* "Federal Food Programs: 1990–2006." Table 551. Washington, DC: U.S. Department of Commerce.

U.S. Department of Agriculture, Food and Nutrition Service. 2009a. "Annual Summary of Food and Nutrition Service Programs." Washington, DC: U.S. Department of Agriculture. http://www.fns.usda.gov/pd/annual.htm.

―――. 2009b. "Supplemental Nutrition Assistance Program Participation and Costs." Washington, DC: U.S. Department of Agriculture. http://www.fns.usda.gov/pd/SNAPsummary.htm.

U.S. Department of Housing and Urban Development. 1999. *The Widening Gap: New Findings on Housing Affordability in America*. Washington, DC: Department of Housing and Urban Development.

―――. 2005. *Affordable Housing Needs 2003: Report to Congress*. Washington, DC: Department of Housing and Urban Development.

―――. 2007. *Affordable Housing Needs 2005: Report to Congress*. Washington, DC: Department of Housing and Urban Development.

―――. 2008. *The Third Annual Homeless Assessment Report to Congress*. Washington, DC: Department of Housing and Urban Development.

U.S. General Accounting Office. 1999. *Medicaid Enrollment: Amid Declines, State Efforts to Ensure Coverage after Welfare Reform Vary*. GAO/HEHS-99-163. Washington, DC: U.S. General Accounting Office.

U.S. Government Accountability Office. 2006. *Defense Acquisitions: Assessments of Selected Major Weapon Programs,* GAO-06-391. Washington, DC: U.S. Government Accountability Office.

U.S. House of Representatives, Committee on Agriculture. *2008 Farm Bill Nutrition Title: Promoting Health and Fighting Hunger in the United States*. Fact Sheet. Washington, DC: U.S. Government Printing Office.

U.S. House of Representatives, Committee on Ways and Means. 1998. *Green Book*. Washington, DC: U.S. Government Printing Office.

―――. 2002. "Workforce Investment Act." Section 15, (969–72) in *2000 Green Book*. Washington, DC: U.S. Government Printing Office.

Weil, Alan, and Kenneth Finegold, eds. 2002. *Welfare Reform: The Next Act*. Washington, DC: Urban Institute Press.

Werner, Alan. 2004. *A Guide to Implementation Research*. Washington, DC: Urban Institute Press.

Wheaton, Laura, and Elaine Sorenson. 2007. "The Potential Impact of Increasing Child Support Payments to Families." Perspectives on Low-Income Working Families Brief 5. Washington, DC: The Urban Institute.

Wholey, Joseph S., Harry P. Hatry, and Kathryn E. Newcomer. 2004. *Handbook of Practical Program Evaluation*, 2nd ed. San Francisco: Jossey-Bass.

Williamson, Stephanie, Catherine A. Jackson, and Jacob A. Klerman. 1997. "Welfare Waivers State-Specific Descriptions." Santa Monica, CA: Rand Corporation.

Wilson, William Julius. 1996. *When Work Disappears: The World of the New Urban Poor*. New York: Random House.

―――. 1987. *The Truly Disadvantaged: The Inner City, the Underclass, and Public Policy*. New York: Random House.

Winston, Pamela. 2002. *Welfare Policymaking in the States: The Devil in Devolution.* Washington, DC: Georgetown University Press.

Wolfe, Barbara, and Scott Scrivner. 2005. "The Devil May Be in the Details: How the Characteristics of SCHIP Programs Affect Take-Up." *Journal of Policy Analysis and Management* 24(3): 499–522.

Zedlewski, Sheila R. 2004. *Recent Trends in Food Stamp Participation: Have New Policies Made a Difference?* Washington, DC: Urban Institute. *Assessing the New Federalism* Policy Brief B-58.

Zedlewski, Sheila R., and Sarah Brauner. 1999. *Declines in Food Stamp and Welfare Participation: Is There a Connection?* Washington, DC: The Urban Institute. *Assessing the New Federalism* Discussion Paper 99-13.

Zedlewski, Sheila R., and Amelia Gruber. 2001. *Former Welfare Families Continue to Leave the Food Stamp Program.* Washington, DC: The Urban Institute. *Assessing the New Federalism* Discussion Paper 01-05.

Zedlewski, Sheila R., Gina Adams, Lisa Dubay, and Genevieve Kenney. 2006. *Is There a System Supporting Low Income Working Families?* Washington, DC: Urban Institute. http://www.urban.org/url.cfm?ID=311282.

Zedlewski, Sheila R., David Merriman, Sarah Staveteig, and Kenneth Finegold. 2002. "TANF Funding and Spending across the States." In *Welfare Reform: The Next Act,* edited by Alan Weil and Kenneth Finegold (225–46). Washington, DC: Urban Institute Press.

Zunz, Oliver, Leonard Schoppa, and Nobuhiro Hiwatari. 2002. *Social Contracts under Stress: The Middle Classes of America, Europe, and Japan at the Turn of the Century.* New York: Sage Publications.

About the Authors

Martha R. Burt has been at the Urban Institute for more than 30 years, where she served as the director of the Social Services Research Program, conducting research and writing about policies on welfare, homelessness, hunger, teen pregnancy and parenting, and social services. As part of the *Assessing the New Federalism* project, Dr. Burt directed the analysis of how public systems for welfare, child care, and child protective services had changed after three years of welfare reform. Her third book on homelessness—*Helping America's Homeless: Emergency Shelter or Affordable Housing?*—analyzes the policy implications of findings from the National Survey of Homeless Assistance Providers and Clients. Dr. Burt has also directed work on the impact of federal and state policy changes on the well-being of children and youth, on hunger among the elderly, and on service issues related to domestic violence. In relation to violence against women, she has examined coordinated community response to domestic violence, what TANF programs are doing to recognize and accommodate domestic violence as a barrier to work, and the effects of STOP funding through the Violence Against Women Act on justice system activities and effectiveness. Dr. Burt's research has also focused on policies and services for at-risk youth and persons with serious mental illness. She developed a widely used method to estimate the national and local public costs of teenage childbearing, and is the coauthor of a highly regarded book discussing the policy issues involved in teenage childbearing—*Private Crisis, Public Cost.*

Demetra Smith Nightingale is a principal research scientist and member of the faculty at the Institute for Policy Studies at Johns Hopkins University, where she teaches graduate courses on social policy and program evaluation. Her research concentrates on employment, skills training, social assistance, women and family issues, immigration, youth development, and welfare reform. Much of her research involves evaluating the implementation of public programs and the impacts of programs and services on individuals and families. Her studies have analyzed programs in every state in the United States as well as social and economic policies in Argentina, Chile, Russia, and China. She is the author of dozens of books and articles; among her books are *Reshaping the American Workforce in a Changing Economy,* with Harry Holzer (2007), and *The Low-Wage Labor Market: Challenges and Opportunities for Self-Sufficiency,* co-edited with Kelleen Kaye (2000). Before joining Johns Hopkins, she was at the Urban Institute for 29 years, most recently as principal research associate and program director in the Labor and Social Policy Center. She is also a senior research affiliate with the National Poverty Center at the University of Michigan, affiliate faculty with the Johns Hopkins Population Center, a senior research consultant with the Urban Institute, and a senior consultant with the World Bank (Social Protection Division).

Index